Authors
& Artists
for Young
Adults

ISSN 1040-5682

Authors & Artists for Young Adults

VOLUME 74

THOMSON

GALE

Detroit • New York • San Francisco • New Haven, Conn. • Waterville, Maine • London

THOMSON

GALE

Authors and Artists for Young Adults, Volume 74

Project Editor
Robert James Russell

Editorial
Bev Baer, Dana Ferguson, Amy Fuller, Allison Green, Michelle Kazensky, Lisa Kumar, Kathy Meek, Jennifer Mossman, Joseph Palmisano, Mary Ruby, Amanda Sams, Marie Toft

Permissions
Beth Beaufore

Imaging and Multimedia
Lezlie Light, Robyn Young

Composition and Electronic Capture
Tracey L. Matthews

Manufacturing
Cynde Bishop

LIBRARY OF CONGRESS CATALOG CARD NUMBER 89-641100

ISBN-13: 978-0-7876-7793-0
ISBN-10: 0-7876-7793-0
ISSN 1040-5682

Printed in the United States of America
10 9 8 7 6 5 4 3 2 1

Contents

Introduction

Authors and Artists for Young Adults is a reference series designed to serve the needs of middle school, junior high, and high school students interested in creative artists. Originally inspired by the need to bridge the gap between Gale's *Something about the Author*, created for children, and *Contemporary Authors*, intended for older students and adults, *Authors and Artists for Young Adults* has been expanded to cover not only an international scope of authors, but also a wide variety of other artists.

Although the emphasis of the series remains on the writer for young adults, we recognize that these readers have diverse interests covering a wide range of reading levels. The series therefore contains not only those creative artists who are of high interest to young adults, including cartoonists, photographers, music composers, bestselling authors of adult novels, media directors, producers, and performers, but also literary and artistic figures studied in academic curricula, such as influential novelists, playwrights, poets, and painters. The goal of *Authors and Artists for Young Adults* is to present this great diversity of creative artists in a format that is entertaining, informative, and understandable to the young adult reader.

Entry Format

Each volume of *Authors and Artists for Young Adults* will furnish in-depth coverage of approximately twenty-five authors and artists. The typical entry consists of:

—A detailed biographical section that includes date of birth, marriage, children, education, and addresses.

—A comprehensive bibliography or filmography including publishers, producers, and years.

—Adaptations into other media forms.

—Works in progress.

—A distinctive essay featuring comments on an artist's life, career, artistic intentions, world views, and controversies.

—References for further reading.

—Extensive illustrations, photographs, movie stills, cartoons, book covers, and other relevant visual material.

A cumulative index to featured authors and artists appears in each volume.

Compilation Methods

The editors of *Authors and Artists for Young Adults* make every effort to secure information directly from the authors and artists through personal correspondence and interviews. Sketches on living authors and artists are sent to the biographee for review prior to publication. Any sketches not personally reviewed by biographees or their representatives are marked with an asterisk (*).

Highlights of Forthcoming Volumes

Among the authors and artists planned for future volumes are:

John James Audubon	Stanislaw Lem	Elizabeth George Speare
Frank Deford	Jack London	Wislawa Szymborska
Sharon G. Flake	Steven Millhauser	Rick Veitch
Charlotte Perkins Gilman	Nam June Paik	James Whale
James Hilton	O.E. Rolvaag	Jack Williamson
Sarah Orne Jewett	Richard Sala	Robert Wise

Contact the Editor

We encourage our readers to examine the entire *AAYA* series. Please write and tell us if we can make *AAYA* even more helpful to you. Give your comments and suggestions to the editor:

BY MAIL: The Editor, *Authors and Artists for Young Adults,* 27500 Drake Rd., Farmington Hills, MI 48331-3535.

BY TELEPHONE: (800) 347-GALE

Authors and Artists for Young Adults
Product Advisory Board

The editors of *Authors and Artists for Young Adults* are dedicated to maintaining a high standard of excellence by publishing comprehensive, accurate, and highly readable entries on writers, artists, and filmmakers of interest to middle and high school students. In addition to the quality of the entries, the editors take pride in the graphic design of the series, which is intended to be orderly yet appealing, allowing readers to utilize the pages of *AAYA* easily, enjoyably, and with efficiency. Despite the success of the *AAYA* print series, we are mindful that the vitality of a literary reference product is dependent on its ability to serve its readers over time. As critical attitudes about literature, art, and media constantly evolve, so do the reference needs of students and teachers. To be certain that we continue to keep pace with the expectations of our readers, the editors of *AAYA* listen carefully to their comments regarding the value, utility, and quality of the series. Librarians, who have firsthand knowledge of the needs of library users, are a valuable resource for us. The *Authors and Artists for Young Adults* Product Advisory Board, made up of school, public, and academic librarians, is a forum to promote focused feedback about *AAYA* on a regular basis, as well as to help steer our coverage of new authors and artists. The advisory board includes the following individuals, whom the editors wish to thank for sharing their expertise:

Gillian Armstrong

(Photograph by Stephanie L'hostis/Getty Images.)

■ Personal

Born December 18, 1950, in Melbourne, Australia; daughter of a real estate businessman and a school-teacher; married John Pfeffer (a film editor); children: two daughters. *Education:* Studied stage and costume design at Swinbourne College; studied filmmaking at Australian Film and Television School.

■ Addresses

Home—Sydney, Australia. *Agent*—Creative Artists Agency, 9830 Wilshire Blvd., Beverly Hills, CA 90212.

■ Career

Director, producer, art director, and screenwriter. Director of television commercials; also worked as production assistant, assistant designer, and assistant editor of industrial and educational films.

Worked as a waitress. Associated with Women's Film Group, Sydney, Australia. Director of films, including *Old Man and Dog* (short film), 1970; *Roof Needs Mowing* (short film), 1971; *Gretel* (short film), 1973; *Satdee Night* (short film), 1973; *One Hundred a Day* (short film), 1973; *Smokes and Lollies* (documentary), 1975; (and producer) *The Singer and the Dancer*, Columbia, 1976; *My Brilliant Career*, Analysis, 1979; (and co-producer) *Fourteen's Good, Eighteen's Better* (documentary), 1980; *A Busy Kind of Bloke*, 1980; *Touch Wood* (documentary), 1980; *Starstruck*, Cinecom, 1982; *Having a Go* (documentary), 1983; *Not Just a Pretty Face*, 1983; *Mrs. Soffel*, Metro-Goldwyn-Mayer/United Artists, 1984; *High Tide*, Hemdale, 1987; (and producer) *Bingo, Bridesmaids, and Braces* (short documentary), Big Picture, 1988; *Fires Within*, Metro-Goldwyn-Mayer/United Artists Home Video, 1991; *The Last Days of Chez Nous*, Fine Line, 1993; *Little Women*, Columbia, 1994; (and producer) *Not Fourteen Again* (documentary), Beyond Films, 1996; *Oscar and Lucinda*, Fox Searchlight, 1997; *Charlotte Gray*, Warner Bros., 2001; *Unfolding Florence: The Many Lives of Florence Broadhurst*, Film Australia, 2006. Art director, *Promised Woman*, BC Productions, 1974; assistant art director, *The Removalists*, 1975; art director, *The Trespassers*, Filmways, 1975. Also director of the short film *Storytime*, the documentary *A Time and a Place*, and the documentary *Tassie Wood*; assisted on the short film *Zibido*. Appeared in films; roles include nurse, *Promised Woman*, BC Productions, 1974; interviewer, *Smokes and Lollies* (documentary), 1975; interviewer, *Fourteen's Good, Eighteen's Better* (documentary), 1980; and as herself, *A Busy Kind of Bloke*, 1980. Work in television specials include producer and director, *Bob Dylan in Concert*, HBO, 1986; and director, *Hard to Handle: Bob Dylan with Tom Petty and the Heartbreakers*, HBO, 1986.

■ Awards, Honors

Sydney Film Festival Award, best short film, 1976, for *The Singer and the Dancer*; British Critics' Award, best first feature, and seven Australian Film Institute Awards, including best film and best director, all 1980, for *My Brilliant Career*; FACTS Award, best travel commercial, 1982, for American Express television commercial; eleven award nominations, Australian Film Institute, 1993, for *The Last Days of Chez Nous*; Victoria Teachers Federation award for documentary trilogy *Smokes and Lollies, Fourteen's Good, Eighteen's Better*, and *Bingo, Bridesmaids, and Braces*; Australian Film Festival award nomination, best documentary, 1996, for *Not Fourteen Again*.

■ Writings

SCREENPLAYS

Gretel (short film), 1973.
One Hundred a Day 1973.
Smokes and Lollies (documentary), 1975.
Clean Straw for Nothing, 1976.
(With John Pfeffer) *The Singer and the Dancer*, Columbia, 1976.
Fourteen's Good, Eighteen's Better (documentary), 1980.
A Busty Kind of Bloke, 1980.
Touch Wood (documentary), 1980.
Not Just a Pretty Face, 1983.
Not Fourteen Again (documentary; also known as *Now They Are Fourteen* and *Not 14 Again!*), Beyond Films, 1996.

Contributor to periodicals, including *Films in Review*.

■ Sidelights

Filmmaker Gillian Armstrong was the first female in half a century to direct a major feature film in her native Australia. Her 1979 *My Brilliant Career*, about a turn-of-the-century independent woman whose goal was the become a writer, proved an

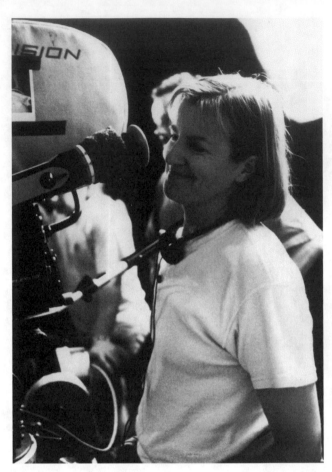

Gillian Armstrong on the set of her 1994 film *Little Women*. (Photograph by Joseph Lederer. The Kobal Collection. Reproduced by permission.)

international success and launched Armstrong's own brilliant career, which has encompassed eight feature length dramas and three feature length documentaries. According to Helen Carter, writing for *Senses of Cinema*, "Armstrong's films are character studies, with human interactions and personal journey at the heart of the narrative." Carter further noted, "With that as her springboard, [Armstrong] has ventured to explore several genres, including musical, gangster and most commonly, period drama." Among her most popular period pieces are, in addition to *My Brilliant Career, Mrs. Soffel, Little Women, Oscar and Lucinda*, and *Charlotte Gray*. As a critic for *International Dictionary of Films and Filmmakers* observed, "Armstrong makes films that resist easy categorization as either 'women's films' or Australian ones. Her films mix and intermingle genres in ways that undermine and illuminate afresh, if not openly subvert, filmic conventions." The same critic went on to note that the pleasures of Armstrong's films "are traditional ones, such as sensitive and delicate cinematography, fluid editing, an evocative feel for setting and costume, and most importantly, a commitment to solid character development and acting." Additionally, the contributor for *International Dictionary of Films and Filmmakers* wrote, Armstrong's work "continually addresses sexual politics and family tensions. Escape from and struggle with traditional sex roles and pitfalls and triumphs therein are themes frequently addressed in her films." Felicity Collins, writing in *The Films of Gillian Armstrong,* observed her movies "have regularly been noted for their rebellious, strong, independent heroines."

Australia as Home and Backdrop

Gillian May Armstrong was born on December 18, 1950, in Melbourne, Australia. The daughter of an amateur photographer father, Armstrong grew up with an appreciation for the visual image. She studied general art, including film and stage and costume design at Swinbourne College, and was among the first graduating class of film directors from the Australian Film and Television School, later the AFTRS. Her earliest works include short dramas, music videos, and documentaries. As a final project for the AFTRS, Armstrong shot the short film, *One Hundred a Day.* Thereafter, commissioned by the Australian Film Corporation, she made a documentary about fourteen-year-old girls in Adelaide, Australia, *Smokes and Lollies.* She subsequently followed this same group of young women, interviewing them at ages eighteen, twenty-six, and thirty-three, and producing the documentaries *Fourteen's Good, Eighteen's Better, Bingo, Bridesmaids and Braces,*

Judy Davis in a scene from the 1979 film *My Brilliant Career.* (Photograph courtesy of The Kobal Collection, 1979. Reproduced by permission.)

A scene from 1994's *Little Women*, with Claire Danes, Trini Alvarado, Winona Ryder, and Kirsten Dunst. (Photograph courtesy of Di Novi/Columbia/The Kobal Collection/Joseph Lederer.)

and the 1996 feature-length documentary, *Not Fourteen Again.* Reviewing the last-named film, Carter called it a "warm, compassionate view of these women and their daughters."

However, it is for her feature-length dramas that Armstrong is best known. Her 1976 film, *The Singer and the Dancer,* was a step toward that goal. Commissioned by the Australian Film Commission, and shot on a minimal budget, the resulting movie was, as described by the critic for *International Dictionary of Films and Filmmakers,* a "precocious study of the toll men take on women's lives that marked the onset of Armstrong's mature style." On the strength of that movie, and her earlier short, *One Hundred a Day,* Armstrong was offered directorial duties on her first feature-length film, *My Brilliant Career.* One of her first innovations on that picture was the casting of, at the time, relative unknown actors in the leads. Sam Neill was cast in the lead male role of Harry Beecham, while the Judy Davis was chosen to play Sybilla Melvin, a young woman who renounces love in order to pursue her ambition of

becoming a professional writer. The film was an international success, earning praise for the young director. Writing in the *New York Times,* Janet Maslin noted that *My Brilliant Career* "marks the beginning of exactly that for both the film's daring, assured, high-spirited Australian director, Gillian Armstrong, and its rambunctious young star." The critic for *International Dictionary of Films and Filmmakers* wrote that *My Brilliant Career* "potently evokes smothered sensuality and conveys sexual tension by small, telling details." Such an early success, however, had its downside for the director. None of her subsequent films, except perhaps for *Little Women,*—another period drama about a self-willed young woman who wants to become a writer—have won such critical acclaim or attention.

Mixes Genres

In an effort to avoid becoming stereotyped as a director of period dramas, Armstrong turned to a contemporary setting with her next film, *Starstruck,* a "high-energy, rock musical," according to Carter. Set in urban, punk-rock Sydney, Australia, the film follows the fortunes of Jackie, who finds fame as a singer, and of Angus, who has dreams of becoming a producer. Maslin, reviewing the work in the *New York Times*, referred to its "dizzy, impudent, high-spirited glory." Maslin went on to call *Starstruck* an "original, and an energetic and funny one at that," as well as a film that "demonstrates [Armstrong's] versatility in no uncertain terms."

Armstrong returned to period drama for her 1984 feature, *Mrs. Soffel,* her first Hollywood film. Based on a true story, the film is set in 1901 in a Pittsburgh prison and features Diane Keaton as Mrs. Soffel, the warden's repressed wife who wants more out of life than domestic chores. Seeking adventure, she engineers the escape of two young murderers, the brothers Ed and Jack Biddle. She joins them in their escape, and for a brief time satisfies her erotic desires and need for adventure before Ed, played by Mel Gibson, is shot. The film was a modest box office hit, but earned generally unfavorable critical reviews. Writing in *People*, Scot Haller noted that the "usually inventive [Armstrong] here sinks in a quicksand of period details and dark-as-night cinematography." Similarly, a *Time* magazine critic found the film "dour and disappointing," while for Vincent Canby, writing in the *New York Times*, the same film was "very strange and maddening." However, the contributor for *International Dictionary of Films and Filmmakers* found *Mrs. Soffel* a "sadly underrated film."

Armstrong returned to Australian settings for the multi-generational *High Tide*, an "unabashedly sentimental weepie, and none the worse for it," according to the *International Dictionary of Films and Filmmakers* writer. Once again starring Judy Davis, the film was a low-budget affair set in a coastal town. Davis plays a singer who abandoned her daughter many years ago for her career, and is now struggling to come back into the daughter's life. For Maslin, writing in the *New York Times,* the film was "much too highly charged, brilliantly photographed and well observed to seem ordinary."

Cate Blanchett and Ralph Fiennes in a scene from the 1997 film *Oscar and Lucinda*. (Directed by Gillian Armstrong. Fox Searchlight/ Australian Film Corp/The Kobal Collection/Philip Le Masurier.)

Winner and Losers

Armstrong's 1991 release, *Fires Within*, was a "fiasco," according to the critic for *International Dictionary of Films and Filmmakers*, "a well-meaning but insipid tale of a Cuban political prisoner and his encounter with his family in Miami." Re-edited without any control from Armstrong, the movie was both a commercial and critical failure. However, her next film, *The Last Days of Chez Nous*, a domestic drama set in contemporary Australia, more than made up for the earlier film's failure. The movie follows the fortunes of a pair of sisters, after one of them becomes involved with the other sister's ex-husband. The contributor for *International Dictionary of Films and Filmmakers* found the movie a "thoughtful, well-acted drama," though Canby, in a *New York Times* review called it an "insufferable relationship movie." Far more positive were the comments of *Entertainment Weekly* writer Owen Gleiberman, who termed the film an "edgy tale of marital breakdown." Gleiberman also praised Armstrong for her "evanescent style of naturalistic storytelling, a way of letting a movie float along on wisps of mood, detail, and interior revelation." Similarly, *Nation* critic Stuart Klawans found *The Last Days of Chez Nous* an "enthralling melodrama full of food, amusements and saturated colors."

Armstrong scored one of her strongest successes with *Little Women*, based on the Louisa May Alcott novel about four sisters growing up during the Civil War in Concord, Massachusetts. Carter called this "Armstrong's most-loved, probably most beautifully crafted, and certainly most successful film." Other critics agreed. Maslin, writing in the *New York Times*, termed it an "enchantingly pretty film [that] is so potent that it prompts a rush of recognition from the opening frame." Maslin also noted that Armstrong is "sentimental without being saccharine." Similar praise came from *Entertainment Weekly* contributor Lisa Schwarzbaum, who found *Little Women* a "graceful, unsentimental, well-made movie," as well as "unselfconsciously beautiful." For David Ansen, writing in *Newsweek*, this "lovely, lived-in [film] . . . will seduce us anew." Likewise, Richard Schickel called *Little Women* an "entrancing film" in a *Time* magazine review.

Armstrong worked from another adapted novel, Australian writer Peter Carey's Booker Prize-winning book, in her 1997 *Oscar and Lucinda*. The "tale of two singular misfits whose fates collide because of a shared passion for gambling," as Ansen described the film in *Newsweek*, it stars Ralph Fiennes, as a lover of horse racing who decides to become a missionary, and Cate Blanchett, who plays an Australian heiress with an independent nature.

Cate Blanchett in the film *Charlotte Gray.* (Warner Bros/Channel 4/The Kobal Collection/Buitendijk, Jaap.)

Ansen praised the film as "handsome, literate and ambitious," but also felt that it "just doesn't jell." Maslin had no such reservations in the *New York Times*, noting the film is directed "exquisitely . . . in a headstrong spirit that recalls [Armstrong's] debut feature." Similarly, for *Variety* critic Emanuel Levy, *Oscar and Lucinda* "is a truly poetic movie whose physical production is just as impressive as its spiritual aspirations."

A further period drama is presented in Armstrong's 2001 World War II epic, *Charlotte Gray*, a film less well received critically. Stephen Holden, writing in the *New York Times*, found the film "lumbering," while *Hollywood Reporter* contributor Kirk Honeycutt thought it a "prosaic muddle" that is "lacking any sort of urgency, suspense or passion." Similarly, *Variety* contributor Todd McCarthy felt the film was a "bland and dour" adaptation of the best-selling novel by Sebastian Faulks.

Armstrong has continued to turn her hand to documentaries, as well, including the 2005 feature, *Unfolding Florence: The Many Lives of Florence Broadhurst,* a "spirited and original documentary," according to a reviewer for *Encore* magazine. The film tells the life story of the Australian design pioneer and feminist idol through interviews, re-enactments, and even animation.

If you enjoy the films of Gillian Armstrong, you may also want to check out the following:

The works of directors Ida Lupino, Jodie Foster, and Lina Wertmuller.

Throughout her career, Armstrong has featured strong, female protagonists and has, as Carter concluded, "made a significant contribution to the Australian film industry and culture and is a role model and inspiration to all filmmakers." Specifically, she influenced other female directors in Australia and New Zealand, including Ann Turner and Jane Campion. Armstrong, though internationally known, is a champion of Australian cinema and identity. As she told the Australian television host George Negus, "We should be proud of the things that makes us Australian and we need to encourage that. . . . The whole world could one day be getting everything from America. I mean, should the only thing we see be CNN? The only movies we see American?"

■ **Biographical and Critical Sources**

BOOKS

Collins, Felicity, *The Films of Gillian Armstrong,* AFI 5-Atom (Melbourne, Victoria, Australia), 1999.
International Dictionary of Films and Filmmakers, Volume 2: Directors, 4th ed., St. James Press (Detroit, MI), 2000.
Women Filmmakers & Their Films, St. James Press (Detroit, MI), 1998.

PERIODICALS

Encore, February, 2006, "'Florence' Unfolds to Packed House at Sundance," p.5.

Entertainment Weekly, March 19, 1993, Owen Gleiberman, review of *The Last Days of Chez Nous,* p. 44; December 23, 1994, Lisa Schwarzbaum, review of *Little Women,* p. 49; June 16, 1995, Meredith Berkman, review of *Little Women,* p. 68; January 16, 1998, Lisa Schwarzbaum, review of *Oscar and Lucinda,* p. 49; January 30, 1998, Lisa Schwarzbaum, review of *Oscar and Lucinda,* p. 47; January 18, 2002, Lisa Schwarzbaum, review of *Charlotte Gray,* p. 55.
Hollywood Reporter, December 17, 2001, Kirk Honeycutt, review of *Charlotte Gray,* p. 8.
Nation, March 29, 1993, Stuart Klawans, review of *The Last Days of Chez Nous,* p. 427; January 23, 1995, Stuart Klawans, review of *Little Women,* p. 107.
National Catholic Reporter, January 20, 1995, Joseph Cunneen, review of *Little Women,* p. 30.
National Review, February 20, 1995, John Simon, review of *Little Women,* p. 72.
New Republic, March 29, 1993, Stanley Kauffmann, review of *The Last Days of Chez Nous,* p. 32.
New Statesman, March 27, 1998, Gaby Wood, review of *Oscar and Lucinda,* p. 44.
Newsweek, January 9, 1995, David Ansen, review of *Little Women,* p. 57; January 12, 1998, David Ansen, review of *Oscar and Lucinda,* p. 61.
New York Times, October 6, 1979, Janet Maslin, review of *My Brilliant Career;* November 10, 1982, Janet Maslin, review of *Starstruck;* December 26, 1984, Vincent Canby, review of *Mrs. Soffel;* February 19, 1988, Janet Maslin, review of *High Tide;* February 26, 1983, Vincent Canby, review of *The Last Days of Chez Nous;* December 21, 1994, Janet Maslin, review of *Little Women;* December 31, 1997, Janet Maslin, review of *Oscar and Lucinda;* December 28, 2001, Stephen Holden, review of *Charlotte Gray.*
O, the Oprah Magazine, January, 2002, "Gillian Armstrong's Magnificent Obsessions," p. 98.
People, January 28, 1985, Scot Haller, review of *Mrs. Soffel,* p. 10; January 9, 1995, Leah Rozen, review of *Little Women,* p. 18.
Time, January 14, 1985, review of *Mrs. Soffel,* p. 66; December 19, 1994, Richard Schickel, review of *Little Women,* p. 74.
Variety, December 8, 1997, Emanuel Levy, review of *Oscar and Lucinda,* p. 110; December 17, 2001, Todd McCarthy, review of *Charlotte Gray,* p. 37; February 27, 2006, Russell Edwards, review of *Unfolding Florence: The Many Lives of Florence Broadhurst,* p. 40.

ONLINE

ABC Online, http://www.abc.net.au/ (July 31, 2003), George Negus, "George Negus Tonight: Gillian Armstrong Interview."

Hollywood.com, http://www.hollywood.com/ (September 27, 2006), "Gillian Armstrong."

Internet Movie Database, http://www.imdb.com/ (September 27, 2006), "Gillian Armstrong."

Popcorn Taxi, http://www.popcorntaxi.com.au/ (November 21, 2001), "Meet Gillian Armstrong."

Senses of Cinema, http://www.sensesofcinema.com/ (September 28, 2006), Helen Carter, "Gillian Armstrong."

Tonya Bolden

■ Personal

Born March 1, 1959, in New York, NY; daughter of Willie J. (a garment center shipping manager) and Georgia C. (a homemaker) Bolden; married (divorced, 1990). *Ethnicity:* African-American. *Education:* Princeton University, B.A. (magna cum laude), 1981; Columbia University, M.A., 1985. *Politics:* Independent. *Religion:* Christian.

■ Addresses

Home—New York, NY. *Agent*—Marie Brown Associates, 412 West 154th St., New York, NY 10032. *E-mail*—Tonbolden@aol.com.

■ Career

Charles Alan, Inc., New York, NY, salesperson, 1981-83; Raoulfilm, Inc., New York, NY, office coordinator, 1985-87; research and editorial assistant to food and wine critic William E. Rice, 1987-88; Malcolm-King College, New York, NY, English instructor, 1988-89; College of New Rochelle School of New Resources, New York, NY, English instructor, 1989-90, 1996-2000. Has worked as an editorial consultant to the MTA Arts for Transit Office, and to Harlem River Press/Writers & Readers Publishing, Inc. Member of Westside Repertory Theatre, 1977-82.

■ Member

New York Council for the Humanities Speakers Bureau.

■ Awards, Honors

Mama, I Want to Sing named a Book for the Teen Age, New York Public Library, 1993; *Just Family* named a Junior Library Guild Selection, 1996; *And Not Afraid to Dare* named a Book for the Teen Age, New York Public Library, 1999; *Thirty-three Things Every Girl Should Know* named one of the Best Books for Young Adults by the American Library Association, 1999; *Strong Men Keep Coming: The Book of African-American Men* named a Book for the Teen Age, New York Public Library, 2000; Coretta Scott King Author Honor Book selection, and James Madison Book Award, both 2006, both for *Maritcha: A Nineteenth-century American Girl.*

■ Writings

The Family Heirloom Cookbook, Putnam (New York, NY), 1990.

(With Vy Higginsen) *Mama, I Want to Sing* (young adult novel), Scholastic (New York, NY), 1992.

Starting a Business from Your Home, Longmeadow Press (Stamford, CT), 1993.

Getting into the Mail-Order Business, Longmeadow Press (Stamford, CT), 1994.

(Editor) *Rites of Passage: Stories about Growing up by Black Writers from around the World*, Hyperion (New York, NY), 1994.

Mail Order and Direct Response, Longmeadow Press (Stamford, CT), 1994.

The Book of African-American Women: 150 Crusaders, Creators, and Uplifters, Adams Media (Holbrook, MA), 1996.

Just Family, Cobblehill Books (New York, NY), 1996.

Through Loona's Door: A Tammy and Owen Adventure with Carter G. Woodson, illustrated by Luther Knox, Corporation for Cultural Literacy (Oakland, CA), 1997.

And Not Afraid to Dare: The Stories of Ten African-American Women, Scholastic (New York, NY), 1998.

(Editor) *Thirty-three Things Every Girl Should Know: Stories, Songs, Poems, and Smart Talk by 33 Extraordinary Women*, Crown (New York, NY), 1998.

(With Mother Love) *Forgive or Forget: Never Underestimate the Power of Forgiveness*, HarperCollins (New York, NY), 1999.

Strong Men Keep Coming: The Book of African-American Men, Wiley (New York, NY), 1999.

(With Eartha Kitt) *Rejuvenate!: It's Never Too Late*, Scribner (New York, NY), 2001.

Rock of Ages: A Tribute to the Black Church, illustrated by R. Gregory Christie, Random House (New York, NY), 2001.

Tell All the Children Our Story: Memories and Mementos of Being Young and Black in America, Harry N. Abrams (New York, NY), 2001.

(Editor) *Thirty-three Things Every Girl Should Know about Women's History: From Suffragettes to Skirt Lengths of the E.R.A.*, Random House (New York, NY), 2002.

(Adaptor) Gail Buckley, *American Patriots: The Story of Blacks in the Military from the Revolution to Desert Storm*, Crown (New York, NY), 2003.

Portraits of African-American Heroes, illustrated by Ansel Pitcairn, Dutton (New York, NY), 2003.

Through Loona's Door: A Tammy and Owen Adventure with Carter G. Woodson, illustrated by Luther Knox, Cedar Grove Books (San Francisco, CA), 2003.

(With Chaka Khan) *Chaka!: Through the Fire*, Rodale (Emmaus, PA), 2003.

The Champ: The Story of Muhammad Ali, illustrated by R. Gregory Christie, Dutton (New York, NY), 2004.

The Book of African-American Women: 150 Crusaders, Creators, and Uplifters, Adams Media (Avon, MA), 2004.

Wake up Our Souls: A Celebration of Black American Artists, Abrams (New York, NY), 2004.

Cause: Reconstruction America, 1863-1877, Knopf (New York, NY), 2005.

Maritcha: A Nineteenth-century American Girl, Abrams (New York, NY), 2005.

M.L. K.: Journey of a King, Abrams (New York, NY), 2005.

(With Mother Love) *Half the Mother, Twice the Love: My Journey to Better Health with Diabetes*, Atria Books (New York, NY), 2006.

Take-off!: American All-Girl Bands during World War II, Knopf (New York, NY), 2007.

Also contributor to books, including *Black Arts Annual*, edited by Donald Bogle, Garland, 1990 and 1992, *Go Girl!: The Black Woman's Book of Travel and Adventure*, Elaine Lee, editor, Eighth Mountain Press, 1997, and *Hands On!: 33 More Things Every Girl Should Know*, edited by Suzanne Harper, Random House, 2001. Contributor of book reviews and articles to *Amsterdam News, Black Enterprise, Essence, Excel, Focus, New York Times Book Review, Small Press,* and *YSB.* Editor, *HARKline* (quarterly newsletter of Harkhomes, a shelter for the homeless in Harlem), 1989-90; editor, *Quarterly Black Review of Books*, 1994-95.

■ Sidelights

Tonya Bolden's books present young people with hopeful and positive life examples. In works such as *Tell All the Children Our Story: Memories and Mementos of Being Young and Black in America* and *Wake up Our Souls: A Celebration of Black American Artists*, Bolden explores the lives of prominent African-American figures. A prolific and award-winning author, she has also founded her own Web site and online newsletter.

Born to Willie and Georgia Bolden on March 1, 1959, in New York City. She took an early interest in literature, often writing stories and poems, a habit that continued into her teen years. "As a child I absolutely adored books," she noted on the Random House Web site. "I loved the journeys they allowed, what they taught me about the world, how they gave my imagination a workout." Bolden attended a public elementary school and a private high school, graduating from The Chapin School in 1977. From 1977 through 1982 Bolden was a company member of the Westside Repertory Theatre, using her skills as an actor, stage manager, and assistant

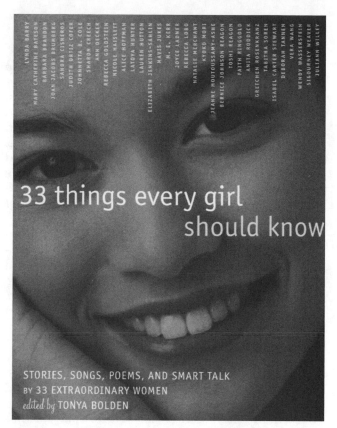

A variety of approaches to life are offered in this 1998 title. (Crown Publishers 1998. Front cover photograph copyright © 1997 by Jim Cummins/FPG International. Used by permission of Crown Publishers, an imprint of Random House Children's Books, a division of Random House, Inc.)

director, and in set construction. Bolden received her bachelor's degree in Slavic languages and literature with a Russian focus, graduating magna cum laude in 1981 from Princeton University. She then earned a master's degree, also in Slavic languages and literature, in 1985 at Columbia University. She later earned a certificate for the advanced study of the Soviet Union from the Harriman Institute at Columbia.

Bolden began her professional career as a salesperson, working for Charles Alan, Inc., a dress manufacturer, in New York City from 1981 to 1983. She also served as liaison between the design, production, and sales departments. In 1985 she moved on to Raoulfilm, Inc. of New York City, working as office coordinator. She also assisted in the research and development of film and literary projects. Bolden moved into the editorial world in 1987 when she worked for food and wine critic William E. Rice, serving as his research and editorial assistant for one year. Also during that year she worked as an

editorial consultant for MTA Arts at the Transit Office. In 1988 Bolden took a position as English instructor at Malcolm-King College; a year later she began teaching English at the College of New Rochelle, School of New Resources, a school for adult learners in New York City.

Makes Literary Debut

Bolden's first book, *The Family Heirloom Cookbook*, was published in 1990 by Putnam. She also published her work as a contributor to *African American History* for publisher Scholastic. In 1993 and 1994 her writings took a business bent and she published *Starting a Business from Your Home* and *Mail-Order and Direct Response*, both by Longmeadow in 1993 and 1994 respectively.

Bolden's writing has not been confined to adult readers; she has published several books for children and adolescents. Bolden's books present young people with hopeful and positive life examples. In *Strong Men Keep Coming: The Book of African-American Men*, she offered more than one hundred short biographies of admirable African-Americans. Her subjects range from well-known people such as W.E.B. DuBois, Jesse Jackson, and Dred Scott, to more obscure figures such as Dave Dinwiddie, a pioneer whose story stretched from Alabama to Oklahoma. Dinwiddie's life contained no groundbreaking discoveries or eye-catching heroism, but his quiet determination to make a good life for himself and his family earned him a spot in Bolden's collection. According to *National Catholic Reporter* contributor Arthur Jones, as a writer Bolden is "quirky" but "not boring." He characterized the author as "a storyteller who editorializes along the way—as good storytellers can without offense." *Strong Men Keep Coming* works both as "an informative read and a textbook," in Jones's opinion. He concluded: "Bolden provided me with insights I didn't have, introduced me to people I didn't know, and the book ended all too soon."

Brave women fill the pages of *And Not Afraid to Dare: The Stories of Ten African-American Women*. The subjects of this book include Ellen Crafts, a light-skinned slave woman who traveled a thousand miles to freedom by posing as an ailing white man attended by a slave, who was really Crafts's husband. Contemporary women such as writer Toni Morrison and athlete Jackie Joyner-Kersee are also profiled. Bolden "writes easily and confidently about her subjects . . . and her compelling stories read like fiction," remarked Lauren Peterson in *Booklist*.

This 2001 history tells what it was like to be young and black in America from Colonial times to the present.
(Scholastic Press, 1998. Copyright © 1998 by Tonya Bolden. Reproduced by permission.)

She coauthored with Vy Higginsen *Mama, I want to Sing* in 1992. Higginsen wrote the hit gospel musical by the same name. The book, a novelization of the musical, is about an eleven-year-old girl torn between pleasing her mother by singing in the church choir and following her dream of popular music. Of this award-winning book, Bolden noted on her Web site, "I had a great time working with the dynamic radio personality Vy Higginsen. . . . Memorable too was meeting the two women on whom the main characters are based."

Her other books authored for young readers include *Just Family*, a novel published by Cobblehill in 1996, *And Not Afraid to Dare: The Stories of Ten African-American Women* by Scholastic in 1998. The latter book's ten biographical sketches portray African American women who were successful in their lives due to their hard work and dedication and who might serve as role models. *Booklist* said of Bolden's work in *And Not Afraid to Dare*, "She writes easily and confidently about her subjects . . . and her compelling stories read like fiction."

Writing for a Young Adult Audience

Bolden has served as editor for several books, including *Rites of Passage: Stories About Growing Up by Black Writers from Around the World* and *Thirty-three Things Every Girl Should Know: Stories, Songs, Poems, and Smart Talk by 33 Extraordinary Women*. In the latter work, Bolden gathered contributions from writers, businesswomen, athletes, artists, and more, all focused on the trials of moving from childhood to adulthood. Communicating with boys, being true to oneself, and dealing with issues such as self-esteem and popularity are all treated. *Booklist* reviewer Shelle Rosenfeld praised *Thirty-three Things Every Girl Should Know*, stating, "Astute, compassionate, sometimes witty, sometimes painfully honest, the pieces are highly readable, entertaining, and educational." In 2002 Bolden published a follow-up titled *Thirty-three Things Every Girl Should Know About Women's History: From Suffragettes to Skirt Lengths of the E.R.A.* The book discusses the role of girls and women in the history of the United States up to the present. "This is a very strong, highly readable offering that gives context to the feminist movement," noted *Booklist* critic Ilene Cooper, and a contributor in Women in Action wrote that *Thirty-three Things Every Girl Should Know About Women's History* "provides an engaging, inspiring, informative look at the role women have played in shaping American history."

In *Rock of Ages: A Tribute to the Black Church*, Bolden explores the history of the Black church from early efforts to freely worship, to the present time and the contributions of the Black Church to American culture. Religion was a powerful force in Bolden's family while she was growing up, and *Rock of Ages* is the author's way of acknowledging the church's role in her life. "The book was in me for years," she told *Bookpage* interviewer Deborah Hopkinson. "I had written a poem about the black church and just put it in a drawer for a long time. I never thought of myself as a poet." When she was later asked to contribute to an anthology, Bolden remembered the poem. "As I looked at it again I realized there was a book in it after all. I also realized it was time to say thank you."

In 2002 Bolden published *Tell All The Children Our Story*, which portrays the lives of African-American children growing up in America, beginning with colonial Jamestown and stretching through the years to the present. Bolden was working on *Tell All The Children Our Story* when the terrorist attacks of September 11, 2001, took place. As many across the nation and the world stood transfixed and grieving, she too found herself trying to comprehend the events, the future, and her place in it. She said in her online newsletter: "In the days immediately following writing was the last thing on my mind. When I thought about what I do for a living I wondered, Does it matter? It was very hard to shake the idea that my work was, well, irrelevant, meaningful in no great way (not when compared with that of firefighters, doctors, nurses, mental health care professionals, and others on the front line of the rescue and recovery efforts)." She found it difficult to keep writing, and had many false starts. Bolden explained in her online newsletter, "I tried to crank stuff out, but nothing I put on paper was close to quality. Day after day I kept going through the motions, and the wastebasket filled up. No matter how hard I tried I couldn't make writing matter." Eventually she found her way and completed the book. The subjects of the book itself helped her in the task. "Most of the subjects had known struggle, adversity, sorrow, pain . . . and gone on to do things with their lives that mattered, and matter still. . . . And if I can tell their stories in a way that will engage the minds of the children, that will

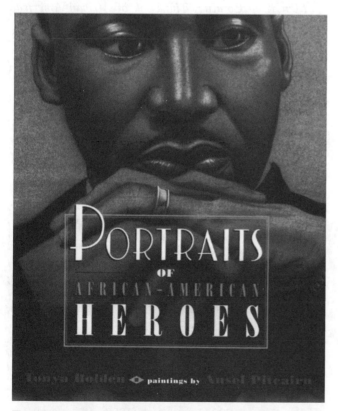

Twenty outstanding black heroes are profiled in this 2003 book. (Puffin Books, 2003. Reproduced by permission of Puffin Books, a division of Penguin Putnam Books for Young Readers.)

give children hope, courage, and a longing to live productive lives, well then, . . . maybe what I do will matter," Bolden said in her online newsletter.

Examining Black History

In *Portraits of African-American Heroes*, Bolden offers biographies of twenty significant historical and contemporary figures. Among the individuals profiled are abolitionist Frederick Douglass, musician Dizzy Gillespie, civil rights leader Martin Luther King, Jr., educator Ruth Simmons, and journalist Charlayne Hunter-Gault. Terry Glover, reviewing the work in *Booklist*, praised the way Bolden presents "keen insights into a subject's personality based on interviews and information drawn from personal memoirs," and a *Kirkus Reviews* critic deemed *Portraits of African-American Heroes* "a fascinating and unique collection." *Wake up Our Souls: A Celebration of Black American Artists* contains of selection of African-American painters, sculptors, photographers, and other artists. Bolden examines not only the artists' lives but their careers as well, and she discusses a representative work from each individual. The author "does a fine job of describing the larger social and political climate in which the artists worked as well as the pervasive discrimination they suffered," according to *Booklist* reviewer Gillian Engberg.

Bolden looks at an important period in U.S. history in *Cause: Reconstruction America, 1863-1877*. The author examines such topics as the Civil Rights Act of 1866, the struggles of freed slaves, and the women's suffrage movement. "Writing from an African American's perspective, Bolden handles the material in an evenhanded manner," observed *Booklist* critic Carolyn Phelan. In *Maritcha: A Nineteenth-century American Girl*, Bolden expands upon a profile originally featured in *Tell All The Children Our Story*. Maritcha Remond Lyons was a free Black child born to a middle-class family in Manhattan in 1848. Her parents' home served as a stop on the Underground Railroad, and she became the first Black student to graduate from Providence High School in Rhode Island. "Bolden draws on a typewritten memoir Maritcha produced late in life and a fine array of photographs, prints, and documents to tell her story," noted Margaret A. Bush in *Horn Book*, and a *Kirkus Reviews* critic remarked that Maritcha's "story provides a valuable glimpse into a history largely forgotten."

If you enjoy the works of Tonya Bolden, you may also want to check out the following books:

James Haskins, *Outward Dreams: Black Inventors and Their Inventions*, 1991.
Lonnie Wheeler, *I Had a Hammer: The Hank Aaron Story*, 1991.
Ellen Levine, *Freedom's Children: Young Civil Rights Activists Tell Their Own Stories*, 1993.

A versatile writer, Bolden has also written study guides for the Carter G. Woodson Foundation Artists-in-the Schools program, including studies of black poet Langston Hughes, on Africa and its people, and on the African contribution to music. She has maintained a busy appearance schedule, visiting schools, book fairs, libraries, book stores, presenting at workshops and serving as author-in-residence, and giving interviews on radio and television. Despite what can be a grueling schedule, she noted in her online newsletter: "I am so grateful to be making a living doing something I love so much."

■ Biographical and Critical Sources

PERIODICALS

American Visions, December, 1997, review of *Through Loona's Door: A Tammy and Owen Adventure with Carter G. Woodson*, p. 34.

Arts & Activities, February, 2005, Jerome J. Hausman, review of *Wake up Our Souls: A Celebration of Black American Artists*, pp. 10-11.

Black Issues Book Review, January, 1999, review of *Thirty-three Things Every Girl Should Know: Stories, Songs, Poems, and Smart Talk by Thirty-Three Extraordinary Women*, p. 56; March-April, 2004, Angela P. Dodson, "300 Years of Black Art," review of *Wake up Our Souls*, p. 37.

Bookbird, summer, 1995, review of *Rites of Passage: Stories about Growing up by Black Writers Around the World*, p. 57.

Booklist, February 15, 1996, Carolyn Phelan, review of *Just Family*, p. 1020; February 15, 1998, Lauren Peterson, review of *And Not Afraid to Dare: The Stories of Ten African-American Women*, p. 993; May

15, 1998, Shelle Rosenfeld, review of *Thirty-three Things Every Girl Should Know*, p. 1611; March 15, 1999, review of *Thirty-three Things Every Girl Should Know*, p. 1297; March 1, 2002, Ilene Cooper, review of *Thirty-three Things Every Girl Should Know about Women's History: From Suffragettes to Skirt Lengths to the E.R. A.*, p. 1146; October 15, 2003, Vanessa Bush, review of *Chaka! Through the Fire*, p. 374; February 15, 2004, Gillian Engberg, review of *Wake up Our Souls: a Celebration of Black American Artists*, p. 1065; March 15, 2004, Terry Glover, review of *The Champ: The Story of Muhammad Ali*, p. 1301; November 15, 2004, John Green, review of *Portraits of African-American Heroes*, p. 575; February 1, 2005, Gillian Engberg, review of *Maritcha: a Nineteenth-Century American Girl*, p. 970; October, 2005, Carolyn Phelan, review of *Cause: Reconstruction America, 1863-1877*, p. 40.

Book Report, September-October, 1996, Karen Sebesta, review of *Just Family*, p. 36; November-December, 1998, Melanie Scalpello, review of *Thirty-three Things Every Girl Should Know*, p. 82, and Sandra B. Connell, review of *And Not Afraid to Dare*, p. 82; May-June, 2002, Ann M.G. Gray, review of *Tell All the Children Our Story*, p. 65.

Book World, January 5, 1997, review of *The Book of African-American Women: 150 Crusaders, Creators, and Uplifters*, p. 13; July 4, 1999, review of *Strong Men Keep Coming: The Book of African-American Men*, p. 11.

Bulletin of the Center for Children's Books, May, 1998, review of *And Not Afraid to Dare*, p. 312; June, 1998, review of *Thirty-three Things Every Girl Should Know*, p. 353.

Children's Book Review Service, April, 1998, review of *And Not Afraid to Dare*, p. 104.

Footsteps, September-October, 2003, review of *American Patriots: The Story of Blacks in the Military from the Revolution to Desert Storm*, p. 49; March-April, 2005, Jason M. Wells, "Crazy about Writing," p. 46.

Horn Book, September, 1995, Rudine Sims Bishop, review of *Rites of Passage*, p. 578; March-April, 2002, Betty Carter, review of *Tell All the Children Our Story*, p. 226; July-August, 2002, Nell D. Beram, review of *Thirty-three Things Every Girl Should Know about Women's History*, p. 483; January-February, 2005, Kathleen Isaacs, review of *The Champ*, pp. 106-107, and Margaret A. Bush, review of *Maritcha*, p. 107.

Horn Book Guide, fall, 1996, review of *Just Family*, p. 290; fall, 1998, review of *Thirty-three Things Every Girl Should Know*, p. 406; review of *And Not Afraid to Dare*, p. 418.

Kirkus Reviews, December 1, 1995, review of *Just Family*, p. 1700; January 1, 1998, review of *And Not Afraid to Dare*, p. 54; March 1, 1998, review of *Thirty-three Things Every Girl Should Know*, p. 335;

December 1, 2002, review of *American Patriots*, p. 1766; December 15, 2003, review of *Portraits of African-American Heroes*, p. 1446; December 15, 2004, review of *Maritcha* and *The Champ*, p. 1198; November 15, 2005, review of *Cause*, p. 1230.

Kliatt, November, 1995, review of *Rites of Passage*, p. 21; May, 1998, review of *Thirty-three Things Every Girl Should Know*, p. 27.

Library Journal, November 15, 1999, Lisa S. Wise, review of *Forgive or Forget: Never Underestimate the Power of Forgiveness*, p. 86.

National Catholic Reporter, January 28, 2000, Arthur Jones, review of *Strong Men Keep Coming*, p. 15.

Publishers Weekly, March 9, 1998, review of *Thirty-three Things Every Girl Should Know*, p. 69; October 4, 1999, review of *Forgive or Forget*, p. 55; July 16, 2001, p. 150; March 11, 2002, review of *Tell All the Children Our Story*, pp. 73-74; July 7, 2003, review of *Chaka*, p. 59; January 3, 2005, review of *The Champ*, p. 55, and review of *Maritcha*, p. 57.

Reading Teacher, March, 1999, review of *And Not Afraid to Dare*, p. 624.

School Arts, November, 2004, Ken Marantz, review of *Wake up Our Souls*, p. 56.

School Library Journal, May, 1996, Susan W. Hunter, review of *Just Family*, p. 110; March, 1998, review of *And Not Afraid to Dare*, p. 228; May, 1998, review of *Thirty-three Things Every Girl Should Know*, p. 150; March, 2002, Carol Jones Collins, review of *Tell All the Children Our Story*, p. 244;

April, 2002, Lee Bock, review of *Thirty-three Things Every Girl Should Know about Women's History*, p. 164; February, 2003, review of *American Patriots*, p. 154; January, 2004, Mary N. Oluonye, review of *Portraits of African-American Heroes*, pp. 140-141; July, 2004, review of *Wake up Our Souls*, p. 117; January, 2005, review of *The Champ*, p. 107; February, 2005, Carolyn Janssen, review of *Maritcha*, p. 145; November, 2005, review of *Cause*, p. 153.

Voice of Youth Advocates, October, 1996, review of *Just Family*, p. 205; June, 1998, review of *And Not Afraid to Dare*, p. 139; August, 1999, review of *Thirty-three Things Every Girl Should Know*, p. 165.

Women in Action, December, 2002, review of *Thirty-three Things Every Girl Should Know about Women's History*, p. 42.

ONLINE

Bookpage Web site, http://www.bookpage.com/ (February, 2002), Deborah Hopkinson, "Tonya Bolden: Capturing Childhood and Community."

Education World, http://www.education-world.com/ (February 19, 2001), "Ten African-American Women Who 'Dared' to Make a Difference."

Random House Web site, http://www.randomhouse.com/ (September 1, 2006), "Tonya Bolden."

Tonya Bolden Web site, http://www.tonyabolden.com (September 1, 2006).

Kate Brian

■ Personal

Born 1974, in NJ; married; husband's name Matt. *Education:* Graduate, Rutgers University. *Hobbies and other interests:* Watching movies, going to the gym, taking night classes.

■ Addresses

Home—Westwood, NJ.

■ Career

Writer.

■ Writings

The Princess and the Pauper, Simon & Schuster Books for Young Readers (New York, NY), 2003.

The V Club, Simon & Schuster Books for Young Readers (New York, NY), 2004, paperback edition published as *The Virginity Club,* Simon Pulse (New York, NY), 2005.

Megan Meade's Guide to the McGowan Boys, Simon & Schuster Books for Young Readers (New York, NY), 2005.

Lucky T, Simon & Schuster Books for Young Readers (New York, NY), 2005.

Sweet 16, Simon & Schuster Books for Young Readers (New York, NY), 2006.

Private, Simon Pulse (New York, NY), 2006.

Invitation Only, Simon Pulse (New York, NY), 2006.

Untouchable, Simon Pulse (New York, NY), 2006.

AS KIERAN SCOTT

Leonardo DiCaprio (biography), Aladdin Paperback (New York, NY), 1998.

Matt Damon (biography), Aladdin Paperback (New York, NY), 1998.

Ultimate Cheerleading (nonfiction), Scholastic (New York, NY), 1998.

James Van Der Beek (biography), Aladdin Paperback (New York, NY), 1999.

How Do I Tell? ("Love Stories" Series), Random House (New York, NY), 1999.

While You Were Gone ("Love Stories" Series), Random House (New York, NY), 1999.

Dance ("Love Stories" Series), Random House (New York, NY), 1999.

Kiss and Tell ("Love Stories" Series), Random House (New York, NY), 1999.

Trust Me ("Love Stories" Series), Random House (New York, NY), 1999.

Cameron Diaz (biography), Chelsea House (New York, NY), 2001.

Selma Hayek (biography), Chelsea House (New York, NY), 2001.

(With Joe Neumaier) *I Was a Mouseketeer!* (nonfiction), Disney Press (New York, NY), 2001.

Jingle Boy (novel), Delacorte (New York, 2003.

I Was a Non-Blonde Cheerleader (novel), Putnam (New York, NY), 2005.

Brunettes Strike Back (novel), Putnam (New York, NY), 2006.

Boys, Blondes, and Basketball (novel), Putnam (New York, NY), 2007.

Also the author, under various pseudonyms, of novelizations of television series, including *Charmed*, *Alias*, and *Everwood*.

■ Adaptations

Princess and the Pauper was optioned for Walt Disney Pictures and Television.

■ Sidelights

Kieran Scott is the author of numerous novels for young adult readers under her own name and using the pseudonym of Kate Brian. Among her most popular titles are *The Princess and the Pauper, The V Club,* and *I Was a Non-Blonde Cheerleader.* Known for her lighthearted humor and readability, Brian has attracted a large fan base to her tales of high school angst. Speaking with an interviewer for *TeenReads. com,* Brian expounded on the use of humor in her books: "I think we all take ourselves too seriously. Plus, I think characters who are able to laugh at themselves and learn from their mistakes and move on are more fun to read about than people who sort of mope around and let things get to them too much. They make for better light comedy, too!"

New Jersey Girl

Born in New Jersey, in 1974, Brian enjoyed reading as a child. Her favorite authors were Laura Ingalls Wilder, who wrote the "Little House" books, and Lucy Maud Montgomery, author of *Anne of Green Gables.* Brian read all the books by both writers over and over. "I think I was supposed to be born in the 1800's as a precocious girl with braids," she told an interviewer for *YA & Kids Books Central.* Brian also enjoyed singing and acting as a youth, and in high school was a cheerleader, an activity that she has used numerous times in her writings. She gradu-

They just can't wait till graduation.

The Virginity Club

formerly titled the v club

KATE BRIAN

Author of THE PRINCESS & THE PAUPER

This 2004 novel tells of four high-school girls who pledge to remain pure to win a scholarship. (Cover photograph copyright © by Michael Frost. Reproduced by the permission of the photographer.)

ated from Rutgers University, majoring both in English and journalism. She began her writing career soon after graduation, penning short biographies of movie stars such as Leonardo DiCaprio, and also contributing several volumes to the Random House romance series, "Love Stories."

Brian's first novels appeared in 2003. As Kieran Scott, she published *Jingle Boy,* and writing as Kate Brian, she released the popular *The Princess and the Pauper.* The former title features a male protagonist, her only book to do so. Paul Nicholas is a Christmas-loving teen, but this Christmas things take a sudden turn for the worse when he sees his girlfriend kissing Santa Claus (a.k.a. Scooby the Skank) at the mall, his father is electrocuted putting up the family's over-abundant light display, and his mother gets fired from her job. Santa himself needs to intervene to set things aright in this "perfect book to read next to a fire with a cup of hot chocolate," according to *TeenReads.com* contributor Carlie Kraft Webber, who concluded that it was "a great book to get—and give!" Reviewing the same novel in *Kliatt*, Michele Winship found the work "silly and full of slap stick," further noting that it "could end up on the big screen as an antidote to the usual Christmas madness."

In *The Princess and the Pauper*, Brian turns the old fairy tale on its head, with a European princess changing places with a poor American girl. Carina is the Crown Princess of the tiny nation of Vineland, and is bored with her cushy life. Visiting Los Angeles, she is anxious to go to a rock concert without her usual chaperones. On a tour of the Rosewood Academy, where her grandmother went to school, Carina makes the acquaintance of the scholarship student, Julia, who bears a remarkable resemblance to the princess. Thus Carina comes up with the plan to switch places: Julia will go to an embassy party, dressed as the princess, while Carina will be able to go to the rock concert. But things do not go as expected, especially when Julia falls in love with the boyfriend of the princess. Heather E. Miller, writing in the *School Library Journal*, praised this "light story generously peppered with modern-day references to movie stars, musical styles, and teenage slang." Similarly, Eva Mitnick, writing in *Booklist*, noted that "although the plot is pure fairy tale, the humor is incisive, . . . and the touch of sweet, G-rated romance will thrill the intended audience." A *Publishers Weekly* reviewer observed that Brian "sets out to capture readers whose literary tastes run to light," and "crowns the tale with an ending worthy of any felicitous fairy tale."

Of Blondes and Virgins

Under her real name, Scott published the 2005 humorous novel, *I Was a Non-Blonde Cheerleader*, featuring brunette Annisa, who moves from New Jersey to Florida and is one of only a handful of non-blondes in the entire school. Even the African-American football coach has dyed his hair blond. She tries out to be a cheerleader and surprisingly wins, the only non-blonde on the squad, and she must deal with attempts at hazing by the other girls because of her outsider status. Scott includes inside information on the techniques of cheerleading and of cheerleading competitions in this book that is "lighthearted fun," according to *Kliatt* contributor Claire Rosser, who also noted that the "rivalries and pranks [are] related with sardonic wit by Annisa."

More praise came from a *Publishers Weekly* contributor, who called the book a "breezy, upbeat celebration of the twin virtues of cheerleading and staying true to one's self." A *Kirkus Reviews* critic commended the "excellent writing" in this book that "should hold young readers' interest throughout." The adventures of Annisa continue in *Brunettes Strike Back* and *Boys, Blondes, and Basketball.*

Writing as Kate Brian, Scott has assembled a succession of popular teen novels. She followed up the success of *The Princess and the Pauper* with the 2004 novel, *The V Club* (published as *The Virginity Club* in its paperback edition). The premise of the novel is a new college scholarship for which purity is one of the requirements. Four friends—Mandy, Kai, Debbie, and Eva—translate this requirement to mean virginity. With $160,000 on the line, these friends go all out to compete for the prize, and complications ensue as boyfriends desire to take relationships to a more intimate level and friendships are strained. A

A teenaged girl finds herself living in a house with seven boys in this 2005 novel. (Cover design by Greg Stadnyk. Cover photograph copyright © 2005 by Michael Frost.)

Kirkus Reviews critic had high praise for *The V Club,* calling it "exceptional chick lit," with "quick pacing, snappy dialogue, clever plotting, authentic characters, and lots of good, clean fun." The same contributor thought Brian was "at the top of her game here." Similarly, *School Library Journal* contributor Catherine Ensley noted that the author's "intuitive understanding of the roller coaster of emotions that teens go through . . . is right on target." A *Booklist* contributor observed that the author's use of alternating points of view allowed her to "represent the full range of teens' attitudes about sex and levels of sexual experience." For a *Publishers Weekly* reviewer, the "feel-good message about remaining true to oneself provides just enough ballast to prevent this fluffy confection form floating entirely away."

In *Megan Meade's Guide to the McGowan Boys,* the author tells the tale of the daughter of military parents who does not want to accompany them to a new posting in South Korea. Instead, she convinces them to allow her to finish high school in the United States by staying with friends, the McGowan family, which has seven sons. Tensions as well as romance arise, as Megan interacts with the boys in this "well-rounded story [that] hits some interesting notes," as *Booklist* contributor Ilene Cooper described it. A critic for *Kirkus Reviews* thought that readers would "enjoy the escapism—if they can overlook the rather formulaic characterizations." In *Lucky T,* Carrie, a fifteen-year-old girl, travels to India in search of her lucky T-shirt that had been given to her by her divorced father and mistakenly donated to charity. She traces the shirt to India and goes there with friends under the guise of volunteering. As the search progresses, Carrie slowly loses her self-centeredness and selfishness as she is exposed to some worldly realities. A *Kirkus Reviews* contributor felt the novel was "sufficiently well-written, with some suspense and comedy, to appeal to a wide range of younger readers." Similarly, *School Library Journal* writer Julie Webb found the book an "enjoyable read in which girl gets the guy, reconciles with her best friend, and learns what matters most in life."

If you enjoy the works of Kate Brian, you may also want to check out the following books:

Lois Lowry, *Your Move, J.P.!,* 1990.
Ann Brashares, *The Sisterhood of the Traveling Pants,* 2001.
Martha Brooks, *True Confessions of a Heartless Girl,* 2002.

Another materialistic teen is presented in *Sweet 16,* in which Teagan Phillips is planning the most expensive, glamorous sixteenth birthday party ever for herself. However, things do not turn out quite how she expected in this novel which takes the young girl into her present, past, and future, much like the character of Scrooge in Charles Dickens's *A Christmas Carol.* The author's 2006 novel, *Private,* inaugurated the "Private" series, which follows the fortunes of Reed Brennan, who wins a scholarship to exclusive Easton Academy and is overjoyed to leave her boring suburban existence behind. Once at Easton she attempts to ingratiate herself with the popular Billings Girls, yet remain true to her own values and to her newfound boyfriend, Thomas Pearson. A *Publishers Weekly* critic concluded: "Readers will no doubt eagerly await the next installment." That next installment, *Invitation Only,* continues Reed's experiences at Easton Academy, now accepted as one of the Billings Girls, and *Untouchable* furthers the series.

Busy on numerous writing projects under two names, Brian finds that creating characters is the best thing about writing. As she noted to the *YA & Kids Books Central* interviewer: "When I'm writing a book my favorite part is creating the characters. I love to get inside their heads and find out who they are and how they think and how they react to different situations." In the same interview, she advised young writers to "carry a notebook and pen with you wherever you go. You never know when an idea is going to strike you or when you might see an interesting person or place and want to write down the details."

■ Biographical and Critical Sources

PERIODICALS

Booklist, October 15, 2003, Eva Mitnick, review of *The Princess and the Pauper,* p. 404; June 1, 2004, review of *The V Club,* p. 1716; September 15, 2005, Ilene Cooper, review of *Megan Meade's Guide to the McGowan Boys,* p. 76;
CosmoGirl!, March, 2006, Kate Brian, "My First Senior Party," p. 176.
Hollywood Reporter, June 25, 2004, Boyrs Kit, "Dis Busy Spin on 'Pauper' Tale," p. 3.
Kirkus Reviews, April 1, 2004, review of *The V Club,* p. 325; January 1, 2005, review of *I Was a Non-Blonde Cheerleader,* p. 56; June 15, 2005, review of *Lucky T,* p. 678; September 15, 2005, review of *Megan Meade's Guide to the McGowan Boys,* p. 1021.
Kliatt, September, 2003, Michele Winship, review of *Jingle Boy;* January, 2005, Claire Rosser, review of *I Was a Non-Blonde Cheerleader;* May, 2005, Myrna Marler, review of *The Virginity Club,* p. 20; Septem-

ber, 2005, Janis Flint-Ferguson, review of *Megan Meade's Guide to the McGowan Boys*, p. 5; January, 2006, Michele Winship, review of *Jingle Boy*.

Publishers Weekly, June 16, 2003, review of *The Princess and the Pauper*, p. 72; April 12, 2004, review of *The V Club*, p. 68; June 14, 2004, review of *The Princess and the Pauper*, p. 65; February 28, 2005, review of *I Was a Non-Blonde Cheerleader*, p. 68; July 25, 2005, review of *The Virginity Club*, p. 79; July 24, 2006, review of *Private*, p. 59.

School Library Journal, August, 2003, Heather E. Miller, review of *The Princess and the Pauper*, p. 154; June, 2004, Catherine Ensley, review of *The V Club*, p. 135; September, 2005, Julie Webb, review of *Lucky T*, p. 198; November, 2005, Amy Patrick, review of *Megan Meade's Guide to the McGowan Boys*, p. 128; June, 2006, Suzanne Gordon, review of *Sweet 16*, p. 148.

ONLINE

Bookburger, http://www.bookburger.typepad.com/ (June 19, 2006), "Kieran Scott."

Penguin Group (USA) Web site, http://us.penguingroup.com/ (August 29, 2006), "Kieran Scott."

SimonSays.com, http://www.simonsays.com/ (August 29, 2006), "Kate Brian."

TeenReads.com, http://www.teenreads.com/ (November, 2003), "Kieran Scott Interview"; (August 29, 2006), Amy Alessio, review of *The V Club*, and Carlie Kraft Webber, review of *Jingle Boy*.

YA and Kids Books Central, http://www.yabookscentral.com/ (July, 2005), "Interviews: Kate Brian."*

Mikhail Bulgakov

■ Personal

Born in 1891 in Kiev, Russia; died of sclerosis, March 10, 1940, in Moscow, U.S.S.R. (now Russia); son of a theologian. *Education:* University of Kiev, medical degree, 1916, graduated with distinction.

■ Career

Physician, 1916-19; writer and dramatist, 1919-1940; journalist and dramatist for newspapers and local theaters in Vladikavkaz, 1919-21; worked as a journalist and editor for various newspapers in Moscow, 1921-25; producer for Moscow Art Theater, 1930-36. *Military service:* Russian Army, 1916-1918, served in frontline military hospitals.

■ Writings

PLAYS

Samooborona, produced at Vladikavkaz, First Soviet Theater, Moscow, Russia, 1920.

Brat'ia Turbinykh, produced at Vladikavkaz, First Soviet Theater, Moscow, Russia, 1920.

Parizhskie kommunary, produced at Vladikavkaz, First Soviet Theater, Moscow, Russia, 1921.

Synov'ia mully, produced at Vladikavkaz, First Soviet Theater, Moscow, Russia, 1921.

Dni Turbinykh, produced at the Moscow Art Theatre, Moscow, Russia, 1926.

Zoikina kvartira, produced at the Vkhtangov Theatre in Moscow, Russia, 1926, translation published as *Zoyka's Apartment,* Smith and Kraus, 1995.

Bagrovyi ostrov, produced at the Kamerny Theatre in Moscow, Russia, 1928.

Kabala sviatosh, 1936.

Posledniye dni, 1943, translation published as *The Last Days (Pushkin)* in *Russian Literature Triquarterly,* 1976.

Beg, 1957.

Blazhenstvo, 1966, translation published as *Bliss* in *Russian Literature Triquarterly,* 1976.

Flight: A Play in Eight Dreams and Four Acts, translation by Mirra Ginsburg, Grove (New York, NY), 1969.

The Early Plays of Mikhail Bulgakov, Ardis (Ann Arbor, MI), 1972, 2nd edition, 1994.

Six Plays, translations by Michael Glenny, William Powell, and Michael Earley, Methuen Drama, 1991.

NOVELS

Belaia gvardiia: Dni Turbinykh, 1927, translation published as *The White Guard,* 1971.

Teatral'nyi roman (unfinished novel), 1965, translation published as *Black Snow: A Theatrical Novel,* 1967.

Master i Margarita, censored edition, 1966, uncensored edition, 1969, translation published as *The Master and Margarita,* 1967, new translation by Diana Burgin and Katherine Tiernan O'Connor, Ardis (Ann Arbor, MI), 1995.

Sobache serdtse, 1969, translation published as *The Heart of a Dog,* 1968.

OTHER

Diavoliada (short stories), 1925, translation published as *Diaboliad, and Other Stories,* 1972.

Zhizn gospodina de Molera (biography), 1962, translation published as *The Life of Monsieur de Moliere,* 1970.

Zapiski iunogo vracha (short stories), 1963, translation published as *A Country Doctor's Notebooks,* 1975.

The Heart of a Dog and Other Stories, translations by Kathleen Cook-Horujy and Avril Pyman, Raduga (Moscow, Russia), 1990.

Manuscripts Don't Burn: Mikhail Bulgakov, A Life in Letters and Diaries, edited by J.A.E. Curtis, Overlook, 1992.

Notes on the Cuff and Other Stories, translation by Alison Rice, Ardis (Ann Arbor, MI), 1992.

■ **Adaptations**

The Master and Margarita was adapted for the theater by Jean-Claude van Italie and published by Dramatists Play Service, 1995; it was also adapted as a 10-part film by Vladimir Bortko for Russian television.

■ **Sidelights**

Considered one of the foremost satirists of early Communist Russia, Mikhail Bulgakov is best known for his novel *Master i Margarita* (*The Master and Margarita*), which is recognized as one of the greatest Russian novels of the twentieth century. Many of Bulgakov's works concern the adjustment of the Russian intellectual class to life under communist rule. Heavily influenced by Nikolai Gogol, Bulgakov combined fantasy, realism, and satire to ridicule modern progressive society in general and the oppressive Soviet system in particular. His works celebrate the nonconformist, and often portray an artist or scientist in conflict with society. Due to official censorship of his manuscripts during his lifetime, Bulgakov's best works remained unpublished until after his death. Amy Singleton Adams,

writing in the *Dictionary of Literary Biography,* explained that "Bulgakov faced daunting obstacles: the chaos of World War I, the Russian Revolution, and the ensuing civil war; disease, poverty, and homelessness during the early 1920s; and political oppression and censorship during his last decade." In opposition to these difficult circumstances, Bulgakov took comfort in his writing. Adams wrote: "For Bulgakov, the written word became a victory over history." Bulgakov's "literary life was a tangled web of frustrations, intrigues and reversals," wrote a critic for the *Economist.* "Most of his plays were never performed; his novels—with the exception of *The White Guard,* an autobiographical chronicle of Russia's civil war—remained unpublished until long after his death. The reason is simply explained: he was among the most intransigent of Bolshevism's opponents."

A Medical Education

Bulgakov was born in 1891 into a Russian family of the intellectual class in the Ukrainian city of Kiev. Music, literature, and theater were important in the family life of the young Bulgakov, as was religion. The family could boast several priests and a famous theologian among its members. Bulgakov's own father was a professor at the Kiev theological academy. He instilled in his son a belief in God and an interest in spiritual matters that he would retain throughout his life. Bulgakov attended Kiev's most prestigious secondary school, the First Kiev Gymnasium, where he earned a reputation for playing practical jokes and inventing stories. Adams recounted: "At school Bulgakov enthralled his classmates with tales that combined fact with fiction so seamlessly that one could not be distinguished from the other. As he did at home, he devised sketches and verbal hoaxes designed to mystify and confuse his listeners." When Bulgakov was sixteen years old, his father died unexpectedly in 1907, leaving behind a wife and seven children. To support the family, Bulgakov's mother worked as a teacher and then as treasurer with the Froebel Society for Furthering the Cause of Education. Although finances were strained, Bulgakov graduated and continued his education as a medical student at the University of Kiev, graduating with distinction in 1916. Assigned to noncombat duty in the Russian army during World War I, Bulgakov worked for several months in frontline military hospitals until he transferred to a remote village, where he served as the only doctor for an entire district. His trials as an inexperienced doctor working under primitive conditions, and the difficulties he faced as an educated man among the ignorant, superstitious peasants, are recorded in the autobiographical

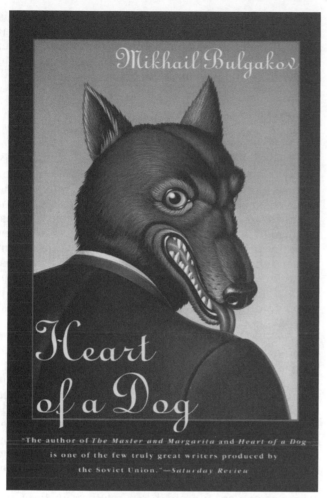

Mikhail Bulgakov

Heart of a Dog

"The author of *The Master and Margarita* and *Heart of a Dog* is one of the few truly great writers produced by the Soviet Union." —*Saturday Review*

A stray dog, crossed with a human criminal, rises to the top of the Soviet bureaucracy in this 1925 novel. (Grove Press, 1968. Reproduced by permission.)

stories published later in *Zapiski iunogo vracha* (*A Country Doctor's Notebooks*). Upon his discharge in 1918 Bulgakov returned to Kiev in time to witness the Bolshevik Red Army, the anti-Bolshevik White Army (pro-Royalist troops), German occupation forces, and Ukrainian nationalists struggling for control of the city, which experienced fourteen violent changes of government in two years. Under Ukrainian nationalist control, the city's Jews were the focus of a terror campaign. When the Red Army took over, the intelligensia were rounded up and murdered. Bulgakov's first novel, *Belaia gvardiia* (*The White Guard*), deals with the life of a family in Kiev during this period.

Bulgakov's time as a doctor led to his first serious writing. Adams explained that "the idea of writing became his sole means of battling his intense feelings of isolation." In 1919 he published his first

story, and the following year he abandoned medicine to devote his time to writing feuilletons for local newspapers and plays for local theaters in the Caucasian city of Vladikavkaz. For a brief time, Bulgakov was head of the literary section of the "People's Commissariat of Enlightenment," set up by the victorious communist government to control public art activities. He was fired when his earlier support for the White Army was discovered. In 1921 he moved to Moscow, where he struggled to support himself and his first wife by editing and writing for various newspapers, a task which he described as "a flow of hopeless grey boredom, unbroken and inexorable." "The true beginning of his writing career," Adams noted, "also marked the start of Bulgakov's lifelong problems with the censorship of the official Soviet literary community and, because writing was now his sole livelihood, with the difficulties of basic survival."

Soviet-Era Plays

Bulgakov did manage to have several short plays staged at the First Soviet Theater. Because the Russian Civil War was still raging, and the communist authorities were more interested in military campaigns against their enemies than with artistic performances, the Russian arts community enjoyed a measure of freedom in the early 1920s that they would not enjoy again until the 1990s. Beginning in 1920, Bulgakov staged the popular success *Brat'ia Turbinykh* (*The Brothers Turbin*), which dramatized events he and his family had undergone in Kiev. His next play, *Glinianye zhenikhi* (*The Clay Bridegroom*) was a lighthearted comedy out of step with communist demands for a politically-committed art. It was not allowed to be staged. Bulgakov learned his lesson. His next play, 1921's *Parizhskie kommunary* (*The Parisian Communards*), celebrated the fiftieth anniversary of the Paris Commune, when leftist radicals had seized the city and held it for several months. Adams found that this play "seemed to alleviate the weight of Bulgakov's bourgeois reputation."

With the partial publication in 1925 of *The White Guard* in the magazine *Rossiya*, Bulgakov gained sufficient respect and popularity as an author to abandon newspaper work. Although his subsequent dramatization of the novel as *Dni Turbinykh* (*Days of the Turbins*) was severely criticized by orthodox communists for sympathetically portraying the officer class of the White Army, it was immediately popular with audiences and became one of Soviet Russia's best-loved plays. Soviet dictator Joseph Stalin himself attended the production fifteen times, viewing the play as ultimately favorable to the

MIKHAIL BULGAKOV

The White Guard

"A writer of fantastic genius."—*Sunday Times*

This 1923 novel tells of the plight of the Turbin family during the battle for Kiev in the Russian Civil War. (McGraw-Hill, Inc, 2000. Reproduced by permission.)

Bolsheviks. By 1929, however, Bulgakov had fallen seriously out of favor with Soviet authorities and his works were banned for their ideological nonconformity.

For the next two years Bulgakov was unable to earn a living, and in 1930, frustrated, depressed, and penniless, he wrote to the Soviet government, asking to be allowed either to work or to emigrate. Stalin personally telephoned Bulgakov three weeks later and arranged for his appointment to the Art Theater as a producer. In 1932, reportedly at Stalin's request once again, *Days of the Turbins* was returned to the stage, making it possible for Bulgakov to have other works published and performed. He remained with the Art Theater until 1936, when he resigned in protest over what he saw as the mishandling of his drama *Kabala sviatosh* (*A Cabal of Hypocrites*), at which time he became a librettist for the Bolshoi Theater. Though publishing little, Bulgakov wrote steadily until his death from nephrosclerosis in 1940.

Battling Soviet Censorship

Bulgakov is believed to have written thirty-six plays, eleven of which survive. Unlike his major prose works, Bulgakov's dramas tend toward the realistic, and are often based on historical events or figures. In direct opposition to Soviet conventions, Bulgakov refused to portray his characters as either wholly positive or negative; rather, they are drawn as individuals with human strengths and frailties. The theme of adjustment to the new Soviet way of life dominates his plays of the 1920s. His best-known drama, *Days of the Turbins*, has been viewed as Moscow's most important theatrical event of the decade and served as the focus for the debate then being waged over the place of art in post-revolutionary society. The play, which deals with the life of a family of Russian intellectuals in Kiev during the Civil War, was the first Soviet play to portray the White intelligentsia as sympathetic figures, rather than the malicious characters common to socialist realist productions. Critical opposition was violent; party critics immediately accused Bulgakov of glorifying the class enemy and denounced the play as counterrevolutionary. Nevertheless, playgoers who had lost relatives in the Civil War identified with the Turbin family and flocked to performances. According to one account, "The women were hysterical; there were tears in the eyes of the men." Bulgakov's next play, *Zoikina kvartira* (*Zoya's Apartment*), concerns the goings-on at a brothel disguised as a sewing shop in Moscow of the 1920s. A comic melodrama, the play satirizes communist institutions and life under Stalin's New Economic Policy. Popular with audiences, it was condemned by Soviet critics for being "pornographic" as well as for failing to convey the proper ideological viewpoint. His next play, *Bagrovyi ostrov* (*The Crimson Island*), a comic attack on censorship, prompted counterattacks on Bulgakov's reputation and was taken out of the Art Theater repertory after only four performances.

Beg (*Flight*), the play considered by some critics to be Bulgakov's best, was not allowed to be staged in the Soviet Union until 1957. In *Flight*, Bulgakov blended comic and tragic situations in eight acts he labelled "dreams" to depict the plight of a group of defeated White generals and a few civilians who elect to emigrate rather than live under communism. Critics have praised *Flight*'s careful construction, character development, and language, as well as its masterful use of stage effects. In *A Cabal of Hypocrites*, based on the life of Moliere, Bulgakov addressed the problem of the artist in a repressive society, a theme that he was to return to in later works. The play is based on one of Bulgakov's literary heroes (Bulgakov once told his wife that Moliere was the first person he would go to see in the afterlife), but is as much fiction as fact, its emphasis being the creator and the creative act rather than historical accuracy. *A Cabal of Hypocrites* was accepted by the Moscow Art Theater in 1931 but was not performed until 1936, after five years of delays and disagreements between Bulgakov and the renowned founder and director of the Art Theater, Konstantin Stanislavsky, over the staging of the play. Bulgakov refused to rewrite crucial scenes and Stanislavsky attempted to make significant changes in the character of Moliere over Bulgakov's protests. *A Cabal of Hypocrites* finally reached the stage after nearly three hundred rehearsals, but closed after seven performances because of hostile critical reception. Pravda criticized Bulgakov's "incorrect" interpretation of history and denounced his "reactionary view of artistic creativity as 'pure' art." Angry and frustrated, Bulgakov resigned from the Art Theater in protest. As his next play, Ivan Vasilevich, was officially proscribed before its premiere, *A Cabal of Hypocrites* was the last of Bulgakov's dramas to be performed in his lifetime.

In addition to his dramas, Bulgakov wrote numerous short stories and novels. His first published collection of stories, *Diavoliada (Diaboliad, and Other Stories)*, was strongly influenced by Gogol: realism dissolves into fantasy and absurdity, and light comic satire erupts into sudden brutality. Included is his best-known story, "Rokovye iaitsa" ("The Fatal Eggs"), in which a well-meaning scientist discovers a red ray that stimulates growth. The ray is appropriated by a bureaucrat to increase the country's chicken population, but through a mix-up produces instead a crop of giant reptiles that ravage the countryside. Critics have read the story as a satirical treatment of the Russian Revolution, or, less specifically, as a commentary on progress and a rejection of revolution in favor of evolution. "The Fatal Eggs" also introduces another of Bulgakov's favorite themes: the consequences of power in the hands of the ignorant. Although written during the same period as *Diaboliad*, Bulgakov's *A Country Doctor's Notebooks* differs radically from these stories as well as from most of his longer fiction in its strict realism and exclusion of the fantastic and grotesque. Another early work, *Sobache serdtse (The Heart of a Dog)*, is included among Bulgakov's most important. Considered one of Soviet Russia's best satirical novellas, the work portrays a scientist's transformation of a dog into a man. The creature develops

reprehensible human qualities, and the scientist changes him back into the good-natured dog he once was. The story, which has obvious thematic parallels to "The Fatal Eggs," has never been published in the Soviet Union because of its counterrevolutionary cast. Critical readings have been similar to those of "The Fatal Eggs": some critics consider it a blatant political satire, equating the operation with the Revolution, while others stress a moral and philosophical interpretation of the conflict between the intellectual scientist and the uneducated masses, and of the disastrous results of interfering with a natural process. Bulgakov's relationship with the Moscow Art Theater, in particular the clashes over the staging of *A Cabal of Hypocrites*, served as the source for his novel *Teatralnyi roman (Black Snow: A Theatrical Novel)*. In this humorous roman a clef of Moscow's theatrical world, Bulgakov portrayed the revered Stanislavsky as a petty tyrant and the Art Theater actors as a group of feuding, scheming egomaniacs. An excellent example of Bulgakov's mature prose, *Black Snow* was unfortunately left unfinished at his death.

Publishes His Masterwork

Bulgakov's acknowledged masterwork, *The Master and Margarita*, developed over a period of twelve years through the drafting of eight separate versions. According to biographers, Bulgakov knew that the novel would be his masterpiece and set aside all other projects during the last years of his illness in order to finish it before his death, dictating final corrections to his wife after he became blind, and adding the epilogue after the manuscript was bound. He gave copies to his wife and to a friend for safekeeping, and they remained a closely guarded secret until Bulgakov's rehabilitation during Nikita Khrushchev's cultural thaw of the late 1950s and early 1960s, a period in which the cult of Stalin was repudiated and the Soviets began to confront some of the murderous excesses of his reign.

The Master and Margarita was finally published in a heavily censored form in two installments in the journal *Moskva* in 1966 and 1967. It caused an immediate sensation and has received an extraordinary amount of critical attention ever since. A blend of satire, realism, and fantasy, the novel is not easily classified or reduced to a single interpretation. "Bulgakov's *The Master and Margarita*," wrote Tabitha McIntosh-Byrd in *Novels for Students*,"-is a novel about novels—an argument for the ability of literature to transcend both time and oppression, and for the heroic nature of the writer's struggle to create that literature." The critic for the *St. James*

Guide to Science Fiction Writers wrote: "In *The Master and Margarita*, reality is infinite, eternal, and transcendent; time and space are relative; man is immortal. Living according to the demands of universal truth is a moral duty for which man is held accountable." Most critics agree that *The Master and Margarita* is composed of three narrative strands. The first concerns the devil (named Woland) and his associates, who visit modern Moscow and create havoc in the lives of the stupid, the scheming, and the avaricious. The second deals with a persecuted novelist (The Master) and his mistress (Margarita), who bargains with Woland for the sake of her beloved. The third level of the book is the Master's novel, a retelling of the story of Pilate and Christ which involved a tremendous amount of research into the history of Jerusalem and early Christian thought. What little negative criticism that has been written on *The Master and Margarita* has focused on the lack of cohesion among these three levels of narrative. The nature of good and evil constitutes a basic philosophical problem in the novel, and much critical attention has been devoted to the nature of Bulgakov's devil, who appears less an evil being in opposition to God than as God's counterpart, whose task it is to punish the corrupt. His relationship with the Master has been seen as a Faustian pact; indeed, references to Johann Wolfgang von Goethe's Faust permeate the novel. Like Bulgakov's characterization of the devil, the portrait of Jesus in *The Master and Margarita* is equally unorthodox; although his character asserts the fundamental beliefs of orthodox Christianity, he complains that everything written about him by his only disciple, Matthew, is inaccurate. With the story of the Master, Bulgakov returns to the theme of the artist in society. He writes that "manuscripts don't burn," asserting his belief that art will endure the vicissitudes of political repression because of its eternal nature, existing as it does apart from the transitory world of political power. Similarly, an important parallel theme to the conflict between the artist and society is developed in the conflict between the spiritual and material worlds, a conflict that in Bulgakov's view ultimately results in the triumph of the spiritual.

Alexander Adabashyan, Oleg Basilashvili and Vladislav Galkin starred in the Russian Television Channel's adaptation of *The Master and Margarita.* (Still from film adaptation with three men talking beneath tree. AP Images.)

Final Years

Bulgakov's last years were filled with suspicion and fear. Government informers were assigned to work in his household and much of his work was refused publication and banned from the stage. "Over the last seven years," Bulgakov wrote in a 1937 letter, "I have created sixteen works in different genres, and they have all perished." Even a play featuring Stalin himself and celebrating the dictator's sixtieth birthday—a desperate move by Bulgakov to get something produced—was rejected by authorities. Government officials held out the hope that he might be allowed an exit visa to leave the country, a hope that never materialized. Bulgakov suffered a nervous collapse and became frightened of walking down the street alone, lest he be taken by the Soviet secret police. Although he is remembered, a critic for *Publishers Weekly* stated, as a "brilliant satirist of life under Stalin," Bulgakov paid a terrible price for taking aim against a totalitarian regime. Following his death in 1940 at the age of 49, Bulgakov was largely forgotten. While *The Master and Margarita* finally appeared in the 1960s, other of his writings were not allowed publication until the 1990s. *Manuscripts Don't Burn: Mikhail Bulgakov, A Life in Letters and Diaries* appeared in 1992 and gathers together neglected early newspaper writings and private diaries, some never seen before and others not reprinted in over seventy-five years. Harvey Pekar in the *Review of Contemporary Fiction* noted that Bulgakov "never accepted Bolshevism, and made this plain as early as November 1919 in a local newspaper article reprinted here." *Notes on the Cuff and Other Stories*, a collection of Bulgakov's early fiction, also appeared in 1992. A critic for *Publishers Weekly* found that the stories' "emotionally charged scenes, naturalistically overwrought dialogue and gallows humor vividly capture the instability of the 1920s."

If you enjoy the works of Mikhail Bulgakov, you may also want to check out the following books:

Yevgeny Zamyatin, *We*, 1920.
Vladimir Voinovich, *Life and Extraordinary Adventures of Private Ivan Chonkin*, 1977.
Gary Shteyngart, *Absurdistan*, 2006.

A. Colin Wright, in an essay for the *Reference Guide to World Literature*, concluded that "Bulgakov is today one of the best-loved writers in the former Soviet Union, seen by many as reflecting the absurdities of that society under Stalinism and—although he died in 1940—of a later period as well." Nadine Natov concluded in her study *Mikhail Bulgakov*: "Courage, moral strength, and creative stamina are the characteristic and most striking features of Mikhail Bulgakov's personality. A talented man gifted with an exuberant imagination and an acute sense of historical reality, Bulgakov added impressive pages to the treasury of Russian literature."

■ Biographical and Critical Sources

BOOKS

Barrat, Andrew, *Between Two Worlds: A Critical Introduction to "The Master and Margarita"*, Clarendon Press (Oxford, England), 1987.

Curtis, J.A.E., *Bulgakov's Last Decade: The Writer as Hero*, Cambridge University Press (Cambridge, England), 1981.

Dictionary of Literary Biography, Volume 272: *Russian Prose Writers between the World Wars*, Thomson Gale (Detroit, MI), 2002.

Edwards, T.R. N., *Three Russian Writers and the Irrational: Zamyatin, Pil'nyak, and Bulgakov*, Cambridge University Press (Cambridge, England), 1982.

Ericson, Jr., Edward E., *The Apocalyptic Vision of Mikhail Bulgakov's "The Master and Margarita"*, Edwin Mellen Press (Lewiston, NY), 1991).

Haber, Edythe C., *Mikhail Bulgakov: The Early Years*, Harvard University Press (Cambridge, MA), 1998.

Hunns, Derek J., *Bulgakov's Apocalyptic Critique of Literature*, E. Mellen Press (Lewiston, NY), 1996.

International Dictionary of Theatre, St. James Press (Detroit, MI), 1993.

Krugovoy, George, *The Gnostic Novel of Mikhail Bulgakov: Sources and Exegesis*, University Press of America, 1991.

Mahlow, Elena N., *Bulgakov's "The Master and Margarita": The Text as a Cipher*, Vantage (New York, NY), 1975.

Milne, Lesley, *"The Master and Margarita": A Comedy of Victory*, Birmingham Slavonic Monographs (Birmingham, England), 1977.

Milne, Lesley, *Mikhail Bulgakov: A Critical Biography*, Cambridge University Press (New York, NY), 1990.

Milne, Lesley, editor, *Bulgakov: The Novelist-Playwright*, Harwood (Luxembourg), 1995.

Natov, Nadine, *Mikhail Bulgakov*, Twayne (Boston, MA), 1985.

Novels for Students, Volume 8, Thomson Gale (Detroit, MI), 2000.

Pittman, Ritta H., *The Writer's Divided Self in "The Master and Margarita"*, St. Martin's Press (New York, NY), 1991.

Proffer, Ellendea, *An International Bibliography of Works by and about Mikhail Bulgakov*, Ardis (Ann Arbor, MI), 1976.

Proffer, Ellendea, *Bulgakov: Life and Work*, Ardis (Ann Arbor, MI), 1984.

Proffer, Ellendea, *A Pictorial Biography of Mikhail Bulgakov*, Ardis (Ann Arbor, MI), 1984.

Reference Guide to Short Fiction, 2nd edition, St. James Press (Detroit, MI), 1999.

Reference Guide to World Literature, 3rd edition, St. James Press (Detroit, MI), 2003.

St. James Guide to Horror, Ghost, and Gothic Writers, St. James Press (Detroit, MI), 1998.

St. James Guide to Science Fiction Writers, 4th edition, St. James Press (Detroit, MI), 1996.

Short Story Criticism, Volume 18, Thomson Gale (Detroit, MI), 1995.

Smeliansky, Anatoly, *Is Comrade Bulgakov Dead?: Mikhail Bulgakov at the Moscow Art Theatre*, translated by Arch Tait, Routledge (New York, NY), 1993.

Terry, Garth M., compiler, *Mikhail Bulgakov in English: A Bibliography, 1891-1991*, Astra Press (Nottingham, England), 1991.

Twentieth-Century Literary Criticism, Thomson Gale (Detroit, MI), Volume 2, 1979, Volume 16, 1985, Volume 59, 2005.

Vozdvizhensky, Vyacheslav, compiler, *Mikhail Bulgakov and His Times: Memoirs, Letters*, translated by Liv Tudge, Progress Publishers (Moscow, Russia), 1990.

Weeks, Laura D., *The Master and Margarita: A Critical Companion*, Northwestern University Press (Evanston, IL), 1996.

Wright, Anthony Colin, *Mikhail Bulgakov: Life and Interpretations*, University of Toronto Press (Toronto, ON), 1978.

PERIODICALS

Booklist, December 15, 1995, Jack Helbig, review of *Zoyka's Apartment*, p. 681.

Canadian American Slavic Studies, summer-fall, 1981, pp. 151-166.

Canadian Slavic Papers, Volume XIV, number 1, 1972, pp. 76-86.

Canadian Slavic Studies, winter, 1969, pp. 615-628.

Commonweal, June 16, 2000, Daria Donnelly, review of *The Master and Margarita*, p. 26.

Economist, June 1, 1991, review of *Manuscripts Don't Burn: Mikhail Bulgakov, A Life in Letters and Diaries*, p. 87.

International Fiction Review, January, 1974, pp. 27-31.

Journal of European Studies, March/June, 1983, pp. 56-74.

Library Journal, April 1, 1997, Michael Rogers, reviews of *Black Snow: A Theatrical Novel*, *A Country Doctor's Notebook*, and *The Heart of a Dog*, p. 134.

Modern Fiction Studies, summer, 1973, pp. 169-178.

New York, May 28, 1990, p. 74.

New Yorker, December 21, 1992, p. 123.

New York Times Book Review, January 3, 1993, p. 3; October 22, 1995, pp. 32-33.

Publications of the Modern Language Association of America, October, 1973, pp. 1162-1172.

Publishers Weekly, July 6, 1992, review of *Notes On the Cuff and Other Stories*, p. 38; October 19, 1992, review of *Manuscripts Don't Burn: Mikhail Bulgakov, A Life in Letters and Diaries*, p. 69; June 26, 1995, review of *The Master and Margarita*, p. 86.

Review of Contemporary Fiction, spring, 1993, Harvey Pekar, review of *Manuscripts Don't Burn: Mikhail Bulgakov, A Life in Letters and Diaries*, p. 282.

Russian Literature Triquarterly, spring, 1973, pp. 533-565; spring, 1978, pp. 123-209 and 219-311.

Russian Review, January, 1974, pp. 20-36; October, 1982, pp. 373-399.

Slavic and East European Journal, Volume XIII, number 3, 1969, pp. 309-325; summer, 1981, pp. 44-55.

Slavic Review, December, 1974, pp. 695-707.

Variety, May 16, 1990, p. 88.

Jonathan Carroll

(Photograph by Joe del Tufo.)

■ Personal

Born January 26, 1949, in New York, NY; son of Sidney (a screenwriter) and June (an actress and lyricist; maiden name, Sillman) Carroll; married Beverly Schreiner (an artist), June 19, 1971; children: Ryder Pierce. *Education:* Rutgers University, B.A. (cum laude), 1971; University of Virginia, M.A., 1973. *Hobbies and other interests:*

■ Addresses

Home—Vienna, Austria. *Agent*—David Higham Associates, 5-8 Lower John St., Golden Square, London W1R 4HA, England.

■ Career

Writer. North State Academy, Hickory, NC, English teacher, 1971-72; St. Louis Country Day School, St. Louis, MO, English teacher, 1973-74; American International School, Vienna, Austria, English teacher, 1974—.

■ Awards, Honors

Emily Clark Balch fellowship in creative writing, University of Virginia, 1972; Book of the Year citation, *Washington Post*, 1983, for *Voice of Our Shadow*; World Fantasy Award, 1988; British Fantasy Award, 1991; Bram Stoker Award, Horror Writers of America, 1996, for best collection; Pushcart Prize, 2006, for story "Home on the Rain."

■ Writings

NOVELS

The Land of Laughs, Viking (New York, NY), 1980.

Voice of Our Shadow, Viking (New York, NY), 1983.

Bones of the Moon, Century (London, England), 1987, Arbor House (New York, NY), 1988.

Sleeping in Flame, Legend (London, England), 1988, Doubleday (New York, NY), 1989.

A Child across the Sky, Legend (London, England), 1989, Doubleday (New York, NY), 1990.

Black Cocktail, illustrated by Dave McKean, Legend (London, England), 1990, St. Martin's Press (New York, NY), 1991.

Outside the Dog Museum, Macdonald (London, England), 1991, Doubleday (New York, NY), 1992.

After Silence, Macdonald (London, England), 1992, Doubleday (New York, NY), 1993.

From the Teeth of Angels, Doubleday (New York, NY), 1994.

Kissing the Beehive, N.A. Talese/Doubleday (New York, NY), 1998.

The Marriage of Sticks, Tor (New York, NY), 1999.

The Heidelberg Cylinder, Mobius New Media (Wilmington, DE), 2000.

The Wooden Sea, Tor (New York, NY), 2001.

White Apples, Tor (New York, NY), 2003.

Glass Soup, Tor (New York, NY), 2005.

OTHER

The Panic Hand (story collection), HarperCollins (London, England), 1995, St. Martin's Press (New York, NY), 1996.

Also author of screenplays, including *The Joker.* Contributor of short stories to periodicals, including *Transatlantic Review, Sport, Cimarron Review, Folio, Christian Science Monitor,* and *Four Quarters,* and of book reviews to *St. Louis Globe-Democrat* and *Cleveland Plain Dealer.*

■ Sidelights

Jonathan Carroll is a fantasy novelist who has won wide acclaim. He is "one of the finest practitioners of contemporary fantasy," according to Charles de Lint in the *Magazine of Fantasy and Science Fiction.* "Carroll is one of the most respected contemporary fantasists, and one of those most accepted by the literary mainstream," Rich Horton wrote in an article for the *SF Site.* "This is due in part to his graceful prose, and in part to the fact that his novels tend to be set in the present day, and to feature fantastical intrusions into otherwise fairly mundane storylines." Many of Carroll's novels begin in ordinary circumstances and then evolve into something quite terrifyingly different. According to Michael Moorcock, writing in the *New Statesman and Society,* "Carroll's books are dangerous. He takes considerable risks and trusts his readers with the nerve and intelligence to follow him. He's a moral visionary whose sturdy, subtle plots are rooted in character, a profound liking for people, a relish for life. Yet he writes about active evil. He uses supernatural fiction to comment upon that evil." Carroll has won the World Fantasy Award, the British Fantasy Award, and the Bram Stoker Award.

An Entertainment Background

Carroll was born in New York City in 1949. He was raised in a creative family. His father, Sidney, was a screenwriter whose credits include *A Big Hand for the Little Lady* and the Paul Newman film *The Hustler.* His mother, June, was an actress and lyricist who appeared in Broadway shows and in films. Because of his parents' involvement in the entertainment industry, Carroll's family life consisted of constant jaunts between the East and West coasts. He rebelled at an early age—calling himself a juvenile delinquent—but credits the death of a teenaged friend, who was shot dead by police, with straightening him out. Carroll attended the Loomis School, a boarding school in Connecticut. This is where he first got interested in writing. His first story was "about an old woman who lives alone in New York, very lonely, and she decides to get a dog," he explained in an article posted at his Web site. The woman eventually kills the dog when he annoys her. Carroll's English teacher was impressed. His father was less impressed, however. He simply advised that "it makes no difference what I write, just so long as I continue writing," Carroll recounted in his Web site article.

Speaking of his early life, Carroll told Rodger Turner in an interview for the *SF Site:* "When I was a boy, I was generally unhappy much of the time because I never really fit in anywhere. I constantly tried with little success to be part of groups I neither liked nor respected. First, I was a semi-hoodlum, then when I was shipped by my worried parents to a tight-assed boy's prep school in Connecticut, I tried being a preppie. Which was really absurd, because from the beginning, I loathed everything that had to do with that group and their values. So what would my younger self say when he heard things'll get better soon? He'd probably say tomorrow is a long time away. And he'd be right because I didn't start being happy and comfortable in my life until I was about nineteen."

Carroll graduated from Rutgers University in 1971. He later earned a masters degree from the University of Virginia. In 1971, he married Beverly Schreiner. The couple have a son, Ryder Pierce. After graduating from Rutgers, Carroll spent several years teaching. He first taught at the North State Academy in Hickory, North Carolina, and then at St Louis County Day School. In 1974, he became an English teacher at the American International School in Vienna, Austria, a position he still holds.

A Town Entranced by Fiction

In *The Land of Laughs,* Carroll's debut novel, a small town has fallen under the influence of a series of children's books. An essayist for the *St. James Guide*

This 1980 novel tells of an entire town ensnared in the magical world of a children's book author. (Patrick Arrasmith,, illustrator. Orb, 2001. Reproduced with permission.)

to Horror, Ghost and Gothic Writers wrote: "The uneasily-allied protagonists of *The Land of Laughs* investigate the background of a writer whose tales they loved as children, and find that the small town where he lived and died is still in the grip of his too-powerful imagination. That grip is far more oppressive than his heart-warming works had implied, although its tightness and sternness both derive from the capacity that his fantasies had to provide an avenue of escape for alienated readers." Jack Sullivan, writing in the *Washington Post Book World*, heralded *The Land of Laughs* as a "beguiling and original novel." Sullivan also observed that the author's "descriptions of his small-town Missouri setting are charming and paradoxically down-to-earth; his characters are engaging, sweet-natured antiquarian oddballs; and his sense of humor is nicely attuned to his fantastic subject matter." An essayist for the *St. James Guide to Fantasy Writers* called *The Land of Laughs* "a strong debut" and Car-

roll' "most perfectly-plotted" novel. Turner, in his review of the novel, called *The Land of Laughs* "a marvel of modern fiction."

Voice of Our Shadow finds Joe Lennox, a successful writer from a New York suburb, living quietly in Vienna, Austria. But Joe is still troubled by the memory of the terrible day years earlier when his brother Ross slipped on the railroad tracks and died. The event tore their small family apart, and Joe's complicity in the tragedy, which began as a taunting game by Ross and his bullying friend, Bobby, has never been revealed. Joe befriends a married couple in Vienna, an essayist for the *St. James Guide to Horror, Ghost and Gothic Writers* explained, "and inconveniently falls in love with the wife. The sudden death of the husband does not serve to make the situation any less complicated; instead, its further development releases a torrent of pent-up guilt left over from the protagonist's troubled relationship with his bullying brother. Penitent though he is for all his past sins, the luckless young man can find no release from the merciless oppression of his long-dead sibling." A critic for *People* found that "at some point his apparently normal characters find themselves in a terrifying, violent and surreal world where the usual rules no longer apply."

Carroll's *Bones of the Moon* tells of Cullen James, who marries her old college friend Danny. While pregnant with the couple's first child, Cullen begins to dream of the strange world of Rondua, which is populated by large talking animals. With her noble son Pepsi, the guide dog Mr. Tracy, and a band of animal helpers, she embarks on a quest to save Rondua from Jack Chili, who bears a disturbing resemblance to murderer Alvin "Axe Boy" Williams, Cullen's real-life neighbor. Increasingly, the boundaries between the two worlds crumble. "Both worlds catapult toward a final collision that's triumphant and tragic at the same time," as a critic for *Publishers Weekly* noted. *Bones of the Moon*, according to an essayist for the *St. James Guide to Horror, Ghost and Gothic Writers*, "is the least downbeat of Carroll's fantasies, striking the most delicate balance between unease and sentimentality."

Sleeping in Flame concerns retired actor and American expatriate Walker Easterling, who meets elegant model Maris York in Vienna. As their relationship deepens, Walker begins to experience bizarre flashes of precognition, as well as disturbing memories of some unknown person's chaotic, abused past. He turns for help to peculiar yet powerful shaman Venasque, who leads him into a maze of past lives, and helps him begin to understand their connection to his present one. As Walker explores the significance of his past, he realizes that old ties still bind him to a malignant entity who theatens his new-found happiness with Maris. "The 'explanation' ultimately provided for his peculiar heritage," wrote an essayist for the *St. James Guide to Horror, Ghost and Gothic Writers*, "can hardly help but seem ill-fitting."

Horror Fiction or Fact?

In *A Child across the Sky* Carroll tells the story of Weber Greston, a filmmaker who searches for lost footage from a horror film made by his deceased friend Philip Strayhorn. He is accompanied by Philip's imaginary playmate from childhood, who has now come to life and claims to be an angel. As his

A small New York town is the scene for a series of miraculous events in this 2001 novel. (Rafal Olbinski, illustrator. A Tor Book, 2001. Reproduced by permission.)

search continues, Weber begins to suspect that Philip made horror films based not on imagination but on fact. *A Child across the Sky*, wrote the essayist for the *St. James Guide to Horror, Ghost and Gothic Writers*, "is the most complicated of Carroll's works, and the most nakedly horrific; the conscientiously nasty-minded double-twist ending is the most effective of all his climaxes." The critic for *Publishers Weekly* concluded that "Carroll's style is elegant; his writing is by turns disturbing, fey, sardonic, grim—frequently within a single paragraph. The unexpected lies at the heart of this novel, and readers seeking a provocative and stimulating—though not always easy—read will be rewarded."

Some of Carroll's earlier characters reappear in *Outside the Dog Museum*. World renowned architect Harry Radcliffe has gone mad. With the help of Venasque, a shaman who appeared in *Sleeping in Flame*, he eventually regains his sanity and accepts a commission to build a Museum for the Sultan of Saru, a small Middle Eastern country. But when war breaks out, the sultan is killed. His son asks that the museum be constructed in Vienna instead, and the payment will be made in magic. The critic for *Publishers Weekly* found that "the picaresque tone, surprisingly, yields at the end to a reprise of a biblical theme, turning this spirited novel into something like a moral tale."

After Silence concerns Max Fischer, who discovers that his girlfriend Lily has lied to him about having a husband, and that her son Lincoln is actually a child whom she kidnapped while an infant. Although Max forgives Lily and tries to establish a stable family, Lincoln's discovery of the truth years later precipitates all three of them on a path toward dissolution and death. *After Silence* "is the most reflective of Carroll's novels, replete with philosophical reveries and aphoristic observations," according to the essayist for the *St. James Guide to Horror, Ghost and Gothic Writers*. The critic for *Publishers Weekly* dubbed *After Silence* as "an electrifing, unforgettable novel."

From the Teeth of Angels finds four characters in Vienna confronted by and struggling with the Angel of Death, who appears to them in ominous dreams. Charles de Lint, writing in the *Magazine of Fantasy and Science Fiction*, found the novel to be "perhaps one of Carroll's darkest outings to date, but it is also filled with moments of great light, hope and courage." "Carroll writes with grace and style," noted Dennis Winters in *Booklist*, "weaving the different strands of his story to their frightening shared climax." Moorcock found that, as the story draws to a close, "we come to realise we have been experiencing a struggle between good and evil as monumental as anything in Milton."

Uncovering an Old Murder

In *Kissing the Beehive,* Carroll tells of author Sam Bayer, who is suffering from writer's block. At a book signing, he meets the lovely Veronica Lake and goes with her and his daughter, Cassandra, to his hometown of Crane's View, hoping to rekindle his writing talent. He hopes, too, to investigate the unsolved murder of a teenaged girl years before. Bayer explores familiar haunts and reconnects with his high school crony Francis McCabe, now an upstanding citizen as Crane's View's police chief. His prying into the old crime awakens the enmity of the murderer, and Bayer must safeguard his new relationship, his beloved daughter, his career, and his life as he tries to nail a disturbed killer. Ted Leventhal in *Booklist* called the novel "a high-quality literary mystery—an enjoyable read." De Lint found *Kissing the Beehive* to be "a novel that will enthrall old fans and win him new ones."

The Marriage of Sticks follows Miranda Romanac, a Manhattan-based rare books dealer, as she attends her high school reunion in Connecticut and discovers that a beloved old boyfriend, James Stillman, has died three years earlier in a tragic accident. Back in New York, thirty-something Miranda feels her previous, carefully ordered existence closing in on her. She kicks over the traces of her old life, becoming involved with a married man, Hugh Oakley, and eventually moving in with him. But Miranda's new reality shifts and dissolves with increasing speed as she experiences disturbing flashes of other lives at once strange and frighteningly familiar: a tormented little girl who died in 1924, a voluptuous artist's mistress, and a vampire with a dangerous gift of immortality. James begins to appear in her dreams, offering kindness and helpful hints, but even he cannot save her from herself and the excruciating choice she must make in order to become whole again. "Carroll realizes characters and settings superbly and propels the story forward compellingly," Ray Olson commented in *Booklist.* A *Publishers Weekly* critic wrote that "Carroll often startles with the deftness of his insights, both personal and metaphysical, and there are many lines that, for their poetry, one wants to cut out and frame."

The Wooden Sea is another surrealist novel that defies easy characterization. The protagonist is Francis McCabe, a small-town police chief. McCabe has a comfortable, happy existence until it is turned upside down by a series of strange coincidences and bizarre events, beginning with the death of a stray dog in his office, that *Library Journal* contributor Jackie Cassada deemed "by turns whimsical and disturbing." As these events are recounted, Elizabeth

In this 2002 novel, a man comes back to life and finds that his knowledge of the afterlife is crucial to the safety of the universe. (Photograph courtesy of Imagestate. Tor, 2003. Reproduced by permission.)

Hand explained in the *Magazine of Fantasy and Science Fiction,* "*The Wooden Sea* cascades into a shimmering, often brilliant shower of strange and beautiful set pieces." "It's not exactly fantasy or science fiction, in spite of the fact that both God and aliens appear in the cast of characters," Bonnie Johnston explained in *Booklist.*

A Return from the Dead

Vincent Ettrich, the protagonist of Carroll's novel *White Apples,* has died and been brought back to life at the beginning of the story. His lover, Isabelle Neukor, is pregnant, and she tells him that their unborn child, Anjo, is behind his return. Beyond bringing people back from the dead, the child has many other powers as well, and it seems that fate intends him to save the universe. However, to do that he needs

Vincent to tell him what Vincent learned while he was dead. Vincent, unfortunately, is unable to remember any of it. According to Moorcock, reviewing the book for the *Guardian*, Carroll "uses no familiar genre tricks to maintain suspense, yet still communicates nail-biting concern for the wellbeing of his central characters and a terrible fear for the fate of the universe." "The novel boasts its share of the fresh perspectives on life and love that Carroll's fans have come to expect," commented a *Publishers Weekly* critic, while Jackie Cassada in a review for the *Library Journal* praised Carroll's "talent for creating characters that seem both unique and familiar."

Glass Soup, the sequel to *White Apples*, is full of "dazzling details and more twists than a bag of pretzels," noted a *Kirkus Reviews* contributor. This volume finds Vincent, Isabelle, and the still-unborn Anjo continuing to fight the forces of Chaos, embodied as John Flannery, a man who seduced several of Isa-

belle's friends and then murdered them. The tale features many of the absurdities for which Carroll's work is known—an octopus drives a tour bus; God is a mosaic made of tiles, but He is also Bob, a stuffed polar bear; Simon, a man who like Vincent has realized that he died but cannot remember it, is constantly accompanied by a foot-high creature named Broximon. *Glass Soup* is "an ambitious retelling of the cosmic struggle between good and evil," wrote a *Publishers Weekly* reviewer, but also "a marvelous comic feast." "Carroll's clever and spellbinding tale," wrote Donna Seaman in *Booklist*, "offers fans and newcomers alike startling perspectives on time and reality, an afterlife made of dreams, a glimmering vision of the divine, and a sweet tribute to love."

"Jonathan Carroll is one of my heroes. For the freedom he gives himself to crowd his pages with imagined and observed reality, cheek to jowl. For his readiness to be silly right after he's broken your heart. He's really created a unique style—sexy, playful, and mordant all at once."—Jonathan Lethem

GLASS SOUP
JONATHAN CARROLL

In this 2005 follow-up to *White Apples*, **the struggle between good and evil continues in a topsy-turvy world.** (Rafal Olbinski, illustrator. A Tor Book, 2005. Reproduced by permission.)

If you enjoy the works of Jonathan Carroll, you may also want to check out the following books:

Philip K. Dick, *Do Androids Dream of Electric Sheep?*, 1968.
Nick Bantock, *The Venetian's Wife: A Strangely Sensual Tale of a Renaissance Explorer, a Computer, and a Metamorphosis*, 1996.
Brian Stableford, *Year Zero*, 2003.

"I love to drop characters into situations which defy reason and the laws they abided by up until five seconds ago," Carroll told Andrew Hedgecock in the *Third Alternative*. "Situations where dogs talk, God appears, aliens drive ambulances, or suddenly we realize we died but are now back in exactly the same life we once had. The question then is how will these people behave faced with those profound realizations/obstacles? Push individuals to extremes way beyond the norm, and you see a great deal about both the good and the bad of human behaviour. When I was a boy I went to a survival school called Outward Bound. Early on, our instructors (a rough lot of ex-soldiers, mountain guides and generally mysteriously shady characters) said, when the going gets tough you're going to see who are the good ones and who are the bad of your fellow students. And that really was true. So I make the going rough for my people beyond the normal three dimensions and then see which of them float and which sink."

Stableford summed up Carroll's work: "By the gruesome standards of modern horror fiction Carroll is extraordinarily subtle, but that gives his work a peculiar effectiveness which is his alone. His narrative voice is original and distinctive—and quite probably inimitable—and the ruminations of his characters, however unreliable they may be as narrators, are possessed of real depth as well as endless fascination."

■ Biographical and Critical Sources

BOOKS

St. James Guide to Fantasy Writers, St. James Press (Detroit, MI), 1996.

St. James Guide to Horror, Ghost and Gothic Writers, St. James Press (Detroit, MI), 1998.

Schweitzer, Darrell, editor, *Discovering Modern Horror Fiction,* Starmont (Mercer Island, WA), 1985.

Zipes, Jack, editor, *The Oxford Companion to Fairy Tales,* Oxford University Press (New York, NY), 2000.

PERIODICALS

Atlanta Journal-Constitution, July 1, 2001, Michael Bishop, "*Wooden Sea* a Zigzag Blend of the Everyday and the Absurd," p. C5.

Book, September-October, 2002, Don McLeese, review of *White Apples,* p. 78.

Booklist, May 1, 1994, Dennis Winters, review of *From the Teeth of Angels,* p. 1581; December 15, 1997, Ted Leventhal, review of *Kissing the Beehive,* p. 685; August, 1999, Ray Olson, review of *The Marriage of Sticks,* p. 2038; December 15, 2000, Bonnie Johnston, review of *The Wooden Sea,* p. 785; September 15, 2002, Whitney Scott, review of *White Apples,* p. 211; September 1, 2005, Donna Seaman, review of *Glass Soup,* p. 58.

Book Page, February, 2001, review of *The Wooden Sea,* p. 10.

Denver Post, March 4, 2001, Robin Vidimos, "*Wooden Sea* a Strangely Credible Adventure."

Edge Magazine, Number 1, March 15, 2000, interview with Carroll.

Entertainment Weekly, February 16, 2001, Rebecca Ascher-Walsh, review of *The Wooden Sea,* p. 92.

Guardian (London, England), May 3, 2003, Michael Moorcock, review of *White Apples,* p. 29.

Hudson Review, summer, 1997, review of *The Panic Hand,* p. 344.

January Magazine, October, 1999, Claude Lelumiere, review of *The Marriage of Sticks;* April, 2001, David Dalgleish, review of *The Wooden Sea.*

Journal of American Culture, fall, 1995, Steffen Hantke, "Deconstructing Horror: Commodities in the Fiction of Jonathan Carroll and Kathe Koja," p. 41.

Kirkus Reviews, July 1, 1980, review of *The Land of Laughs,* p. 850; October 15, 1982, review of *Voice of Our Shadow,* p. 1164; November 1, 1987, review of *Bones of the Moon,* p. 1531; January 15, 1989, review of *Sleeping in Flame,* p. 67; June 1, 1990, review of *A Child Across the Sky,* p. 748; September 15, 1996, review of *The Panic Hand;* July 1, 2002, review of *White Apples,* p. 898; July 1, 2005, review of *Glass Soup,* p. 713.

Library Journal, September 15, 1980, review of *The Land of Laughs,* p. 1883; March 15, 2001, Jackie Cassada, review of *The Wooden Sea,* p. 110; October 15, 2002, Jackie Cassada, review of *White Apples,* p. 97; July 1, 2005, David Keymer, review of *Glass Soup,* p. 64.

Locus, May, 2001, Gary K. Wolfe, review of *The Wooden Sea,* p. 23; September, 2002, Gary K. Wolfe, review of *White Apples,* p. 17; October, 2003, "Jonathan Carroll: Inside the Dog Museum," pp. 6-7, 60-62.

Magazine of Fantasy and Science Fiction, October-November, 1994, Charles de Lint, review of *From the Teeth of Angels,* p. 46; July, 1998, Charles de Lint, review of *Kissing the Beehive,* p. 43; December, 1999, Charles de Lint, review of *The Marriage of Sticks,* p. 28; April, 2001, Charles de Lint, review of *The Heidelberg Cylinder,* p. 29; June, 2001, Elizabeth Hand, review of *The Wooden Sea,* p. 30.

New Statesman and Society, May 6, 1994, Michael Moorcock, review of *From the Teeth of Angels,* p. 36.

New York Times Book Review, January 24, 1988, Elizabeth Gleick, review of *Bones of the Moon,* p. 20; May 17, 1992, Jack Zipes, review of *Outside the Dog Museum,* p. 18; February 11, 2001, Alan Cheuse, review of *The Wooden Sea,* p. 15; June 3, 2001, review of *The Wooden Sea,* p. 27; February 17, 2002, Scott Veale, review of *The Wooden Sea,* p. 20; November 24, 2002, Taylor Antrim, review of *White Apples,* p. 32.

People, February 21, 1983, review of *Voice of Our Shadow,* p.14.

Publishers Weekly, June 15, 1980, review of *The Land of Laughs,* p. 48; October 29, 1982, review of *Voice of Our Shadow,* p. 39; December 11, 1987, Sybil Steinberg, review of *Bones of the Moon,* p. 51; July 20, 1990, Sybil Steinberg, review of *A Child across the Sky,* p. 47; November 15, 1991, review of *Outside the Dog Museum,* p. 65; February 1, 1993, review of *After Silence,* p. 70; March 28, 1994, review of *From the Teeth of Angels,* p. 82; October 7, 1996, review of *The Panic Hand,* p. 60; November 10, 1997, review of *Kissing the Beehive,* p. 56; July 5, 1999, review of *The Marriage of Sticks,* p. 63; January 8, 2001, review of *The Wooden Sea,* p. 47;

April 8, 2002, review of *Bones of the Moon*, p. 211; September 23, 2002, review of *White Apples*, p. 54; August 8, 2005, review of *Glass Soup*, p. 208.

Realms of Fantasy, April, 2001, review of *The Wooden Sea*.

St. Louis Post-Dispatch (St. Louis, MO), October 30, 2002, Dorman T. Shindler, review of *White Apples*, p. E3.

Science Fiction Chronicle, June, 1997, Darrell Schweitzer, interview with Carroll, pp. 7, 38-41, 51-54.

Tales of the Unanticipated, Issue 9, 1991, D.H. Olson, interview with Carroll.

Third Alternative, May, 2003, Andrew Hedgecock, interview with Carroll.

Times (London, England), June 26, 1999, Christina Koning, review of *The Marriage of Sticks*, p. 19.

Tribune Books (Chicago, IL), August 10, 2003, review of *White Apples*, p. 6.

Voice of Youth Advocates, April, 1981, review of *The Land of Laughs*, p. 30; April, 2000, review of *The Marriage of Sticks*, p. 44.

Washington Post, April 25, 1983, Jack Sullivan, review of *Voice of Our Shadow*, p. D2.

Washington Post Book World, May 3, 1981, Jack Sullivan, review of *The Land of Laughs*, p. 4.

ONLINE

Accent Review, http://www.accentreview.com/ (July 15, 2006), Bev Vincent, review of *Glass Soup*.

Alien Online, http://www.thealienonline.net/ (May 13, 2002), Joe Gordon, review of *The Wooden Sea*.

Bookloons, http://www.bookloons.com/ (May 31, 2007), Hilary Williamson, review of *Glass Soup*.

BookSense, http://www.booksense.com/ (May 31, 2007), Gavin J. Grant, interview with Carroll.

InfinityPlus, http://www.infinityplus.co.uk/ (July, 2001), John Grant, review of *The Wooden Sea*; (July, 2002), Gary Couzens, review of *Voice of Our Shadow*; (December 28, 2002), Claude Lalumiere, review of *White Apples*.

Official Jonathan Carroll Web site, http://www.jonathancarroll.com (September 27, 2006).

PopMatters, http://www.popmatters.com/ (May 31, 2007), Mark Dionne, reviews of *The Wooden Sea*.

Rambles: A Cultural Arts Magazine, http://www.rambles.net/ (May 31, 2007), Donna Scanlon, review of *The Wooden Sea* and *The Marriage of Sticks*.

Rocky Mountain News Online, http://www.rockymountainnews.com/ (October 6, 2005), Mark Graham, review of *Glass Soup*.

Ruminator, http://www.ruminator.com/ (October-November, 2005), Susannah McNeely, review of *Glass Soup*.

SFSite.com, http://www.sfsite.com/ (February, 2001), Rodger Turner, interview with Jonathan Carroll; Rodger Turner, review of *The Land of Laughs*; Rich Horton, review of *Voice of Our Shadow*; William Thompson, review of *White Apples*; David Soyka, review of *Outside the Dog Museum*; Rich Horton, review of *The Wooden Sea*; Glen Engel-Cox, review of *Kissing the Beehive*; David Soyka, review of *Glass Soup*.

Strange Horizons, http://www.strangehorizons.com/ (March 5, 2001), Mary Anne Mohanraj, review of *The Marriage of Sticks*.

White Apples Web site, http://www.whiteapples.com/ (January 9, 2003).*

Jean Cocteau

(Photograph courtesy of AP Images.)

■ Personal

Born July 5, 1889, in Maisons-Lafitte, Yvelines, France; died October 11, 1963; buried at Milly-la-Foret, Essone, France, in the garden of the chapel Saint-Blaise-des Simples, which he designed himself; son of Georges (a lawyer) and Eugenie (Lecomte) Cocteau. *Education:* Studied at Lycee Condorcet, Paris; attended private classes.

■ Career

Poet, playwright, novelist, essayist, painter, and director. Founder, with Blaise Cendrars, of Editions de la Sirene, 1918. *Military service:* During World War I, Cocteau went to Rheims as a civilian ambulance driver, and then to Belgium, where he joined a group of marine-riflemen, until it was discovered that his presence was unauthorized; also served for a time with an auxiliary corps in Paris.

■ Member

Academie Francaise, Academie Royale de Belgique, Academie Mallarme, American Academy, German Academy (Berlin), Academie de Jazz (president), Academie du Disque, Association France-Hongrie, National Institute of Arts and Letters (New York; honorary member).

■ Awards, Honors

Prix Louions-Delluc, 1946; Grand Prix de la Critique Internationale, 1950; Grand Prix du Film Avant-garde, 1950, for Orphee; D.Litt., Oxford University, 1956; Commandeur de la Legion d'Honneur, 1961.

■ Writings

POETRY

La Lampe d'Aladin, Societe d'Editions, 1909.
Le Prince frivole, Mercure de France, 1910.
La Danse de Sophocle, Mercure de France, 1912.
Le Cap de Bonne-Esperance, Editions de la Sirene, 1919.
L'Ode a Picasso, Francois Bernouard, 1919.
(With Andre Lhote) *Escales,* Editions de la Sirene, 1920.
Poesies: 1917-20, Editions de la Sirene, 1920.
Vocabulaire, Editions de la Sirene, 1922.
Plain-Chant, Stock, 1923.
Poesie, 1916-23, Gallimard, 1924.

La Rose de Francois, Francois Bernouard, 1924.

Cri ecrit, Imprimerie de Montane (Montpellier), 1925.

Pierre Mutilee, Editions des Cahiers Libres, 1925.

L'Ange heurtebise, Stock, 1925.

Opera: Oeuvres poetiques 1925-27, Stock, 1927, revised edition, 1959, published as *Oeuvres poetiques: 1925-27*, Dutilleul, 1959.

Morceaux choisis, Gallimard, 1932, published as *Poemes*, H. Kaeser (Lausanne), 1945.

Mythologie (poems written on lithographic stones; contains 10 original lithographs by Giorgio di Chirico), Editions de Quatre-Chemins, 1934.

Allegories, Gallimard, 1941.

Leone, Nouvelle Revue Francaise, 1945, translation by Alan Neame published as *Leoun*, [London], 1960.

La Crucifixion, Morihien, 1946.

Le Chiffre sept, Seghers, 1952.

Appogiatures (with a portrait of Cocteau by Modigliani), Editions du Rocher (Monaco), 1953.

Dentelle d'eternite, Seghers, 1953.

Clair-Obscur, Editions du Rocher, 1954.

Poemes: 1916-55, Gallimard, 1956.

(Contributor) Paul Eluard, *Corps memorabiles*, Seghers, 1958.

De la Brouille, Editions Dynamo (Liege), 1960.

Ceremonial espagnol du Phoenix [suivi de] *La Partie d'echecs*, Gallimard, 1961.

Le Requiem, Gallimard, 1962.

Faire-Part (ninety-one previously unpublished poems), foreword by Jean Marais and Claude-Michel Cluny, Librairie Saint-Germain des Pres, 1968.

Vocabulaire, Plain-Chant et autre poemes, Gallimard, 1983.

Poemes (contains *Appogiatures*, *Clair-Obscur*, and *Paraprosodies*), Editions du Rocher, 1984.

Tempest of Stars: Selected Poems, bilingual edition, translated by Jeremy Reed, Enitharmon (London, England), 1992.

Oeuvres poetiques completes, Gallimard, 1999.

NOVELS

Le Potomak, Societe Litteraire de France, 1919, definitive edition, Stock, 1924.

(Self-illustrated) *Le Grand Ecart*, Stock, 1923, reprinted, 1970, translation by Lewis Galantiere published as *The Grand Ecart*, Putnam, 1925, translation by Dorothy Williams published as *The Miscreant*, P. Owen, 1958.

Thomas l'imposteur, Nouvelle Revue Francaise, 1923, revised edition, edited by Bernard Garniez, Macmillan, 1964, translation and introduction by Gal-antiere published as *Thomas the Impostor*, Appleton, 1925, translation by Williams published as *The Impostor*, Noonday Press, 1957.

Les Enfants terribles (also see below), Grasset, 1929, reprinted, 1963, revised edition, edited by Jacques Hardre, Blaisdell, 1969, translation by Samuel Putnam published as *Enfants Terribles*, Harcourt, 1930, translation by Rosamund Lehmann published in England as *The Children of the Game*, Harvill, 1955, same translation published as *The Holy Terrors* (not the same as translation of *Les Monstres sacres*, below), New Directions, 1957.

La Fin du Potomak, Gallimard, 1940.

Deux travestis (contains lithographs by Cocteau), Fournier, 1947.

PLAYS

(With Frederic de Madrazo) *Le Dieu bleu* (ballet), first produced in Paris at the Theatre du Chatelet, June, 1912.

(With Pablo Picasso, Erik Satie, Leonide Massine, and Sergei Pavlovich Diaghilev) *Parade* (ballet), first produced in Paris at the Theatre du Chatelet, May 18, 1917.

(Author of scenario) *Le Boeuf sur le toit ou, The Do Nothing Bar*, with music by Darius Milhaud, first produced in Paris at the Comedie des Champs-Elysees, February 21, 1920.

Les Maries de la tour Eiffel (ballet; first produced in Paris at the Theatre des Champs-Elysses, June 18, 1921), Nouvelle Revue Francaise, 1924, translation by Dudley Fitts published as *The Eiffel Tower Wedding Party*, in *The Infernal Machine, and Other Plays*, New Directions, 1963, translation by Michael Benedikt published as *The Wedding on the Eiffel Tower*, in *Modern French Plays*, Faber, 1964.

Antigone (based on the play by Sophocles), with music by Arthur Honegger, (first produced in Paris at the Theatre de l'Atelier, December 20, 1922), Nouvelle Revue Francaise, 1928, translation by Wildman published in *Four Plays*, MacGibbon & Kee, 1961.

Romeo et Juliette (five-acts and twenty-three tableaux), first produced in Paris at the Theatre de la Cigale, June 2, 1924.

Orphee (one-act tragedy; first produced in Paris at the Theatre des Arts, June 15, 1926), Stock, 1927, translation by Carl Wildman published as *Orphee: A Tragedy in One Act* (first produced in New York at the Living Theatre as *Orpheus*, September 30, 1954), Oxford University Press, 1933, translation by John Savacool published as *Orphee*, New Directions, 1963.

La Voix humaine (also see below; one-act; first produced in Paris at the Comedie-Francaise, February 17, 1930), Stock, 1930, translation by Wildman published as *The Human Voice*, Vision Press, 1951 (produced in New York, 1980).

La Machine infernale (four-act tragedy; first produced in Paris at the Theatre Louis Jouvet, April 10, 1934), Grasset, 1934, reprinted, Livre de Poche, 1974, published in England in French, under the original title, with an introduction and notes by W.M. Landers, Harrap, 1957, translation and introduction by Wildman published as *The Infernal Machine*, Oxford University Press, 1936, translation by Albert Bermel published as *The Infernal Machine*, New Directions, 1963.

Oedipe-Roi (based on the play by Sophocles), first produced in 1937.

Les Chevaliers de la table ronde (four-act; first produced in Paris at the Theatre de l'Oeuvre, October 14, 1937), Gallimard, 1937, reprinted, 1966, translation by W.H. Auden published as *The Knights of the Round Table*, New Directions, 1963.

Les Parents terribles (also see below; three-act; first produced in Paris at the Theatre des Ambassadeurs, November 14, 1938), Gallimard, 1938, reprinted, 1972, revised edition, edited by R.K. Totton, Methuen, 1972, translation by Charles Frank published as *Intimate Relations*, MacGibbon & Kee, 1962, translation by Jeremy Sams published as *Indiscretions*, N. Hern, 1994.

Les Monstres sacres (three-act; first produced in Paris at the Theatre Michel, February 17, 1940), Gallimard, 1940, translation by Edward O. Marsh published as *The Holy Terrors*, MacGibbon & Kee, 1962.

La Machine a ecrire (three-act; first produced in Paris at the Theatre Hebertot, April 29, 1941), Gallimard, 1941, translation by Ronald Duncan published as *The Typewriter*, Dobson, 1957.

Renaud et Armide (three-act tragedy; first produced in Paris at the Comedie-Francaise, April 13, 1943), Gallimard, 1943.

L'Aigle a deux tetes (also see below; three-act; first produced in Paris at the Theatre Hebertot, November, 1946), Gallimard, 1946, reprinted, 1973, translation by Duncan published as *The Eagle Has Two Heads*, Funk, 1948, translation by Wildman published as *The Eagle with Two Heads*, MacGibbon & Kee, 1962.

(Adaptor) Tennessee Williams, *Un Tramway nomme desir* (first produced in Paris at the Theatre Edouard VII, October 17, 1949), Bordas, 1949.

Bacchus (three-act; first produced in Paris at the Theatre Marigny, December 20, 1951), Gallimard, 1952, translation by Mary C. Hoeck published as *Bacchus: A Play*, New Directions, 1963.

(Translator and adaptor) Jerome Kilty, *Cher menteur* (first produced in Paris at Theatre de l'Athenee, October 4, 1960), Paris-Theatre, 1960.

L'Impromptu du Palais-Royal (first produced in Tokyo, May 1, 1962), Gallimard, 1962.

OPERA

Oedipus rex: Opera-oratorio en deux actes d'apres Sophocle, Boosey & Hawkes, 1949.

FILMS

(And director) *Le Sang d'un Poete* (produced, 1932), Editions du Rocher, 1948, augmented edition, 1957, translation by Lily Pons published as *The Blood of a Poet*, Bodley Press, 1949.

La Comedie du bonheur, produced, 1940.

Le Baron fantome (appeared also as actor), produced, 1942.

L'Eternel retour (produced, 1944), Nouvelles Editions Francaises, 1948.

Les Dames du Bois du Boulogne, produced, 1944.

(And director) *La Belle et la bete* (based on a fairy tale by Mme. Leprince de Beaumont; produced, 1945), Editions du Rocher, 1958, bilingual edition, New York University Press, 1970.

Ruy Blas (adaptation of the play by Victor Hugo; produced, 1947), Editions du Rocher, 1947.

La Voix humaine (adaptation of the play), produced, 1947.

(And director) *L'Aigle a deux tetes* (adaptation of the play), produced, 1947.

Noces de sable, produced 1948.

(And director) *Les Parents terribles* (adaptation of the play; produced, 1948), Le Monde Illustre, 1949, translation and adaptation by Charles Frank produced under title *Intimate Relations* (also known as *Disobedient*), 1952.

Les Enfants terribles (adaptation of the novel), produced, 1948.

(And director) *Orphee* (Cocteau speaks a few lines as *author*; produced, 1949), Andre Bonne, 1951.

(And director) *Santo Sospiro* (short film), produced, 1951.

Ce Siecle a cinquante ans (short film), produced, 1952.

La Coronna nagra, produced, 1952.

(And director) *Le Rouge est mis* (short film), produced, 1952.

(And director) *Le Testament d'Orphee* (produced, 1959), Editions du Rocher, 1959.

NONFICTION

Le Coq et l'arlequin (with a portrait of Cocteau by Picasso), Editions de la Sirene, 1918, translation by Rollo H. Myers published as *Cock and Harlequin: Notes Concerning Music*, Egoist Press (London), 1921.

Dans le ciel de la patrie, Societe Spad, 1918.

Le Secret professionnel, Stock, 1922.

Dessins, Stock, 1923, translation published as *Drawings,* Dover, 1972.

Picasso, Stock, 1923.

Lettre a Jacques Maritain, Stock, 1926, published as *Lettre a Maritain: Reponse a Jean Cocteau* (including response by Maritain), Stock, 1964.

Le Rappel a l'ordre, Stock, 1926, translation by Myers published as *A Call to Order,* Faber & Gwyer, 1926, reprinted, Haskell House, 1974.

Romeo et Juliette: Pretexte a mise en scene d'apres le drame de William Shakespeare, Se Vend au Sans Pareil, 1926.

Le Mystere laic (an essay on indirect study), Editions de Quatre Chemins, 1928, published *Essai de critique indirecte: Le mystere laic-Des beaux arts consideres comme un assassinat,* introduction by Bernard Grasset, Grasset, 1932.

(Published anonymously) *Le Livre blanc,* Les Quatre Chemins (Paris), 1928, reprinted, B. Laville, 1970, translation published as *The White Paper,* Olympia Press (Paris), 1957, Macaulay, 1958, translation with an introduction by Crosland, containing woodcuts by Cocteau, published as *Le Livre blanc,* P. Owen, 1969, revised edition published as *Le Livre blanc suivi de quatorze textes erotiques inedits; illustre de dix-huit dessins,* Persona (Paris), 1981.

(Self-illustrated) *Opium: Journal d'une desintoxication,* Stock, 1930, reprinted, 1972, translation by Ernest Boyd published as *Opium: The Diary of an Addict* (contains twenty-seven illustrations by Cocteau), Longmans, Green, 1932, translation by Margaret Crosland and Sinclair Road published as *Opium: The Diary of a Cure,* P. Owen, 1957, revised edition, 1968, Grove, 1958.

(Self-illustrated) *Portraits-Souvenir, 1900-1914,* Grasset, 1935, translation by Crosland published as *Paris Album, 1900-1914,* W.H. Allen, 1956.

(Contributor) Gea Augsbourg, *La Vie de Darius Milhaud,* Correa, 1935.

60 dessins pour "Les Enfants terribles," Grasset, 1935.

Mon premier voyage: Tour du monde en 80 jours, Gallimard, 1936, translation by Stuart Gilbert published as *Round the World Again in Eighty Days,* G. Routledge, 1937, translation by W.J. Strachan published as *My Journey Round the World,* P. Owen, 1958.

Dessins en marge du texte des "Chevaliers de la table ronde," Gallimard, 1941.

Le Greco, Le Divan, 1943.

Portrait de Mounet-Sully (contains sixteen drawings by Cocteau), F. Bernouard (Paris), 1945.

La Belle et la bete: Journal d'un film, Janin, 1946, translation by Ronald Duncan published as *Diary of a Film,* Roy, 1950, revised edition published as *Beauty and the Beast: Diary of a Film,* Dover, 1972.

Poesie critique (poetry criticism), edited by Henri Parisot, Editions des Quatre Vents, 1946, published in two volumes, Gallimard, 1959.

(With Paul Claudel, Paul Eluard, and Stephane Mallarme) *De la musique encore et toujours!,* preface by Paul Valery, Editions du Tambourinaire, 1946.

La Difficulte d'etre, P. Morihien, 1947, translation by Elizabeth Sprigge published as *The Difficulty of Being,* introduction by Ned Rorem, P. Owen, 1966, Coward, 1967.

Le Foyer des artistes, Plon, 1947.

L'Eternel retour, Nouvelles Editions Francaises, 1947.

Art and Faith: Letters between Jacques Maritain and Jean Cocteau, Philosophical Library, 1948.

(Self-illustrated) *Drole de menage,* P. Morihien, 1948.

Lettre aux Americains, Grasset, 1949.

(Editor) *Almanach du theatre et du cinema,* Editions de Flore, 1949.

Maalesh: Journal d'une tournee de theatre, Gallimard, 1949, translation by Mary C. Hoeck published as *Maalesh: Theatrical Tour in the Middle East,* P. Owen, 1956.

(Editor) *Choix de lettres de Max Jacob a Jean Cocteau: 1919-1944,* P. Morihien, 1949.

Dufy, Flammarion, 1950.

(With Andre Bazin) *Orson Welles,* Chavane, 1950.

Modigliani, F. Hazin (Paris), 1950.

(With others) *Portrait de famille,* Fini, 1950.

Jean Marais, Calmann-Levy, 1951, reprinted, 1975.

Entretiens autour de cinematographe, recueillis par Andre Fraigneau, A. Bonne, 1951, translation by Vera Traill published as *Cocteau on Film: A Conversation Recorded by Andre Fraigneau,* Roy, 1954, reprinted, Dover, 1972.

Journal d'un inconnu, Grasset, 1952, translation by Alec Brown published as *The Hand of a Stranger,* Elek Books (London), 1956, Horizon, 1959, translation by Jese Browner published as *Diary of an Unknown,* Paragon House, 1988.

Reines de la France, Grasset, 1952.

(With Julien Green) *Gide vivant* (includes commentary by Cocteau and excerpts from the diary of Green), Amiot-Dumont, 1952.

Carte blanche (prose sketches with drawings, watercolors and photographs by Cocteau), Mermod (Lausanne), 1953.

(With others) *Prestige de la danse,* Clamart, 1953.

Discours de reception de M. Jean Cocteau a l'Academie francaise et reponse de M. Andre Maurois, Gallimard, 1955.

Look to the Glory of Your Firm and the Excellence of Your Merchandise, for If You Deem These Good, Your Welfare Becomes the Welfare of All, translated by Lewis Galantiere, Draeger (Montrouge), c1955.

Aux confins de la Chine, Edition Caracteres, 1955.

Colette: Discours de reception a l'Academie Royale de Belgique, Grasset, 1955 (extracts in English published in *My Contemporaries*, 1967.

Lettre sur la poesie, Dutilleul, 1955.

Le Dragon des mers, Georges Guillot, 1955.

(Contributor) *Marbre et decoration*, Federation Marbriere de France, 1955.

Journals (contains sixteen drawings by Cocteau), edited and translated with an introduction by Wallace Fowlie, Criterion Books, 1956.

Adieu a Mistinguett, Editions Dynamo, 1956.

Art et sport, Savonnet (Limoges), 1956.

Impression: Arts de la rue, Editions Dynamo, 1956.

(Author of introduction and notes) Jean Dauven, compiler, *Jean Cocteau chez les sirens: Une experience de linguistic sur le discours de reception a l'Academie francaise de M. Jean Cocteau* (illustrations by Picasso), Editions du Rocher, 1956.

Temoignage (with portrait and engraving by Picasso), P. Bertrand, 1956.

Le Discours de Strasbourg, Societe Messine d'Editions et d'Impressions (Metz), 1956.

Le Discours d'Oxford, Gallimard, 1956, translation by Jean Stewart published as *Poetry and Invisibility*, in *London Magazine*, January, 1957.

(With Louis Aragon) *Entretiens sur le Musee de Dresde*, Cercle d'Art, 1957, translation published as *Conversations on the Dresden Gallery*, Holmes, 1983.

Erik Satie, Editions Dynamo, 1957.

La Chapelle Saint Pierre, Villefranche sur Mer, Editions du Rocher, 1957.

La Corrida du premier mai, Grasset, 1957.

Comme un miel noir (in French and English), L'Ecole Estienne, 1958.

(With Roloff Beny and others) *Merveilles de la Mediterranee*, Arthaud, 1958.

Paraprosodies precedees de 7 dialogues, Editions Du Rocher, 1958.

(Contributor) G. Coanet, *De bas en haut*, La Societe Messine d'Editions et d'Impressions (Metz), 1958.

La Salle des mariages, Hotel de ville de Menton, Editions du Rocher, 1958.

La Canne blanche, Editions Estienne, 1959.

Gondole des morts, All'Insegne del Pesce d'Oro (Milan), 1959.

Guide a l'usage des visiteurs de la Chapelle Saint Blaise des Simples, Editions du Rocher, 1960.

De la brouille, Editions Dynamo, 1960.

Notes sur "Le Testament d'Orphee," Editions Dynamo, 1960.

(Editor) *Amedeo Modigilani: Quinze dessins*, Leda, 1960.

Decentralisation, [Paris], 1961.

Du Serieux, [Paris], 1961.

(With others) *Insania pingens*, Ciba (Basle), 19611961, published as *Petits maitres de la folies*, Clairfontaines (Lausanne), 1961.

Le Cordon ombilical, Plon, 1962.

Picasso: 1916-1961 (with twenty-four original lithographs by Picasso), Editions du Rocher, 1962.

Discours a l'Academie royale de langue et de litterature francaises, Editions Dynamo, 1962.

Hommage, Editions Dynamo, 1962.

Interview par Jean Breton (preceded by two poems by Cocteau, Malediction au laurier, and Hommage a Igor Stravinsky), [Paris], 1963.

Adieu d'Antonio Ordonez, Editions Forces Vives, 1963.

(Contributor) *La Comtesse de Noailles*, Librairie Academique Perrin, 1963.

(Contributor) *Exposition les peintres temoins de leur temps* (catalog), Musee Galliera (Paris), 1963.

(Contributor) *Toros muertos*, Editions Forces Vives, 1963.

La Mesangere, De Tartas, 1963.

Jean Cocteau: Entretien avec Roger Stephane (interview), J. Tallandier, 1964.

(Contributor) *Exposition Lucien Clergue* (catalog), Le Musee (Luneville), 1964.

Entretien avec Andre Fraigneau (interview), preface by Pierre de Boisdeffre, Union Generale d'Editions, 1965.

Pegase, Nouveau Cercle Parisien du Livre, 1965.

My Contemporaries, translated, edited, and introduced by Crosland, P. Owen, 1967, Chilton, 1968.

Entre Radiguet et Picasso, Editions Hermann, 1967.

Professional Secrets: The Autobiography of Jean Cocteau (not related to 1922 book), translated by Richard Howard, edited by Robert Phelps, Farrar, Straus, 1970.

Lettres a Andre Gide avec quelques reponses d'Andre Gide, La Table Ronde, 11970.

(With Raymond Radiguet) *Paul et Virginie*, Edition Speciale, 1973.

Lettres a Milorad, 1955-1963, Editions Saint-Germain-des-Pres, 1975.

Correspondence avec Jean-Marie Magnan, Belfond, 1981.

Le Passe defini I, 1951-1952, journal, edited by Pierre Chanel, Gallimard, 1983, translation by Richard Howard published as *Past Tense: The Diaries of Jean Cocteau*, Volume 1, Harcourt, 1986.

Lettres a Jacques Maritain, Stock, 1984.

Le Passe defini II, 1953, journal, edited by Chanel, Gallimard, 1985.

Souvenir Portraits: Paris in the Belle Epoque, translated by Jesse Browner, Paragon House (New York, NY), 1990.

(With Georges Feydeau) *Thirteen Monologues*, translated by Peter Meyer, Oberon (London, England), 1996.

Round the World Again in 80 Days, translated by Stuart Gilbert, Tauris Parke (London, England), 2000.

OMNIBUS VOLUMES

Call to Order (contains *Cock and Harlequin, Professional Secrets*, and other critical essays), translated by Rollo H. Myers, Holt, 1923, reprinted, Haskell House, 1974.

Oedipe-Roi [and] Romeo et Juliette, Plon, 1928.

Jean Cocteau (contains a study of Roger Lannes, poems, and a bibliography), Seghers, 1945, revised edition, 1969.

Oeuvres completes, 11 volumes, Marguerat, 1947–1951.

Theatre, 2 volumes, Gallimard, 1948, augmented edition, 2 volumes, Grasset, 1957.

Poemes (contains *Leone, Allegories, La Crucifixion,* and *Neige*), Gallimard, 1948.

Theatre de Poche, P. Morihien, 1949, published as *Nouveau theatre de poche*, Editions du Rocher, 1960.

Anthologie poetique de Jean Cocteau, Le Club Francais du Livre, 1951.

Venise images par Ferruccio Leiss [and] L'Autre face de Venise par Jean Cocteau, D. Guarnati (Milan), 1953.

Le Grand ecart [and] La Voix humaine, Club des Editeurs, 1957.

Impression [with] Arts de la rue [and] Eloge de l'imprimerie, Editions Dynamo, 1957.

Cocteau par Lui-meme, edited by Andre Fraigneau, Editions du Seuil, 1957.

Five Plays (contains *Orphee, Antigone, Intimate Relations, The Holy Terrors,* and *The Eagle with Two Heads*), Hill & Wang, 1961.

Orpheus, Oedipus Rex, [and] The Infernal Machine, translated with a foreword and introductory essay by Wildman, Oxford University Press, 1962.

Four Plays (contains *Antigone, Intimate Relations, The Holy Terrors,* and *he Eagle with Two Heads*), MacGibbon Kee, 1962.

Les Enfants terribles [and] Les Parents terribles, Club des Librairies de France, 1962.

Special Cocteau: Les Maries de la Tour Eiffel [and] Les Chevaliers de la table ronde, [Paris], 1966.

Opera [with] Le Discours du grand sommeil, preface by Jacques Brosse, Gallimard, 1967.

The Infernal Machine, and Other Plays, New Directions, 1967.

Opera [with] Plain-Chant, Livre de Poche, 1967.

Le Cap de Bonne-Esperance [with] Le Discours du grand sommeil, Gallimard, 1967.

Pages choisies, edited by Robert Prat, Hachette, 1967.

Opera [with] Des mots, De mon style, Tchou, 1967.

Two Screenplays: The Blood of a Poet [and] The Testament of Orpheus, translated by Carol Martin-Sperry, Orion Press, 1968.

Screenplays and Other Writings on the Cinema (contains *The Blood of a Poet, Beauty and the Beast,* and *Testament of Orpheus*), Orion Press, 1968.

White Paper [with] The Naked Beast at Heaven's Gate, the latter by P. Angelique, Greenleaf Classics, 1968.

Three Screenplays: L'Eternal retour, Orphee, La Belle et la bete, translated by Carol Martin-Sperry, Orion Press, 1968.

Cocteau's World: An Anthology of Writings by Jean Cocteau, translated and edited by Margaret Crosland, P. Owen, 1971, Dodd, 1973.

Du cinematographie (collected works), edited by Andre Bernard and Claude Gauteur, P. Belfond, 1973.

Entretiens sur le cinematographie, edited by Bernard and Gauteur, P. Belfond, 1973.

Mon Premier voyage, Des beaux-arts consideres comme un assassinat, Lettre a Maritan, Vialetay, 1973.

Orphee: Extraits de la tragedie d'Orphee ainsi que des films Orphee et Le Testament d'Orphee, Bordas, 1973.

Poesie de journalism, 1935-1938, P. Belfond, 1973.

Also author of *Sept dialogues avec le Seigneur qui est en nous*, Editions du Rocher.

OTHER

(Contributor of photographs) Billy Kluver, *A Day with Picasso: Twenty-four photographs by Jean Cocteau*, MIT Press, 1997.

Contributor on the arts to *Paris-Midi*, March to August, 1919; wrote a regular series for *Ce Soir*, 1937-38; founder, with Maurice Rostand and others, of the review *Scheherazade*. Some of Cocteau's manuscripts are housed at the Archives Jean Cocteau, Milly-la-Foret, Essonne, France.

■ Adaptations

There are several recordings of Cocteau's works in French; *Opium: Journal of a Cure* has been adapted for the stage by Roc Brynner and produced in Dublin and London, 1969, and in New York, 1970.

■ Sidelights

Jean Cocteau had a wide-ranging career as a poet, dramatist, screenwriter, and novelist. "Cocteau's willingness and ability to turn his hand to the most disparate creative ventures," James P. Mc Nab wrote in the *Dictionary of Literary Biography,* "do not fit the stereotypical image of the priestlike—or Proust-like—writer single-mindedly sacrificing his life on the altar of an all-consuming art. But the best of his efforts, in each of the genres that he took up, enriched that genre." Among Cocteau's most influential works are *Parade,* a seminal work of the modern ballet, *La Machine infernale,* a play that is still performed some sixty years after it was written, such films as *La Belle et le bete* and *La Sang d'un Poete* (*The Blood of a Poet*), and his novel *Les Enfants terrible,* a study of adolescent alienation. A *National Observer* writer suggested that, "of the artistic generation whose daring gave birth to Twentieth Century Art, Cocteau came closest to being a Renaissance man." Cocteau, according to Annette Insdorf in the *New York Times,* "left behind a body of work unequalled for its variety of artistic expression."

A Problem Child

Thrown out of school as a boy, Cocteau was the problem child of a well-to-do Parisian family. After his father committed suicide when Cocteau was ten, the boy grew closer to his mother, who appears as the dominant female character in much of his later work. As a child Cocteau also formed a lifelong passion for the theatre, which he described many times as being "the fever of crimson and gold." Wallace Fowlie reported: "The atmosphere of the theatre became a world for him. . . . Every detail of a theatre production fascinated him, from the luminously painted backdrop to the women selling caramels in the intermission." Neal Oxenhandler, writing in his book *Scandal and Parade: The Theater of Jean Cocteau,* saw a definite relationship between Cocteau's love for his mother and his love for the theater. Oxenhandler stated: "Cocteau's first experience of the glamor and prestige of the theater was the smell of his mother's perfume and the shimmering beauty of her dresses as she prepared to go out for an evening at the Comedie-Francaise or the Opera. She was the theater."

When Cocteau was eighteen years old, his poems were publicly read in Paris by the actor Edouard de Max and several of his theatre friends. Enamored with the young poet's work, the actors presented a reading at a theatre on the Champs-Elysees. Following this introduction, Cocteau became an active participant in the Paris arts scene. In the period before World War I, he was associated with the avant-garde Cubists, Fauvists and Futurists. Cocteau met and worked with such artists as Pablo Picasso and Erik Satie, published several volumes of poems, began writing plays and ballets, and established himself as a leading member of the French avant-garde. Always a poet first and foremost, Cocteau emphasized from the beginning of his career that, whatever the genre in which he worked, all of his creations were essentially poetry.

Early Success

Cocteau's first early success was the ballet *Parade,* written with composer Erik Satie, painter Pablo Picasso, choreographer Leonide Massine, and Sergei Pavlovich Diaghilev of the Russian Ballet. Telling of a group of mysterious promoters trying unsuccessfully to entice spectators into a circus tent where an undefined spectacle is taking place, *Parade* is generally considered to be the first of the modern ballets. It was also Cocteau's "first public attempt," Alan G. Artner explained in the *Chicago Tribune,* "to express the mysterious and eternal in the everyday." Jacques Guicharnaud and June Beckelman wrote in *Modern French Theatre from Giraudoux to Beckett* that *Parade* "has a theme that might serve as a symbol for the whole of Cocteau's works: Cocteau keeps his public outside. The true spectacle of the inner circus remains forbidden, despite the poet's innumerable invitations to enter. And perhaps that inner circus is no more than an absolute vacuum."

A casual remark made by Diaghilev was Cocteau's inspiration for the ballet. As the two men were walking down a street, Cocteau wondered why it was that Diaghilev was so reserved in his critical judgements of Cocteau's work. The Russian adjusted his monocle and said: "Astonish me." *Parade* was written to do just that. The Futurist-inspired sets and costumes by Picasso and the satirical music of Satie, both of which caused an uproar with the Parisian audience, were complemented by Cocteau's wild scenario involving acrobats, a juggler, and a girl riding a bicycle. "Whatever else Parade may have been," Oxenhandler commented, "it was above all a series of visual surprises." *Parade* is still in the repertories of the Joffrey Ballet and the Metropolitan Opera Ballet.

Another early success was 1921's *Les Maries de la Tour Eiffel* (*The Wedding on the Eiffel Tower*). Written for Les Ballets Suedois, a Swedish ballet troupe working in Paris, the ballet consists of a series of unrelated nonsense scenes set during a wedding reception at the Eiffel Tower. Wild events take place: a camera gives birth to an ostrich; a lion eats several cast members. "The poetry of *Les Maries de la Tour Eiffel,*" Guicharnaud and Beckelman wrote, "consists in replacing traditional coherence by an inner chance that is quite contrary to the logic of everyday

Cocteau on the set of one of his films. (Photograph courtesy of The Kobal Collection. Reproduced by permission.)

reality. 'The scenes fit together like the words of a poem,' says Cocteau in his preface [to the ballet]. Here the poem would be a surrealist divertissement or, to be more explicit, a collage. Its interest lies both in its amusing absurdity and its challenge to accepted forms of poetry and painting." Cocteau claimed that the work was meant to introduce a "classicism of shock" to ballet. Whatever its intentions, *The Wedding on the Eiffel Tower* was denounced by the avant-garde Dadaists of the day as well as by the Parisian middle-class audience.

Cocteau's involvement with the ballet and theatre brought him in the early 1920s into contact with a group of six young composers. Acting as their spokesman, Cocteau brought "Les Six," as they became known, into prominence throughout Europe. Fowlie remarked: "The group of Les Six—Honegger, Poulenc, Milhaud, Taillefer, Auric and Durey—owes [Cocteau] its name and the early support it received in Paris." In addition, Fowlie

related, Cocteau served as an "impresario and interpreter" for such other artists as Satie, Braque, Picasso and Stravinsky, all of whom "owe some of their glory to Cocteau."

During this time Cocteau also began a homosexual relationship with Raymond Radiguet, the young author of several novels. When Radiguet died of typhoid in 1923, Cocteau was distraught. He turned to opium, then a brief reconciliation with the Catholic Church, and finally to a series of young lovers. One of these lovers, Jean Desbordes, inspired a novella entitled *Le Livre blanc.* Published anonymously because Cocteau wished to avoid embarrassing his mother, the book is a frank, first-person account of a homosexual's life in 1920s France. The narrator states that for as long as he can remember, he has had a love for boys. He recalls three important incidents of his early youth: seeing a young farm-boy undressing, two nude gypsy youths relaxing in the trees of his father's estate, and a young servant named Gustave, who rejected his confused advances. One night, while returning to his father's house, a soft-spoken woman named Rose accosts the narrator and they later meet at a hotel. One Sunday at the hotel, Rose introduces the narrator to her nineteen-year-old brother Alfred. The narrator and Alfred carry on an affair without Rose's knowledge. Alfred is actually Rose's pimp. The narrator and Alfred fall in love, but Alfred abandons him to return to his old ways. After a series of disappointing encounters, the narrator gives up on love and decides to join a monastery. He reaches a mountain abbey, and there meets a monk who resembles all the lovers of his past. But even this is a disappointment. The novel ends with the narrator exiling himself from a society that makes his love a vice. "Although the aesthetic interest of *Le Livre blanc* is quite slim," Mc Nab admitted, "it is as rich a compendium of Cocteau's obsessions as any single work he ever wrote." An essayist

for *Gay and Lesbian Literature* found that "*Le Livre blanc*, with its light touch, constant changes of scene, and determined salacity, is reminiscent of eighteenth-century tales. Like eighteenth-century heroes before him, the twentieth-century protagonist of *Le Livre blanc* finally decides that he must leave France, where his sexuality is barely tolerated. But the novella is also 'pure' Cocteau. Many of the images that are more fully developed by Cocteau in later works are found here, from gypsies to mirrors, sailors to centaurs; all are explicitly sexual, undisguised, unsublimated. It becomes clear that sexuality—more precisely homosexuality—is at the heart of all of Cocteau's work, though it is often masked."

Overcomes Drug Addiction

Opium: The Diary of an Addict recounted the facts of Cocteau's opium addiction, for which he twice required hospitalization before being cured. The

A scene from Cocteau's 1930 film *The Blood of a Poet*. (Courtesy of The Kobal Collection, 1930. Reproduced by permission.)

book is based on Cocteau's notes of a three-month hospital stay in late 1928 and early 1929. It is, as Mc Nab described it, "a fascinating account of the stages of withdrawal." Cocteau was treated for his addiction at the Thermes Urbains Sanatorium in Paris. "The Thomist philosopher Jacques Maritain visited him there," Bettina Liebowitz Knapp wrote in her study *Jean Cocteau,* "and spent many hours trying to convince him that a return to Catholicism would lift his depression and bring him new life. Cocteau accepted Maritain's help. When he left the Sanitorium he visited Maritain at his home in Meudon where he was introduced to Father Charles Henrion. Deeply impressed by this priest, Cocteau began taking religious instruction from him, and received the sacraments at his hands. A return to religion, at least for a while, gave him strength and a sense of belonging. Life now had boundaries, order, direction, and most important of all—a future." In addition to the book *Opium,* Cocteau also wrote several poems, collected in *Opera,* in which the opium experience figured prominently. These poems, according to Knapp, "are chiseled in incisive strokes. The feelings of lightness and giddiness are conveyed in harmonious tonalities, a blend of sharp consonants and free-flowing vowels, very nearly concretizing his drug-induced euphoria. During these periods he seemed to attain a kind of second sight that enabled him to discern the invisible from the visible, the inhuman from the human, and to express these visions in dramatic and poignant terms."

During the 1920s Cocteau also devoted his time to writing several novels, a new genre for him. These novels are usually concerned with protagonists who cannot leave their childhoods behind them. In *Le Grand Ecart,* for example, Jacques Forestier finds that beauty always brings him pain, a pattern established when he was a child. As a young man, the pattern continues when he loses his first love to another man, leading Jacques to attempt suicide. Germaine Bree and Margaret Guiton note in *The French Novel from Gide to Camus* that Jacques is "the most directly autobiographical of Cocteau's fictional characters." In addition, as Mc Nab pointed out, the novel anticipates Cocteau's later obsession with childhood.

In *Thomas l'Imposteur,* a novel released only days after *Le Grand Ecart,* Cocteau tells the story of a young boy of sixteen who finds stability and purpose in his life only by joining the French Army during World War I. To enlist in the army, Guillaume Thomas has lied about his age and borrowed a friend's uniform. Soon he is even posing as the

Jean Marais in a scene from the 1950 film *Orphee.* (Courtesy of Andre Paulve/Films du Palais Royal/The Kobal Collection/Corbeau, Roger.)

nephew of a military hero. "Cocteau hastens to add, however, that this is not an ordinary imposture, a vulgar means of 'getting ahead,'"as Bree and Guiton explained. "Guillaume, floating on the edges of a dream, is more at home, more himself, in a fictional than in a real existence." As Mc Nab noted, for Guillaume, "the enemy soldiers are merely a kind of catalyst, allowing his game to go on."

Writes about a Strange Childhood

Les Enfants Terribles (*The Children of the Game*) was begun while Cocteau was in the clinic recovering from his opium addiction. It was first published in 1929. The novel focuses on the doomed relationship between a brother and sister whose isolated existence is threatened and eventually destroyed by the outside world. To escape the loss of their isolation, the two siblings commit a double suicide. "On the one hand," wrote Leon S. Roudiez in *MOSAIC,* "the text extols the impossible values of a lost paradise of childhood; on the other hand, it condemns the contemporary world on account of its ugliness and evil. But Elizabeth and Paul demonstrate that the lost paradise is a myth. . . . The choice between total rejection, which can only be achieved in death, and total compromise, which means corruption of the individual, represents the truth that the text proclaims." Speaking of the book's structure, Bree and Guiton wrote: "Les Enfants terribles . . . has the rigorous economy of means, the geometrical construction, the almost claustrophobic unite de lieu of a classical tragedy. . . . This most ordered of Cocteau's novels also has the strongest poetic impact."

Les Enfants Terribles has won lasting critical acclaim for its haunting evocation of childhood. Knapp praised "the manner in which Cocteau catches and describes with such accuracy the protagonists' innermost thoughts and sensations. . . . The frequent omissions of rational plot sequences, the starkly drawn portraits of the children, the flavor of mystery and excitement which comes with the introduction of the unknown . . ., and the march of Fate . . . lend an enduring haunting quality to the book." Tom Bishop, writing in *Saturday Review*, described *Les Enfants Terribles* as "a haunting novel of youth, classic in form yet highly original in its portrayal of a brother and sister living in a bizarre world of their own." "During the past thirty years," Fowlie stated in *French Literature: Its History and Its Meaning*, "this book has become a classic, both as a novel belonging to the central tradition of the short French novel and as a document of historical-psychological significance." Knapp claimed that *Les Enfants Terribles* was "Cocteau's great work: a novel possessing the force, the tension, poetry, and religious flavor of an authentic Greek tragedy." After publishing *Les Enfants Terribles*, Cocteau essentially gave up long fiction.

During the 1930s Cocteau devoted his time to the theatre, writing two of his most accomplished dramatic works at this time: *La Machine infernale* and *Les Parents terribles*. *La Machine infernale* is an update of the Oedipus legend from ancient Greece. But Cocteau transforms the story into a kind of "Parisian drawing-room comedy," as Joseph Chiari wrote in *The Contemporary French Theatre: The Flight from Naturalism*. This was accomplished by having the characters live in ancient Greece and modern France at the same time, a "time simultaneity," according to Knapp. She explained: Cocteau "succeeded in bringing about such a feat by scenic manipulation. . . . The characters, who lived in the contemporary world, performed on a brightly lit daislike structure placed in the center of the stage; the rest of the area, symbolizing the ancient mytho-

An actor at Cocteau's experimental theatre. (Photograph by Sasha Masour. Copyright © Hulton-Deutsch Collection/Corbis.)

logical, inexorable aspect of existence, was clothed in darkness." Characters speak in contemporary slang, jazz music can be heard in the background, and talk of war and revolution is common. All of these factors successfully mingle the present and the past. "This realism," Knapp believed, "makes disturbingly actual the plight of the entire family—a whole society—which is at the mercy of an inescapable fate." In addition, the blending of present and past was specifically designed to appeal to the Parisian audience. Speaking of the play in *Literary Criticism—Idea and Act: The English Institute, Selected Essays, 1939-1972*, Francis Fergusson found that Cocteau "presents a very ancient myth, the myth of Oedipus, not as a joke, but as a perennial source of insight into human destiny. Yet at the same time the play is addressed to the most advanced, cynical, and even fashionable mind of contemporary Paris.

It is at one and the same time chic and timeless." Oxenhandler, writing in *Jean Cocteau and the French Scene*, declared that *La Machine infernale* "has always been considered Cocteau's greatest work for the theater."

With *Les Parents terribles* Cocteau adopted a Naturalist approach to the theatre. "The characters," Guicharnaud and Beckelman explained, "constantly remind us that they are acting out a play—vaudeville, drama, or tragedy, depending on the moment and situation." The plot revolves around a troubled marriage and a mother's obsessive love for her son. When the son falls in love with a young girl, his mother is distraught. Unknown to both of them, however, is that the girl is also the mistress to the boy's father. The play ends with the mother's suicide. As Oxenhandler noted in his *Scandal and Parade: The Theater of Jean Cocteau*, the play "possesses the chief virtues of good naturalistic theater: psychological depth and insight coupled with a generally liberal and humanitarian view. . . . It is one of the peaks of Cocteau's achievement. . . . But in renouncing the world of myth and poetry where he situates his earlier works [Cocteau] has diminished himself."

The play was first produced at the Theatre des Ambassadeurs in Paris in 1938, where it ran for 200 performances. When the Municipal Council of Paris protested that a play about incest was being performed in a city-owned theatre, however, *Les Parents terribles* moved to the Bouffes Parisiens, where it ran for another 200 performances. In 1941, when a revival of the play was staged in occupied Paris, fascist opponents organized nightly disruptions until the police were forced to close the play. A later attempt to produce the play in Vichy France ended when the Nazi occupiers forbade it.

Tries His Hand at Film

Cocteau's cinematic work began in 1932 with *Le Sang d'un Poete* (*The Blood of a Poet*), a film that C.G. Wallis in the Kenyon Review called "one of the authentic classics of the cinema, in the small group that includes *Caligari*, *Ten Days That Shook the World*, some Rene Clair, and some Chaplin."Divided into four parts, the film follows the poet through a series of hallucinatory experiences which transform him from a naive young man into a "depersonalized poet," as Wallis noted. Cocteau described the film as "a realistic documentary of unreal events."

The protagonist of *Le Sang d'un Poete* speaks to a living statue, steps through a mirror into another realm, gambles for his fate, and—twice—commits suicide. The film ends with the living statue, a woman, rising into an immortal realm accompanied by a bull. "The woman is transformed into an emblematic abstraction, the work of art as posterity sees it, distant, precise, finally made clear if not understandable," Oxenhandler explained. "Looking at *Le Sang d'un Poete* superficially," Wallis wrote, "it is obvious that its aesthetic power resides in its special combination of simplicity of elements, enigma of intention, and a pervading sense of an underlying rationality." Insdorf found that the film can "be appreciated as a voyage through the poet's internal landscape, and as a celebration of film's unique powers." Cocteau, Oxenhandler noted, "repeatedly refused to explain *Le Sang d'un Poete*."

Cocteau's visionary approach to film is also evident in his *La Belle et la bete*, an adaptation of the beauty and the beast legend. Bosley Crowther of the *New York Times* found the film to be "an eminent model of cinema achievement in the realm of poetic fantasy," while Oxenhandler, writing in *Yale French*

A scene from the 1945 film *La Belle et la bete.* (Photograph copyright © Sunset Boulevard/Corbis.)

Studies, claimed that "the camera-work in this beautiful film situates it in that area of imagination where we half believe the impossible, where metaphor is normal speech and miracle is a deeper truth than nature."

La Belle et la bete tells the story of a beautiful maiden who falls in love with a monstrous-looking man. Cocteau's version of the story tells a psychological drama with autobiographical overtones. When the beast discovers that he is loved, he is no longer an outsider, he gains self-knowledge. The film ends with the beast becoming beautiful. "This fable suggest to us . . .," wrote Oxenhandler, "the yearning of a man who has always secretly felt himself an exile from society and dramatizes his triumphant acceptance by society." Crowther believed that "Freudian or metaphysician, you can take from [the film] what you will." He praised it as "a priceless fabric of subtle images. . . . A fabric of gorgeous visual metaphors, of undulating movements and rhythmic pace, of hypnotic sounds and music, of casually congealing ideas."

Cocteau also filmed his plays *Les Parents terribles* and *Les Enfants terribles,* as well as *Orphee* and *Le Testament d'Orphee,* both adaptations of ancient Greek myths. The best of his films, Alan G. Artner wrote in the *Chicago Tribune,* "are masterpieces that equal if not surpass his work in poetry and the theater. Their visions have haunted spectators the world over.""Cocteau," Insdorf stated, "was a boldly personal, stylistically innovative and internationally influential filmmaker. His legacy of elegantly crafted fantasy and dark poetry can be felt in such diverse films as those of Vincent Minnelli and Jacques Demy, as well as David Lynch's 'Elephant Man.'"

In all of his work, Cocteau held true to certain principles of artistic creation. One of these principles was the invocation of mystery. He once explained that "the less a work of art is understood, the less quickly it will open its petals and the less quickly it will wither." Similarly, he believed that "the secret of poetry is to take things from the places in which habit has set them and reveal them from a different angle as though we see them for the first time."

Some of the mystery that Cocteau sought in his art is also found in the enduring public image he created for himself. As he wrote in his *Journal d'un Inconnu,* translated as *Diary of an Unknown,* "Man seeks to escape himself in myth, and does so by any means at his disposal. Drugs, alcohol, or lies. Un-able to withdraw into himself, he disguises himself. . . . He invents. He transfigures. He mythifies. He creates. He fancies himself an artist."

If you enjoy the works of Jean Cocteau, you may also want to check out the following:

Samuel Beckett's play *Waiting for Godot,* and the films of Luis Bunuel and Stan Brakhage.

Evaluations of Cocteau's career note the variety of his work and his prolific creation. Bishop wrote: "Cocteau's output is staggering in quantity and diversity, encompassing novels, plays, poems, films, essays, autobiographical writings, journalism, painting, and a voluminous correspondence. Much of this oeuvre is minor and some is frankly bad, but enough of it is outstanding, either intrinsically or as pure invention. . . . His failures do not diminish his major accomplishments." Doris L. Eder, in an essay for *European Writers,* stated: "Cocteau's most notable achievements during a long, crowded, diverse, and glittering career were in theater and film. . . . He mixed media in a truly creative way. . . . He was a consummate technician and innovator." "One overlooks a lot in the case of Cocteau," Artner stated, "from narcissism and opium addiction to some less than sterling behavior during the Occupation. One overlooks it because he worked so very hard at becoming a poet and achieved it so irresistibly in film and in the ballet theater." Bree, writing in *Contemporary Literature,* called Cocteau "one of the most versatile and talented personalities France has produced in our own time, a poet, essayist, novelist, playwright, film-maker, draftsman, and animator whose accomplishments have yet to be assessed." Summarizing Cocteau's reputation, Drew Jones in the *Dictionary of Literary Biography* stated: "Cocteau was a true visionary, producing acclaimed works in more genres than any other single artist of the twentieth century."

■ Biographical and Critical Sources

BOOKS

Anderson, Alexandra and Carol Saltus, editors, *Jean Cocteau and the French Scene,* Abbeville Press, 1984.

Bernard, Andre and Claude Gauteur, *Entretiens sur le cinematographe*, Belfond, 1973.

Bree, Germaine and Margaret Guiton, *The French Novel from Gide to Camus*, Harcourt, 1962.

Brown, Frederick, *An Impersonation of Angels: A Biography of Jean Cocteau*, Viking, 1968.

Chanel, Pierre, *Album Cocteau*, Tchou (Paris, France), 1970.

Chiari, Joseph, *The Contemporary French Theatre: The Flight from Naturalism*, Rockliff, 1958, reprinted, Gordian Press, 1970.

Cocteau, Jean, *Professional Secrets: The Autobiography of Jean Cocteau*, translated by Richard Howard, edited by Robert Phelps, Farrar, Straus, 1970.

Contemporary Literary Criticism, Thomson Gale (Detroit, MI), Volume 1, 1973, Volume 8, 1978, Volume 15, 1980, Volume 16, 1981, Volume 43, 1987.

Crosland, Margaret, *Jean Cocteau*, Knopf, 1956.

Crowson, Lydia, *The Esthetic of Jean Cocteau*, University Press of New England, 1978.

Dictionary of Literary Biography, Thomson Gale (Detroit, MI), Volume 65: *French Novelists, 1900-1930*, 1988, Volume 258: *Modern French Poets*, 2002; Volume 321: *Twentieth-Century French Dramatists*, 2006.

Dubourg, Pierre, *La Dramaturgie de Jean Cocteau*, Bernard Grasset, 1954.

European Writers, Scribner (New York, NY), 1990.

Evans, Arthur B., *Jean Cocteau and His Films of Orphic Identity*, Art Alliance, 1975.

Fifield, William, *Jean Cocteau*, Columbia University Press, 1974.

Fowlie, Wallace, editor and translator, *The Journals of Jean Cocteau*, Criterion, 1956.

Fowlie, *Jean Cocteau: The History of a Poet's Age*, Indiana University Press, 1966.

Fowlie, *French Literature: Its History and Its Meaning*, Prentice-Hall, 1973.

Fraigneau, Andre, *Jean Cocteau: Entretiens autour du cinematographe*, Andre Bonne, 1951, translation by Vera Traill published as *Cocteau on the Film: A Conversation Recorded by Andre Fraigneau*, Dobson, 1954.

Fraigneau, Andre, *Cocteau par lui-meme*, Editions du Seuil, 1957, translation by Donald Lehmkuhl published as *Cocteau*, Grove, 1961.

Fraigneau, Andre, *Jean Cocteau: Entretiens avec Andre Fraigneau*, preface by Pierre de Boisdeffre, Union Generale d'Editions, 1965.

Gay and Lesbian Literature, St. James Press (Detroit, MI), 1994.

Gilson, Rene, *Jean Cocteau*, Seghers, 1964, Crown, 1969.

Guicharnaud, Jacques and June Beckelman, *Modern French Theatre from Giraudoux to Beckett*, Yale University Press, 1961.

International Dictionary of Ballet, St. James Press (Detroit, MI), 1993.

International Dictionary of Films and Filmmakers, 4th edition, St. James Press (Detroit, MI), 2000.

International Dictionary of Theatre, St. James Press (Detroit, MI), 1993.

Kihm, Jean-Jacques and Elizabeth Sprigge, *Jean Cocteau: The Man and the Mirror*, Coward-McCann, 1968.

Knapp, Bettina Liebowitz, *Jean Cocteau*, Twayne, 1970.

Lannes, Roger and Henri Parisot, *Jean Cocteau*, Seghers, 1945.

Magnan, Jean-Marie, *Cocteau*, Desclee de Brouwer (Paris, France), 1968.

Mauriac, Claude, *Jean Cocteau ou la verite du mensonge*, Odette Lieutier, 1945.

Millecam, Jean-Pierre, *L'Etoile de Jean Cocteau*, Editions du Rocher, 1952.

Mourgue, Gerard, *Jean Cocteau*, Editions Universitaires, 1965.

Oxenhandler, Neal, *Scandal and Parade: The Theatre of Jean Cocteau*, Rutgers University Press, 1957.

Peters, Arthur King, *Jean Cocteau and Andre Gide: An Abrasive Friendship*, Rutgers University Press, 1973.

Reference Guide to World Literature, 2nd edition, St. James Press (Detroit, MI), 1995.

Ries, Frank W. D., *The Dance Theatre of Jean Cocteau*, University of Michigan Research Press (Ann Arbor, MI), 1986.

Saul, Julie, editor, *Jean Cocteau—The Mirror and the Mask: A Photo-Biography*, Godine (Boston, MA), 1992.

Sprigge, Elizabeth and Jean-Jacques Kihm, *Jean Cocteau: The Man and the Mirror*, Gollancz, 1968.

Steegmuller, Francis, *Cocteau: A Biography*, Little, Brown, 1970.

Styan, J. L., *Modern Drama in Theory and Practice: Symbolism, Surrealism and the Absurd*, Volume 2, Cambridge University Press, 1981.

Tsakiridou, Cornelia A., editor, *Reviewing Orpheus: Essays on the Cinema and Art of Jean Cocteau*, Bucknell University Press, 1997.

West, Paul, *The Modern Novel*, Volume I, Hutchinson University Library, 1963.

Wimsatt, W. K., editor, *Literary Criticism—Idea and Act: The English Institute, Selected Essays, 1939-1972*, University of California Press, 1974.

PERIODICALS

Adam, Number 300, 1965.

American Imago, summer, 1976.

American Scholar, summer, 1989, Renee Winegarten, "Reappraisal: In Pursuit of Cocteau."

Bright Lights Film Journal, October, 2000, Gary Morris, "A Black Silence Almost as Violent as Laughter: Jean Cocteau's Orphic Trilogy."

Cahiers Jean Cocteau, Numbers 1-10, 1969-1985.

Chicago Tribune, May 17, 1988; July 2, 1989.

Choice, November, 1973.

Classical and Modern Literature, summer, 1998, H. Dwight Page, "The Resurrection of the Sophoclean Phoenix: Jean Cocteau's 'La Machine Infernale,'" pp. 329-343.

Commentary, April, 1971.

Commonweal, November 17, 1967.

Contemporary Literature, Volume 9, number 2, 1968, p. 251.

Dalhousie French Studies, Number 59, 2002, Henry Cohen, "Cocteau's 'Les parents terribles' as an Ironic Remaniement of Racine's 'Phedre,'" pp. 56-66.

Dance Scope, fall-winter, 1976-77, pp. 52-67.

Empreintes (Brussels), May, 1950; June, 1950; July, 1950.

Film Comment, winter, 1971-72, George Amberg, "The Testament of Jean Cocteau," pp. 23-27.

Films and Filming, July, 1960, p. 21.

Films in Review, June-July, 1951, Jean R. Debrix, "Cocteau's 'Orpheus' Analyzed: Its Chief Virtue Is What It Tried to Do," pp. 1823.

French Review, spring, 1974, pp. 162-170.

French Studies Bulletin, winter, 2004, Nicholas de Villiers, "The Retrospective Closet-Effect: Jean Cocteau and Roland Barthes," pp. 14-20.

Interview, December, 1994, p. 66.

Kenyon Review, winter, 1944, C.G. Wallis, "The Blood of a Poet," pp. 24-42.

London Magazine, March, 1967.

Los Angeles Times, February 12, 1989.

Modern Drama, March, 1976, pp. 79-87.

MOSAIC, spring, 1972, pp. 159-166.

Nation, October 19, 1970, p. 379.

National Observer, June 12, 1967.

New Yorker, September 27, 1969.

New York Times, December 24, 1947, p. 12; May 13, 1984; April 17, 1988; September 22, 1989.

New York Times Book Review, December 25, 1966.

Paris Review, summer-fall, 1964, William Fifield, "Jean Cocteau: An Interview," pp. 13-37.

Paris-Theatre, February, 1954.

Romanfilm, 1946.

Saturday Review, September 19, 1970.

La Table Ronde, October, 1955.

Time, September 28, 1970, p. 77.

Times (London, England), November 28, 1984; April 4, 1985; April 2, 1987.

Times Literary Supplement, October 6-12, 1989.

Variety, May 16, 1994, p. 48.

Yale French Studies, Number 5, 1950; Number 17, 1956, Neal Oxenhandler, "Poetry in Three Films of Jean Cocteau," pp. 14-20.

Yale Romantic Studies, April, 1961.

ONLINE

RogerEbert.com, http://rogerebert.suntimes.com/ (May 14, 2000), Roger Ebert, review of *Orpheus*

Senses of Cinema, http://www.sensesofcinema.com/ (July-August, 2003), Julia Levin, "The Blood of a Poet."*

(Photograph by Todd Chalfant. AP Images.)

Lee Falk

Personal

Original name Leon Gross; changed name to Lee Falk; born April 28, 1911, in St. Louis, MO; died of congestive heart failure, March 13, 1999, in New York, NY; son of Albert and Eleanor Aleina Gross; married Louise Kanaseriff (divorced); married Constance Morehead Lilienthal (divorced); married Elizabeth Moxley (a stage director), December 31, 1976; children: (first marriage) Valerie, (second marriage) Diane, Conley. *Education:* University of Illinois, B.A.

Career

Cartoonist, comic strip creator. King Features Syndicate, New York, NY, creator of comic strips *Mandrake the Magician,* 1934-99, and *The Phantom,* 1936-99. Producer and director of summer theatres, 1940-60. Advertising copywriter, St. Louis, MO, 1934-38. Director of radio shows. *Military service:* U.S. Army Signal Corps, 1944-45.

Member

National Cartoonists Society, Newspaper Comics Council, Dramatists Guild, Actors Equity Association, Players.

Awards, Honors

Yellow Kid Award, Comics Conference, Lucca, Italy, 1971; Lifetime Achievement Award, Ministry of Culture, Italy; Adamson Award, Sweden, for best foreign comics creator, 1977; Golden Adamson, Sweden, 1986; Silver T-Square Award, 1986; City of St. Louis created a Lee Falk Day in 1994.

Writings

(With Ray Moore) *The Phantom: The Prisoner of the Himalayas,* edited by Len Brown, Nostalgia Press (New York, NY), 1969.

(With Phil Davis) *Mandrake the Magician: Mandrake in Hollywood,* edited by Len Brown, Nostalgia Press (New York, NY), 1970.

The Story of the Phantom: The Ghost Who Walks, fifteen volumes, Avon (New York, NY), 1972.

Killer's Town, Avon (New York, NY), 1973.

The Golden Circle, Avon (New York, NY), 1973.

The Mysterious Ambassador, Avon (New York, NY), 1973.

The Vampires and the Witch, Avon (New York, NY), 1974.

The Curse of the Two-Headed Bull, Avon (New York, NY), 1975.

The Phantom Sundays: The Nazi Menace, Movie Publisher Services, 1989.

The Official Mandrake Sundays, Movie Publisher Services, 1989.

The Phantom: The Inexorables, 1942/43 Daily Strips, Pacific Comics Club, 1992.

The Phantom and *Mandrake the Magician* comic strips have been collected in many book-length editions.

OTHER

(With Alan Cranston) *The Big Story* (play), 1940.
The Passionate Congressman (play), 1945.
(With John LaTouche) *Happy Dollar* (musical play), 1950.
Eris and Home at Six (plays), Dramatists Play Service (New York, NY), 1971.
Mandrake and the Enchantress (musical play), 1974.

Also author of *Mandrake the Magician* and other stage plays.

■ Adaptations

Several Phantom novels, written by ghost writers, were published by Avon. The Phantom appears in several feature films, including the 1943 *The Phantom* serial, the 1996 *Phantom,* starring Billy Zane, and the upcoming film *The Ghost Who Walks.* In 1994, the Phantom appeared in the Hearst Entertainment animated television series *Phantom 2040,* set fifty years in the future and featuring the grandson of the present-day Phantom. *Mandrake the Magician* was adapted for a film in 1942 by Columbia Pictures Corp., and as a television series in 1954. The characters of Mandrake and Phantom teamed with Flash Gordon for the 1986 animated television series, *Defenders of the Earth.* A musical stage play featuring the Phantom was produced in Sweden in 1985; the character also appeared in the Norwegian play *Fantomets glade bryllup* ("Phantom's Happy Wedding"). The Phantom appears in the video games *Phantom 2040, Defenders of the Earth,* and *The Phantom: The Ghost Who Walks.*

■ Sidelights

American cartoonist and comic strip creator Lee Falk was a legend in his own time. Creator of *Mandrake the Magician,* which premiered in 1934, and *The Phantom,* which first appeared in 1936, Falk amazingly continued to write both strips until his death in 1999, making him the last active comic strip writer from the Golden Age of comic strips of the

1930s. This longevity played against Falk, since many of his readers assumed he had long ago retired and no longer created the daily strips. In 1996, Jonathan Mandell wrote in the *Los Angeles Times* that "both Falk and the Phantom are legendary figures, both have been around a long, long time—and people aren't sure that either really exists." In the same article, Falk, then an octogenarian, jokingly noted: "Sixty million people read [*The Phantom*] every day. . . . Every taxi driver in Stockholm knows the Phantom. Dock workers in Trinidad. Shoeshine boys in Naples. And people in New York go, 'So what are you doing these days, Lee?'"

What he was doing was what he had been up to for six decades, writing daily and Sunday comic strips for both *Mandrake the Magician,* and *The Phantom.* As Joseph Szadkowski noted in the *World & I,* Falk was a "founding father of the American comic strip industry," and a person who was "a step ahead of his time for more than six decades." Szadkowski dubbed Falk a "master of sequential literature, the art of telling an in-depth, sometimes very detailed, continuing story in panel form." For Elaine Woo, writing an obituary of Falk in the *Los Angeles Times,* he was "a pivotal figure in the history of comics." Ironically, however, it was the theater, and not the world of comics, in which Falk sought his real success.

Success as a College Student

Born Leon Gross in St. Louis, Missouri, in 1911, the future cartoonist later took the name of Falk and shortened his given name to Lee. His father died when Falk was a baby, and he was brought up by his mother and stepfather, Albert Epstein. He demonstrated an early interest in writing. After serving as the editor of his high school newspaper, he continued with literary pursuits at the University of Illinois, where he majored in literature and contributed stories, poetry, and articles to the school paper.

As a sophomore in college, Falk had the idea of the comic strip which eventually became *Mandrake the Magician,* featuring the eponymous superhero who uses his powers of prestidigitation, his quick wit, and his ability to instantly hypnotize to fight evil. "I came up with the story of Mandrake the Magician because I loved magicians like Houdini and the great adventurers, like Marco Polo," Falk told Szadkowski. "Mandrake is a conglomeration of the great magicians, adventurers, and detectives I have always enjoyed reading about." Falk took his character's name from a poem by John Donne,

A newspaper page featuring Falk's first comic strip character, the master illusionist Mandrake the Magician ("Mandrake the Magician" created by Lee Falk Either, photograph. Copyright © King Features Syndicate.)

where he first heard of the mandrake root, used in medieval times as a cure-all. Mandrake was a first, as Don Markstein noted on *Don Markstein's Toonopedia:* "The first super-powered, costumed crime fighter in comics was not Superman. It was Mandrake the Magician."

Falk drew two weeks of the comic strip following the adventures of his crime-fighting magician, then put it aside for a time. However, he was encouraged by Harry Tuthill, a professional comic strip creator living in St. Louis, to try and find a buyer for his strip. Still in college, Falk visited New York with his father and made the rounds of syndicated publishers. He also visited numerous stage producers, having also brought along several plays he had written. Falk's plan was to follow the career of whichever product sold first. The comic strip won out when King Features Syndicate purchased it as a regular daily strip.

Because Falk was still in college, the contract specified that *Mandrake the Magician* would begin syndication upon the youthful cartoonist's graduation. Falk set about developing story lines for the strip, and also found an older artist, Phil Davis, to draw the strip, as he realized he would not be able to keep up with the daily work of both writing and drawing. Davis would continue drawing the strip until his death in 1964, and was then replaced by Harold "Fred" Fredericks, Jr. *Mandrake the Magician* debuted on June 11, 1934, and from the start it proved popular. The following year a Sunday page was added, and an assistant, Ray Moore, was brought on to help with the inking. Falk himself continued to develop and write the stories for the rest of his life.

Though Falk had traveled little himself, he used exotic locations in his comic strip. After all, Mandrake was said to have developed his mental powers from years of training in Tibet. Among Mandrake's teachers were Luciphor, also known as Cobra, who ultimately used his special powers for evil purposes and became one of Mandrake's main nemeses. Mandrake is partnered in the strip with Lothar, an African prince who gave up his throne to help Mandrake battle evil. As Markstein noted, Lothar is "American comics' first seriously-treated black character." Szadkowski also commented on the special role of this character: "Nonwhite action heroes have been rare in comic and superhero history. Lothar is unique: He is a very real, intelligent partner—not just a sidekick." Mandrake also teams up with a female hero, Narda, a princess of a mythical European kingdom who, like Lothar, gives up her throne to fight evil. Mandrake and Narda had one of the longest engagements in history,

finally marrying in 1998. The strip has remained popular for over six decades, published in more than two hundred newspapers in eight languages worldwide. "Now, as when it debuted," observed Szadkowski, "*Mandrake* is admired for its tightly constructed plots, excellent dialogue, drama, and suspense."

The Phantom and Beyond

The prolific Falk did not allow himself to be satisfied with his early success. In fact, he believed that his comic strip would probably not last more than a few years. In the early years of *Mandrake the Magician*, Falk worked as a copy writer at a St. Louis advertising agency, where he eventually became vice president. He also continued to write stories and stage plays. In 1936 he came up with the idea for another comic strip, *The Phantom*. A crime fighter like Mandrake, the Phantom was among the first superheros to battle criminals while hiding his

Falk (right) with French director Alain Resnois at the Comic Strips Congress in 1965. (Photograph courtesy of David Lees/ Time Life Pictures/Getty Images.)

The 1943 film serial *The Phantom* **had Tom Tyler as the jungle hero.** (Photograph courtesy of The Kobal Collection.)

identity behind a mask. Falk teamed with Moore for the artwork, and later artists have included Wilson McCoy, Bill Lignante, Sy Barry, and Fredericks. "The longstanding international success of the strip was due to Falk's solid storylines and the talent of these men," according to Ed Rhoades, writing on *Lee Falk's Phantom* Web site.

Indeed, as with *Mandrake the Magician, The Phantom* also was an instant success. In creating this popular strip, Falk was inspired and influenced by such fictional characters as Edgar Rice Burroughs's Tarzan and Mowgli from Rudyard Kipling's *The Jungle Book.* He also blended myths and legends from El Cid to King Arthur, and elements of Greek and Norse folklore. As Rhoades noted: "The tale of the Phantom was a blend of mystical elements and realism. Drawing on the influence of classic literature, mythology, history, current events, and theatre, Falk provided something for everyone." The Phantom's purple skintight costume was inspired by Robin Hood, and this costuming effect was later copied by most comics superheroes.

Initially, Falk intended his superhero to be a playboy who dons the mask to fight crime and evil. Then he decided on another approach. The Phantom would be only the most recent in a long family line of fighters of evil. The first of these was Kit, son of Christopher Standish, a ship's captain who was slain by pirates four hundred years ago. Kit survives the attack of the pirates, washing up on an Asian (later changed to African) shore. There he is befriended by the Bandar, a tribe of pygmies, and lives in the Bangalla Jungle in Skull Cave, so called because it resembles a human skull. Kit vows to fight evil as the Phantom wherever he may find it. Kit's son carries on the tradition, as do later generations. The current Phantom is the twenty-first member of his family to bear the name. As the centuries go by, and the Phantom in his masked costume appears to remain the same, the legend spreads that he is immortal, and he is referred to as "The Ghost Who Walks." Accompanied by his wolf, Devil, and white horse, Hero, the Phantom is a mysterious figure who strikes fear into the superstitious. Working alone and behind the scenes, the Phantom deals out justice to evildoers in his jungle realm, going after smugglers, pirates, poachers, kidnappers, slavers, and tyrants. On his right hand he wears a skull ring, which leaves a frightening mark on the criminals he punches.

The Phantom became such an international publishing sensation that the comic strip even played a part in world events. During the Second World War, the Norwegians could ignore Nazi propaganda about the destruction of America as long as *The Phantom* continued to be published, for it originated in the United States. Banned, the strip was later smuggled into the occupied country. It was also banned by Benito Mussolini in Italy during the war because it was so popular, stealing affection from Il Duce. The filmmaker Frederico Fellini, a young man and a fan of the strip at the time, created an unlicensed version until the end of World War II.

The Phantom has continued to be an international success. A theme park near Stockholm, Sweden, was named after the masked hero. Over the years, comic books, novels, and movies have been created featuring the Phantom. A host of action figures, T-shirts, games, and collectibles have all made the Phantom an internationally recognized character. Into the twenty-first century, *The Phantom* continues to be the most widely read superhero comic strip in the world, published in fifteen languages in five hundred newspapers worldwide.

Even in the midst of such successes in the world of comics, Falk did not give up his dreams of working in the theater. He eventually operated five theaters,

Billy Zane played the "Ghost Who Walks" in the 1996 film *The Phantom.* (Courtesy of Paramount/The Kobal Collection.)

comic books as well. Fans of his strip, in particular, and comic book fans everywhere owe Lee Falk a debt of gratitude."

If you enjoy the works of Lee Falk, you may also want to check out the following books:

Maxwell Grant, *The Shadow: "The Chinese Disks" and "Malmordo,"* 2006.
Chester Gould, *The Complete Dick Tracy, Volumes 1 and 2,* 2006-07.
Bob Kane, *Batman: The Sunday Classics, 1943-1946,* 2007.

---

producing over three hundred plays and directing one hundred. He also authored numerous plays, including the musicals *Happy Dollar* and *Mandrake the Magician.* Over the years he worked with such famous actors as Marlon Brando, Charlton Heston, Chico Marx, Paul Newman, and Paul Robeson. Though he had had to fudge his biography for King Features as a young writer, saying that he was a seasoned traveler, Falk ultimately made this lie a truth, traveling and working around the world. Married three times and the father of three children, he had only one regret, as Szadkowski quoted: "I never made Broadway, and this was my one disappointment." Falk died of congestive heart failure in 1999. Jay Kennedy, editor in chief of the King Features Syndicate, said at the time of his death that "Lee lived a life as spectacular as those of the characters he created. . . . He was a central figure behind the emergence of adventure comic strips in the 1930s. The popularity of that genre extended to

Falk's legacy in comic strips and comic books is a large one. His were the first costumed and masked superheroes, and they set the pattern for those that followed. However, Falk's heroes used their intelligence rather than physical power and violence in their fight against evil. "I don't believe in violence," Falk told Szadkowski. "The Phantom his never killed anybody in over sixty years. He has never shot an animal except to save someone. Instead of shooting, he will kick the wind out of someone." Neither did Falk's scripts attempt to be didactic. "We don't discuss sex," Falk was quoted by Bryan Shedden on *Deep Woods.* "Religion and politics is minimal. . . . My feeling is that they belong on the editorial page and a comic strip to me is pure entertainment."

■ Biographical and Critical Sources

BOOKS

Horne, M., *The Golden Age of Comics No. 3: The Phantom,* Nostalgia Press (New York, NY) 1969, pp. 3-4.
Illenberger, T., and A. Eyre Keller, editors, *The Cartoonist Cookbook,* Gramercy Publishing Company (New York, NY), 1966, pp. 28-29.
Van Hise, J., *King Comic Heroes,* Pioneer Books (Las Vegas, NV), 1988, pp. 44-65.

PERIODICALS

Chicago Sun-Times, June 7, 1996, Roger Ebert, review of *The Phantom* movie.

Editor & Publisher, December 20, 1986, David Astor, "Fifty Years of Magic and a Masked Man," p. 26.

Los Angeles Times, June 7, 1996, Kenneth Turan, review of "The Phantom," p. 1; June 10, 1996, Jonathan Mandell, "'The Phantom's' Father Is a Pretty Legendary Figure, Too," p. 5.

New York Times, April 15, 1991, Susan Heller Anderson, "Chronicle," p. B7; June 7, 1996, Lawrence Van Gelder, review of *The Phantom.*

People, December 12, 1977, "Do You, Diana, Take This Masked Man to Be Your Lawfully Wedded Phantom?," p. 36.

Washington Post, June 7, 1996, Hal Hinson, review of *The Phantom,* p. D1.

World & I, November, 1995, Joseph Szadkowski, "Father of the Phantom," pp. 136-143.

ONLINE

ChronicleChamber.com, http://www.chroniclechamber.com/ (September 6, 2006), "The Phantom."

Deep Woods, http://www.deepwoods.org/ (September 6, 2006), Bryan Shedden, "Lee Falk: Father of the Phantom."

Don Markstein's Toonopedia, http://www.toonopedia.com/ Don Markstein, "Mandrake the Magician," and "The Phantom."

International Hero Web site, http://www.intenationalhero.co.uk/ (September 6, 2006), "The Phantom, the Ghost Who Walks."

Internet Movie Database, http://www.imdb.com/ (September 6, 2006), "Lee Falk."

Lambiek.net, http://www.lambiek.net/ (September 6, 2006), "Lee Falk."

Lee Falk's Phantom, http://www.geocities.com/athens/8580/phantom/ Ed Rhoades, "Phantom."

Phantom Chronicles, http://haiche.bigcat.net.au/ (September 6, 2006).

OTHER

The Phantom: Comic Strip Crusader (television special), A & E Network, 1996.

OBITUARIES

PERIODICALS

Los Angeles Times, March 16, 1999, Elaine Woo, "Obituaries: Lee Falk; Created 'The Phantom,' 'Mandrake the Magician' Comics," p. 18.

New York Times, March 15, 1999, "Lee Falk, 87, Creator of Comics like 'Mandrake' and 'Phantom,'" p. B8.

Washington Post, March 16, 1999, "Cartoonist Leon Falk Dies," p. B5.

ONLINE

Lee Falk Obituary—Frew Publications, http://www.deepwoods.org/ (September 6, 2006), Jim Shepherd, "Lee Falk 1911-1999."

Rediff on the Net, http://www.rediff.com/ (March 29, 1999), Vir Sangvhi, "Mr. Walker's Last Mile."*

Lawrence Ferlinghetti

(Photograph by Chris Felver. Reproduced by permission.)

■ Personal

Original name Lawrence Ferling; born March 24, 1919, in Yonkers, NY; original family name of Ferlinghetti restored, 1954; son of Charles S. (an auctioneer) and Clemence Ferling; married Selden Kirby-Smith, April, 1951 (divorced, 1976); children: Julie, Lorenzo. *Education:* University of North Carolina, A.B., 1941; Columbia University, M.A., 1947; Sorbonne, University of Paris, doctorat (with honors), 1949. *Politics:* "Now an enemy of the State." *Religion:* "Catholique manque."

■ Addresses

Home—San Francisco, CA. *Office*—City Lights Books, 261 Columbus Ave., San Francisco, CA 94133.

■ Career

Poet, playwright, editor, and painter; worked for Time, New York, NY, post-World War II; taught French in an adult education program, San Fran-cisco, CA, 1951-52; City Lights Pocket Bookshop (now City Lights Books), San Francisco, co-owner, 1953—, founder, publisher, and editor of City Lights Books, 1955—. Participant in literary conferences, art exhibitions, and poetry readings. *Military service:* U.S. Naval Reserve, 1941-45; became lieutenant commander; was commanding officer during Normandy invasion.

■ Awards, Honors

National Book Award nomination, 1970, for *The Secret Meaning of Things;* Notable Book of 1979 citation, *Library Journal,* 1980, for *Landscapes of Living and Dying;* Silver Medal for poetry, Commonwealth Club of California, 1986, for *Over All the Obscene Boundaries;* poetry prize, City of Rome, 1993; San Francisco street named in his honor, 1994; named first poet laureate of San Francisco, 1998; Ivan Sandrof Lifetime Achievement Award, National Book Critics Circle, 2000; Robert Kirsch Award, *Los Angeles Times,* 2001, for body of work; City Lights Books granted landmark status, 2001; PEN Center West Literary Award, 2002, for lifetime achievement; Curtis Benjamin Award for Creative Publishing, Association of American Publishers, 2005; Literarian Award, National Book Foundation, 2005.

■ Writings

(Translator) Jacques Prevert, *Selections from "Paroles,"* City Lights (San Francisco, CA), 1958.

Her (novel), New Directions (New York, NY), 1960.

Howl of the Censor (trial proceedings), edited by J.W. Ehrlich, Nourse Publishing, 1961.

(With Jack Spicer) *Dear Ferlinghetti*, White Rabbit Press, 1962.

The Mexican Night: Travel Journal, New Directions (New York, NY), 1970.

A World Awash with Fascism and Fear, Cranium Press, 1971.

A Political Pamphlet, Anarchist Resistance Press, 1976.

Northwest Ecolog, City Lights (San Francisco, CA), 1978.

(With Nancy J. Peters) *Literary San Francisco: A Pictorial History from the Beginning to the Present*, Harper (New York, NY), 1980.

The Populist Manifestos (includes "First Populist Manifesto"), Grey Fox Press, 1983.

Seven Days in Nicaragua Libre (journal), City Lights (San Francisco, CA), 1985.

Leaves of Life: Fifty Drawings from the Model, City Lights (San Francisco, CA), 1985.

(Translator with others) Nicanor Parra, *Antipoems: New and Selected*, New Directions (New York, NY), 1985.

(Translator, with Francesca Valente) Pier Paolo Pasolini, *Roman Poems*, City Lights (San Francisco, CA), 1986.

Love in the Days of Rage (novel), Dutton (New York, NY), 1988.

(With Alexis Lykiard) *The Cool Eye: Lawrence Ferlinghetti Talks to Alexis Lykiard*, Stride, 1993.

(With Christopher Felver) *Ferlinghetti: Portrait*, Gibbs Smith, 1998.

What Is Poetry?, Creative Arts (Berkeley, CA), 2000.

(Translator, with others) Homero Aridjis, *Eyes to See Otherwise*, New Directions (New York, NY), 2002.

Life Studies, Life Stories: Drawings, City Lights (San Francisco, CA), 2003.

Americus, Book I, New Directions (New York, NY), 2004.

Also author of *Lawrence Ferlinghetti Sits Down with Soheyl Dahi*. Author of narration, *Have You Sold Your Dozen Roses?* (film), California School of Fine Arts Film Workshop, 1957. Contributor to numerous periodicals, including *San Francisco Chronicle*, *Nation*, *Evergreen Review*, *Liberation*, *Chicago Review*, *Transatlantic Review*, and *New Statesman*. Editor, *Journal for the Protection of All Beings*, *Interim Pad*, and *City Lights Journal*. Ferlinghetti's manuscripts are collected at Columbia University, New York, NY, and at the Thomas J. Dodd Research Center, Storrs, CT.

POETRY

Pictures of the Gone World, City Lights (San Francisco, CA), 1955, enlarged edition, 1995.

Tentative Description of a Dinner Given to Promote the Impeachment of President Eisenhower, Golden Mountain Press, 1958.

A Coney Island of the Mind, New Directions (New York, NY), 1958.

Berlin, Golden Mountain Press, 1961.

One Thousand Fearful Words for Fidel Castro, City Lights (San Francisco), 1961.

Starting from San Francisco (with recording), New Directions (New York, NY), 1961, revised edition (without recording), 1967.

(With Gregory Corso and Allen Ginsberg) *Penguin Modern Poets 5*, Penguin (New York, NY), 1963.

Thoughts of a Concerto of Telemann, Four Seasons Foundation, 1963.

Where Is Vietnam?, City Lights (San Francisco), 1965.

To F—Is to Love Again, Kyrie Eleison Kerista; or, The Situation in the West, Followed by a Holy Proposal, F—You Press, 1965.

Christ Climbed Down, Syracuse University (Syracuse, NY), 1965.

An Eye on the World: Selected Poems, MacGibbon & Kee, 1967.

Moscow in the Wilderness, Segovia in the Snow, Beach Books, 1967.

After the Cries of the Birds, Dave Haselwood Books, 1967.

Fuclock, Fire Publications, 1968.

Reverie Smoking Grass, East 128, 1968.

The Secret Meaning of Things, New Directions (New York, NY), 1969.

Tyrannus Nix?, New Directions (New York, NY), 1969.

Back Roads to Far Places, New Directions (New York, NY), 1971.

Love Is No Stone on the Moon, ARIF Press, 1971.

The Illustrated Wilfred Funk, City Lights (San Francisco, CA), 1971.

Open Eye, Open Heart, New Directions (New York, NY), 1973.

Director of Alienation: A Poem, Main Street, 1976.

Who Are We Now? (also see below), City Lights (San Francisco, CA), 1976.

Landscapes of Living and Dying (also see below), New Directions (New York, NY), 1979.

Mule Mountain Dreams, Bisbee Press Collective, 1980.

A Trip to Italy and France, New Directions (New York, NY), 1980.

Endless Life: Selected Poems, New Directions (New York, NY), 1984.

Over All the Obscene Boundaries: European Poems and Transitions, New Directions (New York, NY), 1985.

Inside the Trojan Horse, Lexikos, 1987.

Wild Dreams of a New Beginning: Including "Land-scapes of Living and Dying" and "Who Are We Now?," New Directions (New York, NY), 1988.

When I Look at Pictures, Peregrine Smith Books, 1990.

These Are My Rivers: New and Selected Poems, 1955-1993, New Directions (New York, NY), 1993.

A Far Rockaway of the Heart, New Directions (New York, NY), 1997.

San Francisco Poems, City Lights (San Francisco, CA), 2001.

How to Paint Sunlight: Lyric Poems and Others, 1997-2000, New Directions (New York, NY), 2001.

PLAYS

Unfair Arguments with Existence: Seven Plays for a New Theatre (contains *The Soldiers of No Country* [produced in London, England, 1969], *Three Thousand Red Ants* [produced in New York, NY, 1970; also see below], *The Alligation* [produced in San Francisco, 1962; also see below], *The Victims of Amnesia* [produced in New York, NY, 1970; also see below], *Motherlode, The Customs Collector in Baggy Pants* [produced in New York, NY, 1964], and *The Nose of Sisyphus*), New Directions (New York, NY), 1963.

Routines (includes *The Jig Is Up, His Head, Ha-Ha,* and *Non-Objection*), New Directions (New York, NY), 1964.

Three by Ferlinghetti: Three Thousand Red Ants, The Alligation, [and] The Victims of Amnesia, produced in New York, NY, 1970.

EDITOR

Beatitude Anthology, City Lights (San Francisco, CA), 1960.

Pablo Picasso, *Hunk of Skin*, City Lights (San Francisco, CA), 1969.

Charles Upton, *Panic Grass*, City Lights (San Francisco, CA), 1969.

City Lights Anthology, City Lights (San Francisco, CA), 1974, reprinted, 1995.

City Lights Pocket Poets Anthology, City Lights (San Francisco, CA), 1995.

RECORDINGS

(With Kenneth Rexroth) *Poetry Readings in "The Cellar,"* Fantasy, 1958.

Tentative Description of a Dinner to Impeach President Eisenhower, and Other Poems, Fantasy, 1959.

Tyrannus Nix? and Assassination Raga, Fantasy, 1971.

(With Gregory Corso and Allen Ginsberg) *The World's Greatest Poets 1*, CMS, 1971.

Lawrence Ferlinghetti Live at the Poetry Center, Poetry Center, 2003.

City Lights Voices: The Berlin Tapes, 2004.

■ Adaptations

The poem "Autobiography" was choreographed by Sophie Maslow, 1964; *A Coney Island of the Mind* was adapted for the stage by Steven Kyle Kent, Charles R. Blaker, and Carol Brown and produced at the Edinburgh Festival, Scotland, 1966; a poem was adapted for television by Ted Post on Second Experiment in Television, 1967.

■ Sidelights

As poet, playwright, publisher, and spokesman, Lawrence Ferlinghetti helped to spark the San Francisco literary renaissance of the 1950s and the subsequent "Beat" movement. Ferlinghetti was one of a group of writers—labeled the "Beat Generation"—who felt strongly that art should be accessible to all people, not just a handful of highly educated intellectuals. His career has been marked by a constant challenge to the status quo in art; his poetry engages readers, defies popular political movements, and reflects the influence of American idiom and modern jazz. In *Lawrence Ferlinghetti: Poet-at-Large*, Larry Smith noted that the author "writes truly memorable poetry, poems that lodge themselves in the consciousness of the reader and generate awareness and change. And his writing sings, with the sad and comic music of the streets."

Ferlinghetti performed numerous functions essential to the establishment of the Beat movement while also creating his own substantial body of work. His City Lights bookstore provided a gathering place for the fertile talents of the San Francisco literary renaissance, and the bookstore's publishing arm offered a forum for publication of Beat writings. He also became "America's best-selling poet of the twentieth century," according to Paul Varner in *Western American Literature*. As Smith noted in the *Dictionary of Literary Biography*, "What emerges from the historical panorama of Ferlinghetti's involvement is a pattern of social engagement and literary

Ferlinghetti has operated City Lights Books since 1953. (Photograph courtesy of City Lights Books, Inc. Reproduced by permission.)

experimentation as he sought to expand the goals of the Beat movement." Smith added, however, that Ferlinghetti's contribution far surpasses his tasks as a publisher and organizer. "Besides molding an image of the poet in the world," the critic continued, "he created a poetic form that is at once rhetorically functional and socially vital." *Dictionary of Literary Biography* essayist Thomas McClanahan likewise contended that Ferlinghetti "became the most important force in developing and publicizing antiestablishment poetics."

A Troubled Upbringing

Ferlinghetti was born Lawrence Monsanto Ferling, the youngest of five sons of Charles and Clemence Ferling. His father, an Italian immigrant, had shortened the family name upon arrival in America. Only years later, when he was a grown man, did Ferlinghetti discover the lengthier name and restore it as his own.

A series of disasters struck Ferlinghetti as a youngster. Before he was born, his father died suddenly. When he was only two, his mother suffered a nervous breakdown that required lengthy hospitalization. Separated from his brothers, Lawrence went to live with his maternal uncle, Ludovic Monsanto, a language instructor, and Ludovic's French-speaking wife, Emily. The marriage disintegrated, and Emily Monsanto returned to France, taking Lawrence with her. During the following four years, the youngster lived in Strasbourg and spoke only French.

Ferlinghetti's return to America began with a stay in a state orphanage in New York; he was placed there by his aunt while she sought work in Manhattan. The pair were reunited when the aunt found a position as governess to the wealthy Bisland family in Bronxville. Young Ferlinghetti endeared himself to the Bislands to such an extent that when his aunt disappeared suddenly, he was allowed to stay. Surrounded by fine books and educated people, he was encouraged to read and learn fine passages of literature by heart. His formal education proceeded first in the elite Riverdale Country Day School and later in Bronxville public schools. As a teenager he was sent to Mount Hermon, a preparatory academy in Massachusetts.

Ferlinghetti enrolled at the University of North Carolina in 1937. There he majored in journalism and worked with the student staff of the Daily Tarheel. He earned his bachelor's degree in the spring of 1941 and joined the U.S. Navy that fall. His wartime service included patrolling the Atlantic coast on submarine watch and commanding a ship during the invasion of Normandy. After his discharge Ferlinghetti took advantage of the G.I. Bill to continue his education. He did graduate study at Columbia University, receiving his master's degree in 1948, and he completed his doctoral degree at the University of Paris in 1951.

Moves to San Francisco

Ferlinghetti left Paris in 1951 and moved to San Francisco. For a short time he supported himself by teaching languages at an adult education school and by doing freelance writing for art journals and for the *San Francisco Chronicle.* In 1953 he joined with Peter D. Martin to publish a magazine, *City Lights,* named after a silent film starring actor Charlie Chaplin. In order to subsidize the magazine, Martin and Ferlinghetti opened the City Lights Pocket Book Shop in a neighborhood on the edge of Chinatown.

Before long the City Lights Book Shop was a popular gathering place for San Francisco's avant-garde writers, poets, and painters. "We were filling a big need," Ferlinghetti told the *New York Times Book Review.* "City Lights became about the only place around where you could go in, sit down, and read books without being pestered to buy something. That's one of the things it was supposed to be. Also, I had this idea that a bookstore should be a center of intellectual activity; and I knew it was a natural for a publishing company too."

In addition to his new career as an entrepreneur, Ferlinghetti was busy creating his own poetry, and in 1955 he launched the City Lights Pocket Poets publishing venture. First in the "Pocket Poets" series was a slim volume of his own, *Pictures of the Gone World.* In *Lawrence Ferlinghetti,* Smith observed that, from his earliest poems onwards, the author writes as "the contemporary man of the streets speaking out the truths of common experience, often to the

This bestselling 1955 poetry collection established Ferlinghetti's reputation. (Cover photograph from the Bettmann Archive. New Directions, 1958. Reproduced by permission of New Directions Publishing Corp and Bettmann/Corbis.)

reflective beat of the jazz musician. As much as any poet today he. . . sought to make poetry an engaging oral art." McClanahan wrote: "The underlying theme of Ferlinghetti's first book is the poet's desire to subvert and destroy the capitalist economic system. Yet this rather straightforward political aim is accompanied by a romantic vision of Eden, a mirror reflecting the Whitmanesque attempts to be free from social and political restraints."

These sentiments found an appreciative audience among young people of the mid-twentieth century, who were agonizing over the nuclear arms race and cold war politics. By 1955 Ferlinghetti counted among his friends such poets as Kenneth Rexroth, Allen Ginsberg, and Philip Whalen, as well as the novelist Jack Kerouac. Ferlinghetti was in the audience at the watershed 1955 poetry reading "Six

Poets at the Six Gallery," at which Ginsberg unveiled his poem *Howl*. Ferlinghetti immediately recognized *Howl* as a classic work of art and offered to publish it in the "Pocket Poets" series. The first edition of *Howl and Other Poems* appeared in 1956 and sold out quickly. A second shipment was ordered from the publisher's British printer, but U.S. customs authorities seized it on the grounds of alleged obscenity. When federal authorities declined to pursue the case and released the books, the San Francisco Police Department arrested Ferlinghetti on charges of printing and selling lewd and indecent material.

Ferlinghetti engaged the American Civil Liberties Union for his defense and welcomed his court case as a test of the limits to freedom of speech. Not only did he win the suit on October 3, 1957, he also benefitted from the publicity generated by the case. In the *Dictionary of Literary Biography*, Smith wrote: "The importance of this court case to the life and career of Ferlinghetti as well as to the whole blossoming of the San Francisco renaissance in poetry and the West Coast Beat movement is difficult to overestimate. Ferlinghetti and Ginsberg became national as well as international public figures leading a revolution in thinking as well as writing. The case solidified the writing into a movement with definite principles yet an openness of form."

Publishes *A Coney Island of the Mind*

For Ferlinghetti, these "principles" included redeeming poetry from the ivory towers of academia and offering it as a shared experience with ordinary people. He began reading his verses to the accompaniment of experimental jazz and reveled in an almost forgotten oral tradition in poetry. In 1958 New York's New Directions press published Ferlinghetti's *A Coney Island of the Mind*, a work that has since sold well over one million copies in America and abroad. In his *Dictionary of Literary Biography* piece, Smith called *A Coney Island of the Mind* "one of the key works of the Beat period and one of the most popular books of contemporary poetry. . . . It launched Ferlinghetti as a poet of humor and satire, who achieves an open-form expressionism and a personal lyricism." Walter Sutton offered a similar assessment in *American Free Verse: The Modern Revolution in Poetry*. Sutton felt that the general effect of the book "is of a kaleidoscopic view of the world and of life as an absurd carnival of discontinuous sensory impressions and conscious reflections, each with a ragged shape of

its own but without any underlying thematic unity or interrelationship." Sutton added, "To this extent the collection suggests a Surrealistic vision. But it differs in that meanings and easily definable themes can be found in most of the individual poems, even when the idea of meaninglessness is the central concern."

In *Lawrence Ferlinghetti*, Smith suggested that the poems in *A Coney Island of the Mind* demonstrate the direction Ferlinghetti intended to go with his art. The poet "enlarged his stance and developed major themes of anarchy, mass corruption, engagement, and a belief in the surreality and wonder of life," to quote Smith. "It was a revolutionary art of dissent and contemporary application which jointly drew a lyric poetry into new realms of social—and self-expression. It sparkles, sings, goes flat, and generates anger or love out of that flatness as it follows a basic motive of getting down to reality and making

Ferlinghetti reading his poetry in the basement of City Lights Books in 1980. (Photograph copyright © Roger Ressmeyer/Corbis.)

of it what we can." Smith concluded: "Loosely, the book forms a type of 'Portrait of the Artist as a Young Poet of Dissent.' There are some classic contemporary statements in this, Ferlinghetti's—and possibly America's—most popular book of modern poetry. The work is remarkable for its skill, depth, and daring."

If certain academics grumbled about Ferlinghetti's work, others found it refreshing for its engagement in current social and political issues and its indebtedness to a bardic tradition. "Ferlinghetti has cultivated a style of writing visibly his own," claimed Linda Hamalian in the *American Book Review*. "He often writes his line so that it approximates the rhythm and meaning of the line. He also has William Carlos Williams' gift of turning unlikely subjects into witty poems. . . . He introduces the unexpected, catching his readers open for his frequently sarcastic yet humorous observations." Poetry contributor Alan Dugan maintained that the poet "has the usual American obsession, asking, 'What is going on in America and how does one survive it?' His answer might be: By being half a committed outsider and half an innocent Fool. He makes jokes and chants seriously with equal gusto and surreal inventiveness, using spoken American in a romantic, flamboyant manner."

Two collections of Ferlinghetti's poetry provide insight into the development of the writer's overarching style and thematic approach: *Endless Life: Selected Poems* and *These Are My Rivers: New and Selected Poems, 1955-1993*. Ferlinghetti chose selections from among his eight books of poetry and his work in progress, written over twenty-six years, for inclusion in *Endless Life*. The poems reflect the influences of e. e. cummings, Kenneth Rexroth, and Kenneth Patchen and are concerned with contemporary themes, such as the antiwar and antinuclear movements. Some critics have dismissed Ferlinghetti "as either sentimental or the literary entrepreneur of the Beat generation," noted John Trimbur in *Western American Literature*, the critic adding that he feels such labels are unjustified. Ferlinghetti writes a "public poetry to challenge the guardians of the political and social status quo for the souls of his fellow citizens," Trimbur maintained, noting that the poet does so while "risking absurdity." In *World Literature Today*, J. Martone acknowledged that while Ferlinghetti has produced heralded poetry, some of that poetry is stagnant. "Ferlinghetti never moves beyond—or outgrows—the techniques of [his] early poems," maintained Martone, adding that "his repertoire of devices (deliberately casual literary allusion, self-mockery, hyperbole) becomes a bit

tedious with repetition." However, Joel Oppenheimer praised the poet in the *New York Times Book Review*, contending that Ferlinghetti "learned to write poems, in ways that those who see poetry as the province of the few and the educated had never imagined."

Ferlinghetti focuses on current political and sexual matters in *These Are My Rivers*. As Rochelle Ratner noted in *Library Journal*, the poems are experimental in technique, often lacking common poetic devices such as stanza breaks, and they appear in unusual ways on the page, "with short lines at the left margin or moving across the page as hand follows eye." Yet, despite its visual effect, Ashley Brown commented in *World Literature Today*, "Ferlinghetti writes in a very accessible idiom; he draws on pop culture and sports as much as the modern poets whom he celebrates." Ratner averred that "Ferlinghetti is the foremost chronicler of our times." Indeed, the collection shows "Ferlinghetti still speaking out against academic poetry just as he did when the Beat Movement began," remarked Varner in *Western American Literature*. "Ferlinghetti, always the poet of the topical now, still sees clearly the 1990s," the critic added.

In 1997, Ferlignhetti published the collection *A Far Rockaway of the Heart*, which is to some degree a follow-up to *A Coney Island of the Mind*. Containing one hundred and one poems, each about a page in length, the collection examines the changes that Ferlinghetti and the country have undergone in the forty years since *A Coney Island of the Mind* was published. A *Publishers Weekly* critic dubbed the book "a glorious rant against mediocrity, greed, capitalism and boring poetry." According to Janet St. John in *Booklist*, the new collection offers "a far more personalized narrative of familial, poetical, and social history" than did *A Coney Island of the Mind*. Jack Foley, reviewing the title for the *Alsop Review*, concluded: "What higher praise can we give *A Far Rockaway of the Heart* than to say that it is a worthy successor to its predecessor?"

Writes Plays and Novels

Drama has also proved a fertile ground for Ferlinghetti. He carried his political philosophies and social criticisms into experimental plays, many of them short and surrealistic. In *Lawrence Ferlinghetti*, Smith contended that the writer's stint as an experimental dramatist "reflects his stronger attention to irrational and intuitive analogy as a means

Ferlinghetti reads a poem at the National Book Awards ceremony in New York City in 2005. (Photograph by Henny Ray Abrams. AP Images.)

filled with phallic symbols and prophetic visions of desire. At once existential, absurd, symbolic, expressionistic, cinematic and surrealistic in vision and form, *Her* is controlled, as all of Ferlinghetti's work is, by a drive toward expanded consciousness." Smith concluded, "The book is truly a spirited, though somewhat self-mocking, projection of the optimistic goals the Beat and San Francisco poetry movements placed on a grand imaginative scale."

Ferlinghetti published another novel in 1988, *Love in the Days of Rage*. This chronicles a love affair between an expatriate American painter named Annie, and a Parisian banker of Portuguese extraction named Julian. Their relationship takes place against the backdrop of 1968 Paris, during the student revolution that took place during that year. Though at first Annie thinks Julian is conservative, because of his clothing style and occupation, he eventually reveals his involvement in a subversive plot—which she supports him in. Alex Raksin, discussing *Love in the Days of Rage* in the *Los Angeles Times Book Review*, praised the work as an "original, intense novel" in which Ferlinghetti's "sensitivity as a painter. . . is most apparent." Patrick Burson, critiquing for the *San Francisco Review of Books*, explained that "*Love in the Days of Rage* challenges the reader on several stylistic levels as it attemps to mirror the anarchistic uprising of '68 which briefly united intellectuals, artists, and proletariats in common cause." Burson went on to conclude that the book is "an uneven ride, at times maddeningly confused, but noble in intent and final effect."

of suggesting the 'secret meaning' behind life's surface. Though the works are provocative, public, and oral, they are also more cosmic in reference, revealing a stronger influence from Buddhist philosophy." In *Dialogue in American Drama*, Ruby Cohn characterized the poet's plays as "brief sardonic comments on our contemporary lifestyle. . . . The themes may perhaps be resolved into a single theme—the unfairness of industrial, consumer-oriented, establishment-dominated existence—and the plays are arguments against submission to such existence."

In 1960 Ferlinghetti's first novel, *Her*, was published. An autobiographical, experimental work that focuses on the narrator's pursuit of a woman, the novel received very little critical comment when it was published. According to Smith in the *Dictionary of Literary Biography*, *Her* "is an avant-garde work that pits character and author in a battle with the subjective relativity of experience in a quest for ideals; a surrealistic encounter with the subconscious—

If you enjoy the works of Lawrence Ferlinghetti, you may also want to check out the following books:

Allen Ginsberg, *Howl*, 1956.
Jack Kerouac, *On the Road*, 1957.
Gregory Corso, *The Happy Birthday of Death*, 1960.

Ferlinghetti, who continues to operate the City Lights bookstore, travels frequently to give poetry readings. His paintings and drawings have been exhibited in San Francisco galleries; his plays have been performed in experimental theaters. In 2001 readers saw the arrival of two books by Ferlinghetti: *How to Paint Sunlight: Lyric Poems and Others, 1997-2000* and *San Francisco Poems*. As Smith observed in the *Dictionary of Literary Biography*, Ferlinghetti's life and writing "stand as models of the existentially authentic and engaged. . . . His work exists as a vital challenge and a living presence to the contemporary artist, as an embodiment of the strong, anticool, compassionate commitment to life in an absurd time." *New York Times Book Review* correspondent Joel Oppenheimer cited Ferlinghetti's work for "a legitimate revisionism which is perhaps our best heritage from those raucous [Beat] days—the poet daring to see a different vision from that which the guardians of culture had allowed us." *New Pages* contributor John Gill concluded, reading a work by Ferlinghetti "will make you feel good about poetry and about the world—no matter how mucked-up the world may be."

■ Biographical and Critical Sources

BOOKS

The Beat Generation: A Gale Critical Companion, Thomson Gale (Detroit, MI), 2003.

Charters, Ann, *Kerouac: A Biography,* Straight Arrow Books (San Francisco, CA), 1973.

Charters, Samuel, *Some Poems/Poets: Studies in American Undeground Poetry since 1945,* Oyez (Berkeley, CA), 1971.

Cherkovski, Neeli, *Ferlinghetti: A Biography,* Doubleday (New York, NY), 1979.

Cohn, Ruby, *Dialogue in American Drama,* Indiana University Press, 1971.

Concise Dictionary of American Literary Biography: The New Consciousness, 1941-1968, Thomson Gale (Detroit, MI), 1987.

Contemporary American Dramatists, St. James Press (Detroit, MI), 1994.

Contemporary Dramatists, 4th edition, St. James Press (Detroit, MI), 1988.

Contemporary Literary Criticism, Thomson Gale (Detroit, MI), Volume 2, 1974, Volume 6, 1976, Volume 10, 1979, Volume 27, 1984, Volume 111, 1998.

Contemporary Poets, 7th edition, St. James Press (Detroit, MI), 2001.

Dictionary of Literary Biography, Thomson Gale (Detroit, MI), Volume 5: *American Poets since World War II,* 1980, Volume 16: *The Beats: Literary Bohemians in Post-War America,* 1983.

Ehrlich, J.W., *Howl of the Censor,* Nourse Books (San Carlos, CA), 1961.

Everson, William, *Archetype West: The Pacific Coast as a Literary Region,* Oyez (Berkeley, CA), 1976.

Felver, Christopher and Lawrence Ferlinghetti, *Ferlinghetti: Portrait,* Gibbs Smith, 1998.

Kherdian, David, *Six Poets of the San Francisco Renaissance: Portraits and Checklists,* Giligia Press (Fresno, CA), 1967.

Meltzer, David, *The San Francisco Poets,* Ballantine (New York, NY), 1971.

Modern American Literature, 5th edition, St. James Press (Detroit, MI), 1999.

Ogar, Richard, editor, *The Poet's Eye: A Tribute to Lawrence Ferlinghetti and City Lights Books,* Friends of the Bancroft Library (Berkeley, CA), 1997.

Parkinson, Thomas, *Poets, Poems, Movements,* UMI Research Press, 1987.

Phillips, Lisa, editor, *Beat Culture and the New America, 1950-65,* Flammarion (New York, NY), 1995.

Poetry Criticism, Volume 1, Thomson Gale (Detroit, MI), 1991.

Reference Guide to American Literature, 4th edition, St. James Press (Detroit, MI), 2000.

Rexroth, Kenneth, *American Poetry in the Twentieth Century,* Herder & Herder, 1971.

Rexroth, Kenneth, *Assays,* New Directions (New York, NY), 1961.

Silesky, Barry, *Ferlinghetti: The Artist in His Time,* Warner Books (New York, NY), 1990.

Skau, Michael Walter, *Constantly Risking Absurdity: The Writings of Lawrence Ferlinghetti,* Whitston (Troy, NY), 1989.

Smith, Larry R., *Lawrence Ferlinghetti: Poet-at-Large,* Southern Illinois University Press (Carbondale, IL), 1983.

Stephenson, Gregory, *The Daybreak Boys: Essays on the Literature of the Beat Generation,* Southern Illinois University Press, 1990.

Sutton, Walter, *American Free Verse: The Modern Revolution in Poetry,* New Directions (New York, NY), 1973.

Tytell, John, *Naked Angels: The Lives and Literature of the Beat Generation,* McGraw-Hill (New York, NY), 1976.

Vale, V., *Real Conversations 1,* Re/Search Publications (San Francisco, CA), 2001.

Vrana, Stan A., *Interviews and Conversations with 20th-Century Authors Writing in English: An Index, Series II,* Scarecrow Press (Metuchen, NJ), 1986.

Watson, Steven, *The Birth of the Beat Generation: Visionaries, Rebels, and Hipsters, 1944-1960,* Pantheon Press (New York, NY), 1995.

PERIODICALS

America, August 20, 1977, review of *Who Are We Now?,* p. 80; April 25, 1998, Edward J. Ingebretsen, review of *A Far Rockaway of the Heart,* p. 29.

American Book Review, March-April, 1984, review of *Endless Life: Selected Poems*, p. 8; July, 1990, review of *Love in the Days of Rage*, p. 19.

American Literature, March, 1982, review of *Literary San Francisco: A Pictorial History from Its Beginnings to the Present Day*, p. 154.

American Poetry Review, September-October, 1977, review of *Who Are We Now?*, p. 45.

Another Chicago Magazine, Number 16, 1986, "A Conversation: Lawrence Ferlinghetti," pp. 118-130.

Antioch Review, winter, 1981, review of *Literary San Francisco*, p. 133.

Arizona Quarterly, autumn, 1982.

Berkeley Barb, April 7, 1967, Richard Ogar, "My Escape from Siberia: An Interview with Lawrence Ferlinghetti," pp. 8-9.

Bloomsbury Review, March-April, 2003, Ray Gonzalez, "Tracing the Public Surface: An Interview with Lawrence Ferlinghetti," pp. 13, 18-19.

Booklist, December 1, 1973, review of *Open Eye, Open Heart*, p. 365; January 15, 1975, review of *City Lights Anthology*, p. 480; February 15, 1977, review of *Who Are We Now?*, p. 877; February 15, 1979, review of *Northwest Ecolog*, p. 907; October 1, 1979, review of *Landscapes of Living & Dying*, p. 212; December 1, 1980, review of *Literary San Francisco*, p. 499; September 15, 1988, review of *Love in the Days of Rage*, p. 119; November 15, 1995, Ray Olson, review of *City Lights Pocket Poets Anthology*, p. 532; May 15, 1997, Janet St. John, review of *A Far Rockaway of the Heart*, p. 1557.

Books & Culture, March, 1998, review of *A Far Rockaway of the Heart*, p. 35.

Bulletin of Bibliography, June, 1994, Bill Morgan, "Lawrence Ferlinghetti: An Updated Bibliography, 1980-1993," pp. 111-154.

Carleton Miscellany, spring, 1965, review of *Routines*, p. 112.

Chicago Tribune, May 19, 1986; September 13, 1988.

Chicago Tribune Book World, February 28, 1982.

Choice, June, 1965, review of *Routines*, p. 226; March, 1974, review of *Open Eye, Open Heart*, p. 87; April, 1977, review of *Who Are We Now?*, p. 199; January, 1979, review of *Northwest Ecolog*, p. 1516; December, 1980, review of *Literary San Francisco*, p. 527.

Concerning Poetry, Number 20, 1987, Michael Skau, "The Poet as Poem: Ferlinghetti's Songs of Myself," pp. 57-71.

Critique, Volume 19, number 3, Michael Skau, "Toward Underivative Creation: Lawrence Ferlinghetti's *Her*," 1978.

Enclitic, Volume 11, number 2, 1989, John O'Kane, "Lawrence Ferlinghetti: Anarchism and the Poetry Revolution," pp. 47-58.

Explicator, winter, 2001, Marilyn Ann Fontane, "Ferlinghetti's 'Constantly Risking Absurdity,'" p. 106.

Georgia Review, winter, 1989.

Guardian, April 16, 1998, p. T20.

Kirkus Reviews, January 15, 1969, review of *The Secret Meaning of Things*, p. 78; August 15, 1973, review of *Open Eye, Open Heart*, p. 928; June 15, 1980, review of *Literary San Francisco*, p. 812.

Library Journal, June 15, 1958, Gerald D. McDonald, "Lawrence Ferlinghetti: A Coney Island of the Mind"; November 15, 1960; April 1, 1969, review of *The Secret Meaning of Things*, p. 1504; September 15, 1973, review of *Open Eye, Open Heart*, p. 2556; January 15, 1975, review of *City Lights Anthology*, p. 128; December 1, 1976, review of *Who Are We Now?*, p. 2494; December 15, 1979, review of *Landscapes of Living & Dying*, p. 2651; August, 1980, Bonnie Jo Dopp, p. 1635; May 1, 1981, Susan Mernit, review of *Endless Life*, p. 977; October 1, 1988, William Gargan, review of *Love in the Days of Rage*, p. 100; October 1, 1993, Rochelle Ratner, review of *These Are My Rivers: New and Selected Poems, 1955-1993*, p. 98; March 15, 1998, p. 107; July, 2004, review of *Americus, Book I*, p. 87.

Life, September 9, 1957.

Listener, February 1, 1968.

Los Angeles Times, July 20, 1969; March 18, 1980; September 27, 1985.

Los Angeles Times Book Review, August 24, 1980; October 19, 1980; March 24, 1985; September 4, 1988, Alex Raksin, review of *Love in the Days of Rage*, p. 4.

Midwest Quarterly, autumn, 1974; summer, 1983, Robert Dana, "An Interview with Lawrence Ferlinghetti," pp. 412-440.

Minnesota Review, July, 1961.

Modern Drama, Number 22, 1979, Michael Skau, "Toward a Third Stream Theatre: Lawrence Ferlinghetti's Plays," pp. 29-38.

Mother Jones, July-August, 2003, Dennis McNally, "The Beat Goes On: City Lights and San Francisco Have Changed a Lot in the Last 50 Years, but Lawrence Ferlinghetti's Corner Bookstore Is Still the Coolest Room in Town," p. 76.

Nation, October 11, 1958.

New Pages, spring-summer, 1985.

New Republic, February 22, 1975, review of *City Lights Anthology*, p. 33.

New Statesman, April 14, 1967, review of *Her*, p. 513; December 1, 1967, review of *Eye on the World*, p. 779.

New York Times, April 14, 1960; April 15, 1960; April 16, 1960; April 17, 1960; February 6, 1967; February 27, 1967; September 13, 1970; September 21, 1980, Doris Grumbach, review of *Literary San Francisco*, p. 16.

New York Times Book Review, September 2, 1956; September 7, 1958; April 29, 1962; July 21, 1968; September 8, 1968; September 21, 1980; November 1, 1981, Joel Oppenheimer, review of *Endless Life,* p. 40; November 6, 1988, Richard Goodman, review of *Love in the Days of Rage,* p. 22; November 6, 1994.

Observer (London, England), November 1, 1959; April 9, 1967.

Parnassus, spring-summer, 1974.

Poetry, November, 1958; July, 1964; May, 1966, review of *Routines,* p. 125; November, 1972, review of *The Secret Meaning of Things,* p. 105.

Poetry Review, summer, 1992, Tony Curtis, interview with Ferlinghetti, pp. 22-27.

Prairie Schooner, fall, 1974, review of *Open Eye, Open Heart,* p. 275; summer, 1978.

Publishers Weekly, January 13, 1969, review of *The Secret Meaning of Things,* p. 90; August 13, 1979, review of *Landscapes of Living & Dying,* p. 60; April 3, 1981, Genevieve Stuttaford, review of *Endless Life,* p. 66; August 5, 1988, Sybil Steinberg, review of *Love in the Days of Rage,* p. 71; September 26, 1994, review of *These Are My Rivers,* p. 59; November 27, 1995, review of *City Lights Pocket Poets Anthology,* p. 67; March 31, 1997, review of *A Far Rockaway of the Heart,* p. 69; September 28, 1998, John High, "Bookstore Owner Named Poet Laureate," p. 24; March 12, 2001, review of *How to Paint Sunlight: Lyric Poems and Others, 1997-2000,* p. 85; October 29, 2001, review of *Love in the Days of Rage* p. 35; March 22, 2004, review of *Americus, Book I,* p. 81.

Pulpsmith, autumn, 1984, "Pulpsmith Interviews Lawrence Ferlinghetti," pp. 132-142.

Punch, April 19, 1967.

Renascence, spring, 1966, James A. Butler, "Ferlinghetti: Dirty Old Man?," pp. 115-123.

Review of Contemporary Fiction, fall, 1990, S.E. Gontarski, "Lawrence Ferlinghetti on Grove Press," pp. 128-131.

San Francisco Chronicle, March 5, 1961.

San Francisco Oracle, February, 1967, pp. 2-3, 6-17, 29-34, 40-41.

San Francisco Review of Books, September, 1977; fall, 1988, Patrick Burnson, "Passionate Spring," p. 44.

Saturday Review, October 5, 1957; September 4, 1965.

Sewanee Review, fall, 1974.

Small Press Review, September, 1995, Larry Smith, review of revised edition of *Pictures of the Gone World,* p. 12.

Sunday Times (London, England), June 20, 1965.

Times (London, England), October 27, 1968.

Times Literary Supplement, April 27, 1967; November 25, 1988.

Virginia Quarterly Review, autumn, 1969, review of *The Secret Meaning of Things,* p. R133; spring, 1974.

Washington Post Book World, August 2, 1981.

West Coast Review, winter, 1981.

Western American Literature, spring, 1982, review of *Endless Life,* p. 79; winter, 1995, review of *These Are My Rivers,* p. 372.

Whole Earth Review, winter, 1988, interview with Ferlinghetti, p. 115; summer, 1999, Lawrence Ferlinghetti, "A Far Rockaway of the Heart," p. 38.

Wilson Library Bulletin, June, 1958, Peter Thomas Conmy, "The Literary Background of the San Francisco Bay Area," pp. 720-725.

Wisconsin Studies in Contemporary Literature, summer, 1967, L.A. Ianni, "Lawrence Ferlinghetti's Fourth Person Singular and the Theory of Relativity," pp. 392-406.

World Literature Today, summer, 1977, review of *Who Are We Now?,* p. 450; spring, 1982, review of *Endless Life,* p. 348; autumn, 1989, Michael Leddy, review of *Wild Dreams of a New Beginning,* pp. 683-684; autumn, 1994, Ashley Brown, review of *These Are My Rivers,* p. 815; winter, 1998, Lee Oser, "A Far Rockaway of the Heart," p. 138.

ONLINE

Alsop Review, http://www.alsopreview.com/index2.html/ (May 25, 2007), Jack Foley, review of *A Far Rockaway of the Heart.*

City Lights Web site, http://www.citylights.com/ (October 12, 2006), "Lawrence Ferlinghetti."*

(Photograph copyright © 2001 by Jeri Goodkind.)

■ Personal

Born in 1948, in Omaha, NE; married; wife's name Jeri. *Education:* Studied drawing at the Omaha School of Fine Arts. *Hobbies and other interests:* Walking in the woods, painting.

■ Addresses

Home—Mount Desert Island, ME; Henderson, NV. *Agent*—Russell Galen, Scovil, Chichak, Galen Literary Agency, Inc., 381 Park Ave. S., Ste. 1020, New York, NY 10016.

■ Career

Author. First worked in his parents' mail-order business before moving on to careers as an artist, hypnotherapist, violin maker, carpenter, restorer of rare artifacts, and wildlife artist.

■ Writings

"SWORD OF TRUTH" SERIES

Wizard's First Rule, Tor Books (New York, NY), 1994.
Stone of Tears, Tor Books (New York, NY), 1995.

Terry Goodkind

Blood of the Fold, Tor Books (New York, NY), 1996.
Temple of the Winds, Tor Books (New York, NY), 1997.
Soul of the Fire, Tor Books (New York, NY), 1999.
Faith of the Fallen, Tor Books (New York, NY), 2000.
The Pillars of Creation, Tor Books (New York, NY), 2001.
Debt of Bones, Gollancz (London, England), 2001.
Naked Empire, Tor Books (New York, NY), 2003.
Chainfire, Tor Books (New York, NY), 2005.
Phantom, Tor Books (New York, NY), 2006.

■ Adaptations

The "Sword of Truth" novels are being developed as a television mini-series by director Sam Raimi.

■ Sidelights

Best-selling fantasy author Terry Goodkind is known for his "Sword of Truth" series, which has sold over twenty million copies worldwide. In an article for *InfinityPlus,* John D. Owen explained some of Goodkind's appeal to his many readers: "Goodkind manages to do two things with each volume. He first tells a near-enough complete story each time, based around the same set of characters but coming to a satisfactory conclusion each time, leaving the reader with some sense of closure for each volume. . . . Secondly, Goodkind cranks up the tension with each story, escalating the stakes each time, placing his protagonists in ever greater peril, but with commensurate rewards." According to Russ Allbery, in an article posted at the *Eagle* Web site, "It feels like he's in love with the feel of a mythic world, gets a thrill out of writing every scene, and treats each archetype like it's the first time he's ever gotten to think about it." William E. Perry, in a review posted at the *Objectivist Center* Web site, noted: "If you have never read a Goodkind novel, consider doing so. . . . Goodkind writes fantasy—but it is fantasy that is actually about life on earth. This earth." Goodkind incorporates his own ideas about freedom, morality, and individual responsibility into the themes of his novels. Speaking with John C. Snider in an interview for *Sci-Fi Dimensions,* Goodkind explained: "When you say that freedom is a value, that's kind of a vague abstraction. My purpose in writing my novels is to make those abstracts, like 'freedom' and 'individuality' come to life through characters and stories. When you bring values to life that way, you are ennobling mankind. You are inspiring people."

Success as a writer came late for Goodkind. He was forty–six years old when his debut novel, *Wizard's First Rule,* was published in 1994. He is living evidence that good teachers really do make a difference. As a boy, he had been made to hate reading because most adults chastised him for being so slow at it. It was not that the young Goodkind disliked the stories that were in books; he had a great deal of difficulty sorting out the words. He had dyslexia, though he did not learn this until later. His teachers—most of them, anyway—taught him that what was important in reading and writing was getting the grammar and spelling correct. In addition, students were judged on how many books they could read, whether they were literary works or not. Goodkind liked to read adventure stories, such as the Edgar Rice Burroughs books, which he found in his local library.

But then in his senior year of high school Goodkind met Ann Hansen, his English composition teacher. "This teacher read the stories I wrote for her class and saw something more than a collection of misspelled words," the author recalled in an online interview with James Frenkel posted at the *Tor Books* Web site. "Although she admonished me over my poor spelling and grammatical errors, she also told me that there was something beyond the mechanics of writing that was profoundly important. She saw the story. She encouraged me to write stories. She let me touch something noble. This changed my

Goodkind begins his "Sword of Truth" series with this 1994 novel. (Tom Doherty Associates, Inc., 1994. Copyright © 1994 by Terry Goodkind. Reproduced by permission.)

world." Although he was constantly dreaming up stories and writing them in his head all the time he was growing up, Goodkind did not write down many of his tales. Writing was not a practical pursuit, and so he searched for another career.

Always a good artist, Goodkind had been drawing ever since he could remember, and he started selling his work when he was in high school. He later worked as a wildlife artist, as well as becoming involved in other artistic professions, including making violins and restoring rare artifacts. In addition, he had stints as a hypnotherapist and cabinet maker. But he told Stacy Trevenon in *Half Moon Bay Review,* "All these things were in search of writing. . . . The thing you desire most is the last thing you get to because you're afraid to fail at it."

Begins Writing in Maine

Goodkind felt ready to write only when he was about forty-five years old. By that time, he had already moved from his home in Omaha to his favorite state, Maine, a place he had fallen in love with just after finishing high school. There, using his skills as a carpenter, he built his own home. It is just the sort of house one would expect from a creative mind. Along with the expected wood-paneled library, he has an office with panels hand painted to look like granite, and a kitchen with cabinets made out of a heavy, stonelike material. His home is decorated with objects showing his interest in antiquities, including masks from Indonesia, medieval weaponry, and a variety of antiques.

It was while building his private sanctuary in the Maine woods that Goodkind finally decided to

Richard Cypher must train to become a wizard in this 1995 novel. (Tom Doherty Associates, Inc., 1995. Copyright © 1995 by Terry Goodkind. Reproduced by permission.)

write his first novel. "I don't think I could have written what I did any earlier," the author told Lynn Flewelling in a *Bangor Daily News* article. "I had to live this long, had the experiences I've had, to create what I do. I knew I wanted to write for years, but I had to be ready so I wouldn't blow it. The move to Maine was the final step." In an online *Barnes & Noble* author chat, Goodkind related how the character of Mother Confessor Kahlan Amnell came to him: "I was building my house at the time Kahlan first came to me, and I let the story grow in my mind for a year when I finished the house. Then I started writing, and it took thirteen months to write *Wizard's First Rule*. Ten weeks after I wrote the end, I had an agent and the book was sold and auctioned for the highest price ever paid for a first fantasy novel." Goodkind received a $275,000 two-book deal from Tor for *Wizard's First Rule* and his then-unfinished *Stone of Tears*. "I hate telling that story to people who've been struggling for years. . . .," the author told Flewelling. "They look at me and I kind of back up in case they go for my throat."

An Instant Success

Goodkind's success as a writer was immediate, with the first book in what was to become the "Sword of Truth" series quickly becoming a best seller, and the author gathering a loyal following of readers. Goodkind's books are traditional fantasy quest tales in which the forces of Good are pitted against the Dark. There is mystery, magic, and romance aplenty, plus what some say is the author's particular strength: strong characters. The hero of *Wizard's First Rule* is Richard Cypher, a simple woodsman who loves living in the forest. His life quickly becomes complicated when he meets Kahlan Amnell, who has fled her kingdom from the evil wizard Darken Rahl. Richard, whose father has just been slain for refusing to reveal the location of the Book of Counted Shadows, learns that he has inherited magical abilities, and that he must become a Seeker and wield the Sword of Truth in a fight against Rahl. Together with Kahlan and the kindly wizard Zedd, Richard sets out for the Midlands to defeat Rahl. He does so by using the "Wizard's First Rule"—the knowledge that people are stupid. Richard tricks Rahl into thinking he is opening the magical Box of Orden which will give Rahl dominion over all the world. The mistake proves fatal to Rahl, who turns out to be Richard's real father, therefore revealing Richard Cypher to be Richard Rahl and explaining the source of Richard's magical abilities.

Wizard's First Rule is a rather dark story, full of bloodshed, torture, and other violent scenes. Some have commented on this grim aspect of Goodkind's

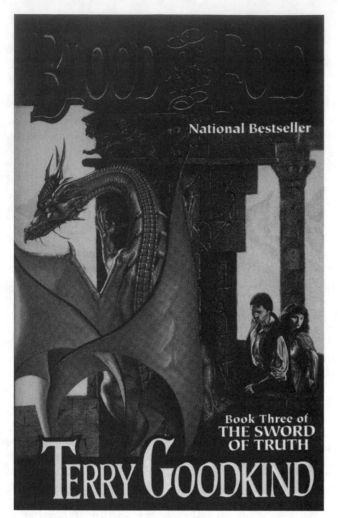

The "Sword of Truth" continues in this 1996 fantasy.
(Tom Doherty Associates, Inc., 1996. Copyright © 1996 by Terry Goodkind. Reproduced by permission.)

work, to which he has responded that, though he is writing fantasy, when it comes to the realities of the ugliness of war he wishes to remain realistic. Goodkind explained to Snider: "The reason I'm graphic in depicting battle scenes is because I want to be clear that war is not glorious. . . . It's about defending yourself against people that want to kill you."

Goodkind's novel has yet another theme: the use of magic as a metaphor for technology. Some of the characters in his books have an irrational fear of magic, a fear that has the same psychology behind it as the fear many people in the real world have for modern advances. "There is absolutely no difference," the author told Frenkel, "between the forensic psychology of 'My joints be aching because there's a witch down the road who be casting evil spells on me,' and 'My joints are aching because the power lines down the road are emitting low frequency electromagnetic radiation.' None." Goodkind is condemning a similar ignorance in his novel when Kahlan is chased out of her kingdom and persecuted by people who fear her magic.

Even more important to Goodkind, however, are his characters. To him, they are not heroes and heroines living in a fantasy world but more like real people, with real strengths and weaknesses, who just happen to be living in a world where magic is possible. As when Goodkind was building his house and first envisioned the character of Kahlan, the author's characters come to him, bringing their stories with them. "The point of my writing," Goodkind explained in the *Barnes & Noble* online chat, "is how these characters relate to us in terms of their desires, ambitions, and what really matters in their lives. . . . Magic is a new way of looking at emotions that are common to all of us."

Speaking to *Authors and Artists for Young Adults*, Goodkind explained the philosophy behind his fiction: "It is the evil people in the books—the Imperial Order—who, in their devotion to the monstrous philosophy of altruism use the bloody club of self-sacrifice to crush individual liberty and enforce conformity.

"Such altruistic principles are mindlessly pushed by everyone from U.S. politicians and every religion, to Joseph Stalin and Mao Zedong. Because people accept prepackaged philosophy (that's what religion is) they tend to believe that what they are taught is 'the right thing to do.' Self-sacrifice is one of the tools used to strip people of their humanity and their individual choices, to stop them from thinking for themselves, and of getting them to do things like fly airplanes into buildings.

If you enjoy the works of Terry Goodkind, you may also want to check out the following books:

Ayn Rand, *Fountainhead*, 1943.
Robert Jordan, *The Eye of the World*, 1990.
George R.R. Martin, *A Game of Thrones*, 1997.

"Self-sacrifice is swallowed hook, line, and sinker by most people. It's drummed into them from every direction. Through my books I show how people are manipulated with such altruistic notions of self-sacrifice—I demonstrate that self-sacrifice is a corrupt, self-destructive concept."

"I'm writing adventure tales," Goodkind told Snider. "But the philosophy behind them is clearly defined, so that the reader is able to sense, through the character of Richard, a valid sense of life, a noble sense of life. And it's something they want to live up to, because they know it's embracing life, as opposed to the things they're presented with in the world."

■ Biographical and Critical Sources

BOOKS

St. James Guide to Fantasy Writers, St. James Press (Detroit, MI), 1996.

PERIODICALS

Bangor Daily News, November, 1995, Lynn Flewelling, interview with Terry Goodkind.

Booklist, September 1, 1994, Roland Green, review of *Wizard's First Rule,* p. 28; October 1, 1995, Roland Green, review of *Stone of Tears,* p. 254; November 15, 1996, Roland Green, review of *Blood of the Fold,* p. 576; November 1, 1997, Roland Green, review of *Temple of the Winds,* p. 457; May 1, 1999, review of *Soul of the Fire,* p. 1582; February 15, 2000, Whitney Scott, review of *Blood of the Fold,* p. 1128; August, 2000, Roland Green, review of *Faith of the Fallen,* p. 2073.

Bookseller, December 9, 2005, review of *Chainfire,* p. 32.

Half Moon Bay Review, October 23, 1996, Stacy Trevenon, "Top Fantasy Author Terry Goodkind Visits."

Kirkus Reviews, July 1, 1994, p. 892; August 15, 1995, p. 1147; October 1, 1996, review of *Blood of the Fold,* p. 1434; March 1, 1999, review of *Soul of the Fire,* p. 340.

Kliatt, July, 1998, p. 52; January, 1999, review of *Temple of the Winds,* p. 16; March, 2003, Ginger Armstrong, review of *The Pillars of Creation,* p. 34; May, 2005, Hugh Flick Jr., review of *Stone of Tears* audiobook, p. 52.

Library Bookwatch, March, 2005, review of *Chainfire* audiobook.

Library Journal, June, 1994, Carolyn Cushman, review of *Wizard's First Rule,* p. 35; September 15, 1994, Jackie Cassada, review of *Wizard's First Rule,* p. 94; October 15, 1995, Jackie Cassada, review of *Stone of Tears,* p. 91; May 15, 1999, Jackie Cassada, review of *Soul of the Fire,* p. 131; September 15, 1999, December, 2001, Jackie Cassada, review of *Debt of Bones,* p. 181; February 15, 2004, Barbara Perkins, review of *Naked Empire,* p. 179; July 1, 2005, Tim Daniels, review of *Stone of Tears* audiobook, p. 131.

Locus, June, 1994, Carolyn Cushman, review of *Wizard's First Rule,* p. 35; October, 1994, p. 53; February, 1995, p. 76.

New York Times Book Review, August 6, 2006, Dwight Garner, review of *Phantom,* p. 1.

Publishers Weekly, August 29, 1994, review of *Wizard's First Rule,* p. 65; September 25, 1995, review of *Stone of Tears,* p. 48; October 7, 1996, review of *Blood of the Fold,* p. 66; October 13, 1997, review of *Temple of the Winds,* p. 60; April 19, 1999, review of *Soul of the Fire,* p. 66; July 24, 2000, review of *Faith of the Fallen,* p. 73; November 19, 2001, p. 52; December 3, 2001, review of *The Pillars of Creation,* p. 45; December 17, 2001, John F. Baker, "The Selling of Goodkind," p. 13; August 4, 2003, Daisy Maryles, "Building Momentum," briefly discusses author's book *Naked Empire,* p. 18.

Voice of Youth Advocates, February, 1995, Elaine M. McGuire, review of *Wizard's First Rule,* p. 347; June, 1996, Elaine M. McGuire, review of *Stone of Tears,* p. 107; April, 1997, review of *Stone of Tears,* p. 12; April, 2002, p. 51.

ONLINE

Agony Column Book Reviews and Commentary, http://trashotron.com/agony/ (July 28, 2003), Rick Kleffel, review of *Naked Empire.*

Barnes & Noble, http://www.barnesandnoble.com/ (April 13, 1999), interview with Goodkind.

Book Reporter.com, http://www.bookreporter.com/ (October 14, 2006), Stephen Hubbard, review of *Phantom.*

Eagle, http://www.eyrie.org/~eagle (October 13, 2004), Russ Allbery, review of *Faith of the Fallen.*

Fantastic Reviews, http://www.geocities.com/fantasticreviews/ (June, 2005), Gary Romero, review of *Chainfire.*

InfinityPlus, http://www.infinityplus.co.uk/ (October 14, 2006), John D Owen, reviews of *Wizard's First Rule, Stone of Tears, Blood of the Fold,* and *Temple of the Winds.*

Objectivist Center, http://www.objectivistcenter.org/ (October 13, 2006), William E. Perry, "The Randian Fantasies of Terry Goodkind."

Sci-Fi Dimensions, http://www.scifidimensions.com/ (August, 2003), John C. Snider, interview with Terry Goodkind.

SF Reviews.net, http://www.sfreviews.net/ (October 14, 2006), reviews of *Stone of Tears* and *Blood of the Fold.*

Terry Goodkind's Home Page, http://www.terrygoodkind.com (October 14, 2006).

Tor Books Web site, http://www.tor.com/ (October 16, 2006), James Frenkel, interview with Goodkind.

USAToday.com, http://cgi1.usatoday.com/ (August 4, 2003), interactive interview.

Jane Green

■ Personal

Born 1968, in London, England; married David Burke (an investment banker), January, 1999; children: Harrison, Tabitha, Nathaniel, Jasper. *Education:* Attended university.

■ Addresses

Home—Westport, CT.

■ Career

Author, journalist, and public relations professional. *Daily Express,* London, England, journalist.

■ Writings

NOVELS

Straight Talking, Mandarin (London, England), 1997, Broadway Books (New York, NY), 2003.
Jemima J, Penguin (London, England), 1998, published as *Jemima J: A Novel about Ugly Ducklings and Swans,* Broadway Books (New York, NY), 1999.

Mr. Maybe, Broadway Books (New York, NY), 1999.
Bookends, Michael Joseph (London, England), 2000, Broadway Books (New York, NY), 2002.
Babyville, Michael Joseph (London, England), 2001, Broadway Books (New York, NY), 2003.
Spellbound, Michael Joseph (London, England), 2003, published as *To Have and to Hold,* Broadway Books (New York, NY), 2004.
The Other Woman, Viking (New York, NY), 2005.
(With Jennifer Coburn and Liz Ireland) *This Christmas* (novellas), Zebra Books (New York, NY), 2005.
Life Swap, Penguin (London, England), 2006, published as *Swapping Lives,* Viking (New York, NY), 2006.
Second Chance, Viking (New York, NY), 2007.

■ Adaptations

Jemima J.: A Novel about Ugly Ducklings and Swans was adapted for audio cassette, Recorded Books, 2002; *The Other Woman* was adapted for audio cassette, Books on Tape, 2005.

■ Sidelights

Dubbed the "queen of chick lit literati" by *Glamour* magazine, best-selling British author Jane Green built her success on novels centering around witty and attractive young women in their twenties or thirties. Her cast of characters include confident, professional types, yet women who also have an appealing weakness or quirk. They look for a meaningful man in their lives, but if none is available, shopping proves an excellent antidote. As Jennie Bristow noted in the *New Statesman:* "Chick lit is non-aspirational, non-judgmental and thoroughly non-threatening." Green's numerous contributions to the genre are, according to Bristow, "always warm yet perceptive." Green has also extended the genre into the realms of mommy lit, for as she herself began a family, she also had her protagonists go through the hoops of motherhood and family-building. Green's first novel, *Straight Talking,* was published in her native England in 1997, and since then she has published roughly a novel a year, works that have become bestsellers on both sides of the Atlantic.

From Journalism to the Bestseller List

Born in 1968, Green worked for several years after university in public relations and journalism. Writing for London's *Daily Express* in 1997, she made a career change when a new editor came to the paper. "Suddenly I went from writing all the *Sex and the City* kind of stuff about dating and relationships to features about animals," she told Gary Santaniello in an interview for *Westport* magazine. "It was awful." She decided to give up journalism and try to publish a novel. She allowed herself three months for this task, which to most seasoned professional authors seems like the fantasies of a naive beginning writer. In the event, however, a bidding war ensued over the rights to her first work, *Straight Talking.* As she told Santaniello, "When I started writing, I was twenty-seven, I was single, and I was going out with horrific men and having the same relationships over and over again." She went on to note in the same interview, "All I did with my first novel was I sat down and documented it, but it was the first time that women had been able to pick up these kinds of books and say, 'That could be me.'" Green had the good luck to publish her fist novel shortly after the release of the hugely successful *Bridget Jones' Diary,* which announced the arrival of the chick lit genre.

In Green's first novel, *Straight Talking,* Tasha is a glamorous and successful producer of a popular British call-in chat show. Still, Tasha, like her friends has relationship problems, attracted mostly to jerks and losers, while her other male friends consider her a buddy rather than possible lover. Men, the women conclude, are just no good, but "handsome bastards remain must-have accessories," com-

mented a *Kirkus Reviews* critic. Finally, nice but normal Adam makes Tasha question her taste in men. The book became a bestseller in England, but was not published in the United States until 2003, when Green already had a large fan base here. "Fun to read and full of keen relationship observations, this novel is sure to be demanded by Green's numerous fans," stated Karen Core in *Library Journal.* Similar praise came from *People* contributor Marisa Sandora Carr, who found the novel a "witty, satisfying ode to the single-but-looking life."

The title character in *Jemima J* (published in the United States as *Jemima J: A Novel about Ugly Ducklings and Swans,*) is, like Green at one time, a columnist for a small London newspaper. She feels trapped in her job and is passed over for promotion because she is overweight. Jemima becomes involved via the Internet with a fitness expert for

This 1997 novel tells of Tasha, a television producer on the British dating scene. (Photograph by Juniper Pierce. Broadway Books, 2003. Used by permission of the publisher.)

"A total bonbon . . . Green captures the real pain that women feel as they search to find romantic happiness. Put this one in the winner's circle."
—*USA Today*

NATIONAL BESTSELLER

mr. maybe

A NOVEL

Jane Green

BESTSELLING AUTHOR OF JEMIMA J

A young publicist is split between a wealthy boyfriend and a poor one in this 1999 novel. (Photograph by Geoff Spear. Broadway Books, 2002. Used by permission of the publisher.)

California, a long-distance romance that threatens to become up close and forces Jemima to lose a hundred pounds. Finally, Jemima finds love in the right place, with a producer who finally realizes he loves her for who she is and not how she looks. The novel "conveys with sass and humor both the invisibility of the overweight and the shallow perks that accrue to the thin and beautiful," observed Jean Reynolds in a *People* review. Though Nancy Pearl in *Library Journal* found *Jemima J* to be "superficial," even "ridiculous," *Booklist* contributor Kristine Huntley called it "charming, witty, good-hearted fun." A *Publishers Weekly* reviewer likewise stated that "the concept is clever and nicely handled," and remarked that Green "capture[s] the nuances and neuroses of the singles scene with a gimlet eye and an uninhibited voice."

In Green's third novel, *Mr. Maybe*, Libby Mason is a London publicist who finds that she must choose between two eligible bachelors: handsome and fun-loving writer Nick, who is always broke, and wealthy Ed McMahon, generous, obnoxious and deeply in love with Libby. As these two Mr. Maybes vie for Libby's affections, she has to decide what, to her, constitutes the truest form of love. Libby is an "endearingly flawed, contemporary London career girl" who "manages to garner reader sympathy and even a cheer or two," remarked a *Publishers Weekly* reviewer. Although Joseph V. Tirella, writing in *People*, felt that Libby's "gold-digging streak couldn't be more obvious if she carried a pickax," Huntley, writing in *Booklist*, review, called *Mr. Maybe* "a warm, funny novel about a single girl trying to find love."

With *Bookends*, Green "offers a near perfect—and near perfectly clichéd—romantic wish fulfillment fantasy, complete with perfect gay best friend, perfect bookshop, perfect Hugh Grant-like love object, and perfectly coy tricks to keep the lovers apart for 400 pages," according to a *Kirkus Reviews* critic. Four college friends find separate paths in life in this novel. A reviewer for *Publishers Weekly* was also less impressed with this effort from Green, noting that "there are some bright spots, . . . but they are too few and far between."

Chick Lit Grows Up

Green was married in 1999, and began having a family of her own, which grew to four children. In *Babyville*, she portrays this more mature aspect of chick lit. Explaining her shift in subject matter, Green told Peg Tyre of *Newsweek:* "I realized there were only so many books I could write about the same topic." In an interview for the *Bookseller*, Green also addressed this issue, noting that early on in the writing she realized that "the book had to be character driven—it's about people and how their lives are affected by having or not having children, not a book about babies." Lan N. Nguyen wrote in *People*, "Green moves on to what happens after the fairy tale." Three friends look at motherhood from different perspectives as each comes to terms with her feelings regarding children. "There's enough suspense and humor to make up for some clichéd characters," commented a *Publishers Weekly* reviewer, "and Green keeps the dialogue snappy and the pace fast." Green, Nguyen noted, "draws dead-on portraits of the emotional roller coaster each woman is riding."

To Have and to Hold is the American title of Green's *Spellbound*, which offers a further glimpse into life after one says "I do." When Alice, a successful caterer, marries, Joe, she thinks she has found happiness, eager to take his advice on changes in her life. However, she discovers that Joe is a helpless womanizer, and when he is transferred to New York, Alice must decide how much she will sacrifice for her failing marriage. Green herself moved to the United States with her banker husband in 2001, but that was the extent of autobiographical detail included in this book, which became a bestseller both in England and the United States. Some critics were unexcited about the novel. A contributor for *Kirkus Reviews* thought *To Have and to Hold* was "uninspired," and a critic for *Publishers Weekly* noted that the author's style "relies heavily on exposition, and while her prose is clean, her story is padded." However, *Booklist* contributor Huntley felt that the novel demonstrated Green's "mastery of the chick-lit genre."

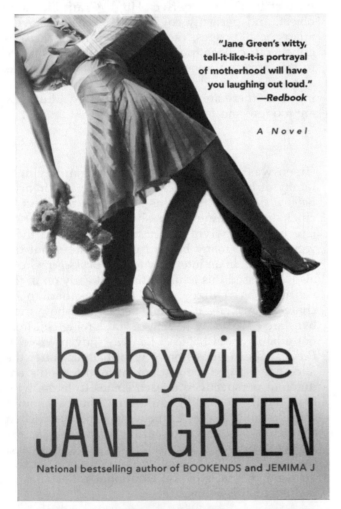

"Jane Green's witty, tell-it-like-it-is portrayal of motherhood will have you laughing out loud."
—Redbook

A Novel

babyville
JANE GREEN
National bestselling author of BOOKENDS and JEMIMA J

This 2003 novel looks at motherhood through the lives of three young women. (Photograph by Wayne Saville. Broadway Books, 2004. Used by permission of the publisher.)

More less than domestic bliss is presented in *The Other Woman*, a story of a recently married woman who hopes to bond with her new in-laws. But quickly her seemingly-perfect mother-in-law becomes something of a monster, interfering in every aspect of the marriage of Ellie and Dan. A columnist for *People* found this a "satisfying tale," and *Booklist* writer Donna Seaman called the same work a "warm and convincing novel." Also writing in *Booklist*, Huntley noted that Green "is particularly adept at producing engaging women's fiction," and that *The Other Woman* was "eminently readable." Similarly, a *Kirkus Reviews* critic called the same novel a "frothy Bridget-Jones-like account of a fashion-savvy newlywed faced with a monster-in-law whose bark is worse than her bite."

Green uses a reality show format for her 2006 title, *Swapping Lives* (titled *Life Swap* in the United Kingdom), the story of dissatisfied Connecticut homemaker, Amber, who switches places with a features director at London's *Poise!* magazine, Vicky, who is single and still looking for the perfect man. Huntley noted in a *Booklist* review that "Vicky and Amber learn to appreciate their own lives thanks to the switch." A *Kirkus Reviews* critic praised Green's high style: "Clothes, bags, shoes, romance, self-acceptance—all we've come to expect and done well enough." For a *Cosmopolitan* reviewer, *Swapping Lives* was a "frisky romp," while for a *Publishers Weekly* contributor it was a "fun but familiar . . . commentary on the cross-Atlantic cultural gap."

In *Second Chance*, Green looks at the effects on family and friends when a 39-year-old man dies. Britisher Tom Fitzgerald has come to America, found a job, gotten married, and had children. But a simple train ride to work ends in tragedy when terrorists attack. Tom's death brings together a wide assortment of friends and family, some of whom have not seen each other in years. The *Publishers Weekly* critic found: "There are few surprises, but the fairy tale ending should appease Green's many fans."

If you enjoy the works of Jane Green, you may also want to check out the following books:

Susan Hubbard, *Lisa Maria Takes Off*, 2005.
Sophie Kinsella, *Shopaholic & Baby*, 2007.
Polly Williams, *Yummy Mummy*, 2007.

Green finds her inspiration for writing in everyday activities, blending some of her personal experi-

In this 2004 novel, a young wife finds that, despite her best efforts to please him, her husband is unfaithful. (Photograph by Juniper Pierce. Broadway Books, 2004. Copyright © 2004 by Jane Green. Used by permission of the publisher.)

ences along with portraits of friends and acquaintances. Speaking with Santaniello, Green noted: "I think my readers have certain expectations, and I think there's usually something glamorous and exciting and big-cityish about my books. . . . I think it would be tough to do something that would be entirely set in the suburbs." However, noting the influence her children have had upon her, she also commented: "In ten years . . . I'll probably be writing about the thrills of having teenagers."

■ Biographical and Critical Sources

PERIODICALS

Book, May-June, 2002, review of *Bookends,* p. 50.

Booklist, April 1, 2000, Kristine Huntley, review of *Jemima J.: A Novel about Ugly Ducklings and Swans,* p. 1412; March 15, 2001, Kristine Huntley, review of *Mr. Maybe,* p. 1332; March 15, 2002, Kristine Huntley, review of *Bookends,* p. 1189; March 1, 2004, Kristine Huntley, review of *To Have and to Hold,* p. 1101; February 1, 2005, Kristine Huntley, review of *The Other Woman,* p. 917; March 1, 2005, Donna Seaman, "Top 10 Women's Fiction," review of *The Other Woman,* p. 1137; March 15, 2006, Kristine Huntley, review of *Swapping Lives,* p. 5.

Bookseller, July 6, 2001, review of *Babyville,* p. 32.

Cosmopolitan, June, 2006, review of *Swapping Lives,* p. 282.

Entertainment Weekly, June 8, 2001, Clarissa Cruz, "Text and the Single Girl: Move over Bridget Jones—The Latest Crop of Chick Lit Is Hitting the Shelves," review of *Mr. Maybe,* p. 68; September 26, 2003, Clarissa Cruz, "Chick-Lit Chic: It's Raining (Mostly Unworthy) Men," review of *Straight Talking,* p. 98; March 4, 2005, review of *The Other Woman,* p. 77; June 16, 2006, review of *Swapping Lives,* p. 79.

Kirkus Reviews, April 15, 2002, review of *Bookends,* p. 515; July 1, 2003, review of *Straight Talking,* p. 875; April 1, 2004, review of *To Have and to Hold,* p. 286; January 15, 2005, review of *The Other Woman,* p. 71; April 15, 2006, review of *Swapping Lives,* p. 370; May 15, 2007, review of *Second Chance.*

Kliatt, September, 2002, Sue Rosenzweig, review of *Jemima J.,* p. 54.

Library Journal, March 1, 2000, review of *Jemima J.,* p. S4; April 15, 2000, Nancy Pearl, review of *Jemima J.,* p. 122; April 15, 2002, Amanda Glasbrenner, review of *Bookends,* p. 125; August, 2003, Karen Core, review of *Straight Talking,* p. 130; April 15, 2004, Core, review of *To Have and to Hold,* p. 124; May 1, 2006, Anika Fajardo, review of *Swapping Lives,* p. 78.

New Statesman, September 24, 2001, Jennie Bristow, "Girls Just Wanna Have Fun," review of *Babyville,* p. 52.

Newsweek, August 4, 2003, Peg Tyre, "Bridget Jones Grows Up: 'Mommy Lit' Takes a Wry, Irreverent Look at Motherhood," p. 52.

People, July 17, 2000, Jean Reynolds, review of *Jemima J.,* p. 45; July 2, 2001, Joseph V. Tirella, review of *Mr. Maybe,* p. 37; June 17, 2002, Julie K.L. Dam, review of *Bookends,* p. 47; June 23, 2003, Lan N. Nguyen, review of *Babyville,* p. 43; October 13, 2003, Marisa Sandora Carr, review of *Straight Talking,* p. 52; April 11. 2005, review of *The Other Woman,* p. 53; July 3, 2006, Lesley Messer, review of *Swapping Lives,* p. 47.

Publishers Weekly, April 10, 2000, review of *Jemima J.,* p. 72; June 11, 2001, review of *Mr. Maybe,* p. 62; August 6, 2001, Daisy Maryles, "Another Brit Lit Hit," p. 19; August 20, 2001, John F. Baker, "Broadway Hot on Green," p. 17; May 6, 2002, review of *Bookends,* p. 33; June 9, 2003, review of *Babyville,* p. 37; July 7, 2003, Daisy Maryles and Dick Donahue, "Here, Chick, Chick, Chick (Behind the Bestsellers)," p. 16; July 21, 2003, review of *Straight Talking,* p. 173; March 1, 2004, review of *To Have and to Hold,* p. 46; May 31, 2004, Daisy Maryles, "Green's Holding"; March 28, 2005, review of *The Other Woman,* p. 56; April 17, 2006, review of *Swapping Lives,* p. 166; April 30, 2007, review of *Second Chance.*

Redbook, July, 2001, review of *Mr. Maybe,* p. G2.

Westport, December, 2004, Gary Santaniello, "Woman of Affairs: Author Jane Green," p. 52.

ONLINE

Chick Lit USA, http://www.chicklit.us/ (July 22, 2004), interview with Jane Green.

Jane Green Home Page, http://www.janegreen.com (August 31, 2006).

Penguin UK Web site, http://www.penguin.co.uk/ (August 31, 2006), "Jane Green."*

(Photograph courtesy of AP Images.)

Amy Heckerling

■ Personal

Born May 7, 1954, in New York, NY; daughter of an accountant; married second husband, Neal Israel (a film director), July, 1984; children: (second marriage) Mollie Sara. *Education:* New York University, B.A., 1975; attended the American Film Institute.

■ Addresses

Home—Beverly Hills, CA. *Agent*—Gersh Agency, 222 N. Canon Dr., Beverly Hills, CA 90210.

■ Career

Producer, director, and writer. Director of films, including *Fast Times at Ridgemont High, Johnny Dangerously, National Lampoon's European Vacation, Look Who's Talking,* and *Look Who's Talking, Too;* director of television series episodes, including *Twilight Zone* and *Fast Times.*

■ Awards, Honors

American Film Institute fellow, 1975; People's Choice Award for Best Comedy, for *Look Who's Talking.*

■ Writings

SCREENPLAYS

(And director) *Look Who's Talking,* Tri-Star Pictures, 1989.
(With husband, Neal Israel; and director) *Look Who's Talking, Too,* Tri-Star Pictures, 1991.
Clueless, Paramount, 1995.
(And director) *Loser,* Columbia Pictures, 2000.
(And director) *I Could Never Be Your Woman,* Bauer Martinez Studios, 2007.

TELEVISION SERIES

(And executive producer and episodic director) *Clueless,* American Broadcasting Company (ABC), 1996.

OTHER

(With Pamela Pettler) *The No-Sex Handbook,* Warner, 1990.

■ Adaptations

The films *Look Who's Talking* and *Look Who's Talking, Too* were adapted as the television series *Baby Talk,* ABC, 1991; *Clueless* was adapted as a television series by ABC in 1996.

■ Sidelights

Amy Heckerling is one of just a handful of women directors who has made a career for herself in the male-dominated world of the American movie industry. She rose to prominence as the director of a raunchy teenage comedy called *Fast Times at Ridgemont High,* which became one of the surprise box office hits of 1982. In the years since, Heckerling's directorial credits have included such "low-brow" but commercially successful movies as *National Lampoon's European Vacation, Clueless, Look Who's Talking,* and *Look Who's Talking, Too* (she also wrote the screenplays for the latter three films). In addition, Heckerling has occasionally worked in television, dabbled in acting, and coauthored a book of humor entitled *The No-Sex Handbook* with Pamela Pettler. However, she remains best known as a writer-director, a vocation in which she feels very much at home. "I'd rather be on a different schedule than the rest of the world and lead a daydreaming life," she told Richard Cohen of *Rolling Stone* in a 1995 interview. "I like to sleep late, avoid the phone, goof with my kid, exercise, and then after dinner I start in."

Heckerling is a native of New York City. She told Luaine Lee in the *Milwaukee Journal Sentinel:* "I really liked *Mad* magazine when I was a kid and thought it would be the coolest thing in the world to work for them." She attended the High School of Art and Design, where she had a bout with anorexia. Heckerling graduated from New York University in 1975 with a B.A. degree. It was during her student days that she saw a 1973 film called *Mean Streets* by fellow New Yorker Martin Scorsese; the experience changed her life. "I worshiped [that film]," Heckerling recalled to Cohen. "Before, it felt like movies were these big splashy things filled with stars that came out of Hollywood. Suddenly there was this movie where I could understand what everybody was saying. I understood their motives, and there was music and energy, and the shooting was cuckoo, and I was going, 'Wow. movies are for me now.'" As a result, Heckerling enrolled in courses at the American Film Institute, where she learned the art of directing by making a series of short films such as *Modern Times, High Finance,* and *Getting It Over With.* This latter effort, a comedy about a nineteen-year-old woman's efforts to lose her virginity, helped Heckerling land a contract at Metro-Goldwyn-Mayer (MGM) studios. Unfortunately for Heckerling, her first project at MGM was aborted by the 1980 Hollywood actors' strike.

After college, Heckerling was married for a time to a musician. But as her film career began to take off, he became more angry. Heckerling explained to Lee: "He said, 'Woman, I want you home, blah, blah, blah.' I said, 'I'm making a movie.' One day it got so bad, I left the house. I never came back." Heckerling's first directing effort for Universal Studios, *Fast Times at Ridgemont High,* was a low-budget, R-rated comedy chronicling a year in the life of a group of California teenagers. The story focused on the adventures of Ridgemont High senior Brad Hamilton, played by the then-unknown Judge Reinhold, and his younger sister Stacy, who was played by Jennifer Jason Leigh. Other up-and-coming young stars in the talented ensemble cast included Phoebe Cates, Forest Whitaker, Eric Stoltz, and Nicolas Cage. However, it was Sean Penn as a stoned surfer named Jeff Spicoli who was the movie's "real scene stealer," as *New York Times* critic Janet Maslin noted. In her review, she described *Fast Times at Ridgemont High* as "a jumbled but appealing teen-age comedy with something of a fresh perspective on the subject." In *New York,* David Denby described the film as "in memory, [standing] out from the Porky's era of teen exploitation like a diamond glistening in the trash." Pulitzer Prize-winning critic Roger Ebert of the *Chicago Sun-Times* was less impressed, giving the film a very definite thumbs down. Ebert described *Fast Times at Ridgemont High* as "sexist," adding that the plot contained "erratic, offensive material that hasn't been thought through."

Although several critics shared Ebert's opinion, *Fast Times at Ridgemont High* was successful at the box office, where it became a cult hit with youthful audiences. The movie's domestic gross alone totaled more than $27 million; that kind of commercial success attracted attention in Hollywood, where Heckerling was suddenly tabbed as one of America's first commercially successful female film directors. But her next film, which she made in 1984 for the Twentieth-Century Fox studio, did little to enhance that reputation. *Johnny Dangerously* was a comedy spoof of 1930s gangster films, starring a talented cast that included Michael Keaton, Joe Piscopo, Maureen Stapleton, and Peter Boyle. Despite Heckerling's best efforts, the film was a flop with audiences and critics alike when it was released in the busy pre-Christmas season. "The movie wants to do for gangster films what *Airplane!* did for *Airport,* and *Top Secret!* did for spy movies. It has its work cut out," Roger Ebert wrote. Ralph Novak of *People* was one of the few reviewers who had anything positive to say, hailing *Johnny Dangerously* as a "good-natured, relaxed parody."

Heckerling did not let the negative press affect her career. She bounced back in 1985 with *National*

Sean Penn and Ray Walston star in the 1982 comedy *Fast Times at Ridgemont High.* (Directed by Amy Heckerling. Courtesy of Universal/The Kobal Collection.)

Lampoon's European Vacation, a comedy that starred Chevy Chase and Beverly D'Angelo. The sequel to *National Lampoon's Vacation* and *National Lampoon's Christmas Vacation*, which Heckerling did not direct, *European Vacation* follows the antics of the all-American Griswald family, led by Chevy Chase and Beverly D'Angelo, as they tour France, England, Italy, and Germany. The movie provided fresh proof of Heckerling's deft commercial touch; *National Lampoon's European Vacation* made more than $12.3 million dollars in its first weekend in theaters and went on to become one of the summer's hits, despite indifferent reviews. David Ansen of *Newsweek* said the movie was a "tacky-looking, mildly amusing, episodic comedy." Janet Maslin of the *New York Times* described it as "a retread" of *National Lampoon's Vacation*, a 1981 hit that had been directed by Harold Ramis.

The same year that *National Lampoon's European Vacation* was released, Heckerling and her second husband, screenwriter-director Neal Israel, had a daughter they named Mollie Sara. Heckerling has said her pregnancy and the birth of her daughter were the inspiration for her next two films. "Anything good that's happened to me in the last five years is because of my kid," she told Richard Lacayo of *People* in a 1991 interview. Heckerling spent the next three years between 1985 and 1988 raising her child and working in television, both as a producer and occasionally as the director of episodes of the *Twilight Zone* and *Fast Times*, a short-lived CBS series that was a spin-off of the film *Fast Times at Ridgemont High*. During this period she also began writing her first movie screenplay. She explained to Daniel Cerone of the *Los Angeles Times*, "When I had Mollie, she would sit on the table in this baby seat and just endlessly look around. . . . My husband and I started to put words in her mouth, what she might be thinking based on her expressions." The end result was a script that became the basis for Heckerling's biggest box office hit, the movie *Look Who's Talking*. That 1989 comedy recounted a baby's humorous thoughts and feelings from the time he was in the womb until he was about two years old.

Bruce Willis provided the voice for Mikey, a wise-cracking infant who is intent on finding a husband for his unmarried mom, played by Kirstie Alley of *Cheers* television sitcom fame. Heckerling wrote the role of the New York cab driver who eventually marries Mikey's mother especially for her friend John Travolta, whose career was at a low point; he had not had a hit in several years. Although the *Look Who's Talking* plot was predictable and the humor sometimes silly, audiences loved the movie and it became a huge hit, breaking box office records for a film opening in the fall, earning Heckerling a People's Choice Award for Best Comedy, and breathing new life into Travolta's career. The reasons were obvious; as Roger Ebert put it, "as a silly entertainment [it] is full of good feeling, and director Amy Heckerling finds a light touch for her lightweight material." Other critics were less kind. "This flabby comedy. . . deserves only one thing:

to fall on its fat one," wrote a reviewer for *Rolling Stone*. Suzanne Moore, writing in *New Statesman & Society*, concurred, stating, "*Look Who's Talking* is as yucky as babyfood."

Yucky or not, *Look Who's Talking* spawned the 1990 sequel *Look Who's Talking, Too* and a 1991 television sitcom titled *Baby Talk*. (There was also a 1994 movie called *Look Who's Talking Now,* which Heckerling co-produced. That film also starred John Travolta and Kirstie Alley in the same roles they had played in the earlier films, but this time there were talking dogs rather than babies.) Neither *Look Who's Talking, Too* nor *Baby Talk* achieved the level of commercial success enjoyed by *Look Who's Talking. Look Who's Talking, Too* follows the adventures of the John Travolta and Kirstie Alley characters after they married. Heckerling again wrote the screenplay, this time in cooperation with Israel, whose earlier writing credits included coauthorship of the phenomenally successful 1984 comedy Police Academy. Working on the premise that if audiences loved a talking baby the first time out, they'd love more of the same a second time around, Heckerling and Israel gave

Chevy Chase meets royalty in this scene from the 1985 comedy *National Lampoon's European Vacation.* (Courtesy of Popperfoto/ Archive Photos, Inc. Reproduced by permission.)

Heckerling directs John Travolta and Kirstie Alley in 1991's *Look Who's Talking Too.* (Directed by Amy Heckerling. Courtesy of The Kobal Collection, 1990. Reproduced by permission.)

Mikey a baby sister, whose voice was supplied by comedian Roseanne Barr. Several other new characters were thrown into the mix for good measure, with Damon Wayans and comic legend Mel Brooks providing the voices. Most critics liked *Look Who's Talking, Too* even less than they liked its predecessor. A reviewer for *Variety*, the entertainment industry weekly newspaper, panned *Look Who's Talking, Too* as a "vulgar sequel" that "overemphasizes toilet humor and expletives. . . ." Ralph Novak of *People* felt much the same way: "Whatever limited charm there was in the original centered on the notion of giving voice to a baby's thoughts. If [*Look Who's Talking*] offered a childish pleasure or two, though, this one is just infantile."

Heckerling's next movie is arguably her best. *Clueless*, which appeared in 1995, was a modern-day version of English writer Jane Austen's classic 1816 novel *Emma*, about a well-intentioned know-it-all matchmaker who is constantly interfering in other people's lives. Heckerling originally wrote the story as a television sitcom pilot for Fox. But when the network rejected it, she followed her agent's advice and turned the story into a film which she also

directed. Heckerling told Cohen of *Rolling Stone*, "I needed a story a girl could go through. I wanted a comedy of manners—so I thought about Jane Austen and remembered how much I loved *Emma* in college. The plot is perfect for any time. Here's a girl, she's rich, she's manipulating people and thinks she knows what's going on but is so into her own world, she doesn't see what everybody else can see." Heckerling set her plot in a Beverly Hills high school in 1995. Emma becomes a hip fifteen-year-old named Cher, played by Alicia Silverstone. That audiences loved the film was clear, for it made more than $20 million in the first week after its release. Critics too were impressed, praising Heckerling's screenplay and direction and lauding Silverstone's performance. In the *Chicago Sun-Times*, Roger Ebert described *Clueless* as a "smart and funny movie" and noted that "Heckerling walks a fine line between satire and put-on, but she finds it, and her dialogue could be anthologized." Reviewer Peter Travers of *Rolling Stone* declared, "Silverstone is a winner. And so is the movie." Ironically, after the success of the big screen version of *Clueless*, the characters and the concept returned to television, the medium for which they were originally intended. Heckerling, acting as executive producer, episodic director, and writer, sold ABC-TV a short-lived weekly half-hour sitcom of the same title. The show aired briefly in 1996.

In 2000 Hecklering returned to the screen with *Loser*, in which freshman Paul Tannek experiences the dark side of contemporary college life. Paul comes from a small town and is the first in his family to attend college. His concerns about passing his courses and paying the high tuition are in sharp contrast to his room mates, whose wealthy families pay the bills. Their concerns revolve around girls and drinking. As Gene Armstrong stated in the *Arizona Daily Star*, Paul's room mates are "abusive, pot-smoking, beer-drinking, date-raping ugly young Americans." Paul eventually meets Dora, a fellow student working as a waitress and having an affair with an older professor. Over the course of the film, their relationship blossoms into love. Armstrong found that the film's "smart plotting and clever dialogue snazzily capture the sort of post-adolescent anxiety that afflicts us when we are learning how to grow up without an instruction manual." Charles

Taylor, in his review for *Salon.com*, concluded: "As clearly as any movie this year, *Loser* says that the most valuable things in a cold world are the relationships we form and sustain."

If you enjoy the works of Amy Heckerling, you may also want to check out the following films:

Three Men and a Baby, 1987.
Father of the Bride, 1991.
You've Got Mail, 1998.

The essayist for *Women Filmmakers & Their Films* concluded that "Heckerling's comic scripts boast fast-paced dialogue and clever humor that occasion-

Alicia Silverstone stars in the 1995 film *Clueless*, **about a rich girl who thinks she knows it all.** (Directed by Amy Heckerling. Copyright © Corbis/Sygma.)

Actor Jason Biggs and Heckerling reviewing footage from the 2000 film *Loser.* (Photograph by Lauren Greenfield. AP Images.)

ally point to the sexism and superficialities of American consumer culture, as they mock and celebrate the insipid yet well-intentioned values of suburbia, even in upscale Beverly Hills. Likewise, they include subversive feminine humor despite their big studio backing. . . . They are well-produced, technically proficient, and engaging works that employ the narrative conventions and formulae that predominate in commercial Hollywood movies. In addition, they are testimony to Heckerling's considerable skill in evoking humorously engaging performances from her actors."

■ **Biographical and Critical Sources**

BOOKS

Cole, Janis, and Holly Dale, *Calling the Shots: Profiles of Women Filmmakers*, Quarry Press (Kingston, ONT, Canada), 1993.

Mayne, Judith, *The Woman at the Keyhole: Feminism and Women's Cinema*, Indiana University Press (Bloomington, IN), 1990.

Quart, Barbara, *Women Directors: The Emergence of a New Cinema*, Praeger (New York, NY), 1989.

Women Filmmakers & Their Films, St. James Press (Detroit, MI), 1998.

PERIODICALS

Arizona Daily Star (Tucson, AZ), July 23, 2000, Gene Armstrong, review of *Loser*, p. E1.

Austin American-Statesman, July 20, 2000, Sharyn Wizda, review of *Loser*, p. E1.

Buffalo News, July 25, 2000, Janet Bossard, review of *Loser*, p. N5.

Chicago Tribune, December 17, 1990.

Entertainment Weekly, October 25, 1996, p. 98.

Los Angeles Times, October 13, 1989, Daniel Cerone, interview with Amy Heckerling; October 26, 1989.

Milwaukee Journal Sentinel, July 24, 2000, Luaine Lee, review of *Loser*, p. 1.

Ms., November, 1985, Z. Klapper, "Movie Directors: Four Women Who Get to Call the Shots in Hollywood," p. 62.

New Statesman & Society, April 13, 1990, Suzanne Moore, review of *Look Who's Talking*, p. 45.

Newsweek, August 12, 1985, David Ansen, review of *National Lampoon's European Vacation*, p. 71.

New York, August 7, 1995, p. 71.

New York Times, September 3, 1982, Janet Maslin, review of *Fast Times at Ridgemont High*; July 27, 1985, Janet Maslin, review of *National Lampoon's European Vacation*, p. 13; October 13, 1989; October 25, 1989; December 1, 1989.

People, January 28, 1985, Ralph Novak, review of *Johnny Dangerously*; May 13, 1985; August 12, 1985, p. 10; February 19, 1990; January 21, 1991, Ralph Novak, review of *Look Who's Talking, Too*, p. 21.

Rolling Stone, October 19, 1989, review of *Look Who's Talking*, p. 29; September 7, 1995, Richard Cohen, "High School Confidential," p. 53; October 8, 1995, Peter Travers, review of *Clueless;* September 7, 1995, Rich Cohen, interview with Heckerling.

San Francisco Chronicle, September 20, 1996, John Carman, review of *Clueless*, p. C1.

Sarasota Herald Tribune, July 21, 2000, George Meyer, review of *Loser*, p. 19.

Time, July 31, 1995, p. 65.

Times (London, England), October 19, 1995, Matt Wolf, interview with Heckerling, p. 35.

Washington Post, October 13, 1989; December 14, 1990.

ONLINE

PopMatters, http://popmatters.com/ (October 14, 2006), Lucas Hilderbrand, review of *Loser*.

Salon.com, http://salon.com/ (July 21, 2000), Charles Taylor, review of *Loser*.*

(Photograph copyright © Rune Hellestad/Corbis.)

Nick Hornby

■ **Personal**

Born April 17, 1957, in Redhill, Surrey, England; divorced; children: three. *Education:* Studied at Cambridge University. *Hobbies and other interests:* Working with his nonprofit organization TreeHouse to raise funds for autistic children.

■ **Addresses**

Home—Highbury, North London, England. *Agent*—Author Mail, Penguin Publicity, 80 Strand, London WC2R 0RL, England.

■ **Career**

Freelance journalist and writer; has worked as a teacher of English as a foreign language (TEFL) and a teacher of English. Cofounder, TreeHouse (nonprofit organization), London, England.

■ **Awards, Honors**

William Hill Sports Book of the Year Award, 1992, for *Fever Pitch;* E.M. Forster Award, American Academy of Arts and Letters, 1999; W.H. Smith fic-

tion award, 2002, for *How to Be Good;* National Book Critics Circle Award nomination for criticism, 2002, for *Songbook;* London Award, 2003.

■ **Writings**

NOVELS

High Fidelity, Riverhead Books (New York, NY), 1995.
About a Boy, Riverhead Books (New York, NY), 1998.
How to Be Good, Riverhead Books (New York, NY), 2001.
A Long Way Down, Riverhead Books (New York, NY), 2005.

OTHER

Contemporary American Fiction (essays), Vision Press (London, England), 1992.
Fever Pitch (memoir), Gollancz (London, England), 1992, Penguin Books (New York, NY), 1994.
(Editor) *My Favourite Year: A Collection of New Football Writing,* Gollancz/Witherby (London, England), 1993.
(Editor, with Nick Coleman) *The Picador Book of Sportswriting,* Picador (London, England), 1996.
Double A-Side: Fever Pitch, High Fidelity, Indigo (London, England), 1997.

Triple Platinum (contains *Fever Pitch, High Fidelity,* and *About a Boy*), Gollancz (London, England), 1999.

(Editor and author of introduction) *Speaking with the Angel* (short stories), Penguin (London, England), 2000.

Songbook (essays), McSweeney's Books (San Francisco, CA/Brooklyn, NY), 2003, published as *31 Songs,* Viking (London, England), 2003.

Otherwise Pandemonium (short stories), Penguin (London, England), 2005.

The Polysyllabic Spree (magazine column collection), McSweeney's Books (San Francisco, CA/ Brooklyn, NY), 2006.

Author of foreword, *A Fan's Notes: A Fictional Memoir by Frederick Exley,* Yellow Jersey (London, England), 1998. Contributor to the London *Sunday Times, Times Literary Supplement, Elle, Vogue, Esquire, Time Out, GQ, Time,* and *Literary Review.* Former music critic for the *New Yorker.* Author of monthly column "Stuff I've Been Reading" for *McSweeney's Believer* magazine.

■ Adaptations

About a Boy and *How to Be Good* were both adapted for audiobooks, Putnam Berkley Audio, 1998 and 2001, respectively; *High Fidelity* was adapted for film, directed by Stephen Frears and starring John Cusack, Touchstone Pictures, 2000; *About a Boy* was adapted for film by Peter Hedges, directed by Chris and Paul Weitz and starring Hugh Grant, Universal, 2002; *Fever Pitch* was loosely adapted for film by Lowell Ganz and Babaloo Mandel, directed by Bobby and Peter Farrelly, and starring Jimmy Fallon and Drew Barrymore, Fox 2000 Pictures, 2005.

■ Sidelights

Nick Hornby is a freelance journalist in England, where he has written on literary topics, football, and—in his fiction as well as his nonfiction—obsession. A writer noted for his sense of humor and earthiness, Hornby has written about his subjects in a way with which some critics strongly identify. According to Jonathan Heawood, quoted in *America's Intelligence Wire* by Thomas Wagner, "Hornby's not the greatest prose stylist since Henry James. He's a rough and ready, get-the-reader writer. Like Graham Greene, he's one of those rare authors who gets away with being a page turner and a writer with something serious to say at the same time." "What Hornby offers to many readers is honesty about emotion and an awareness of the deficiencies of modern men, an awareness that is charming rather than defensive or apologetic," remarked Merritt Moseley in the *Dictionary of Literary Biography.*

Hornby's first novel, *High Fidelity,* was credited with capturing the voice of a generation. "A relaxed and natural writer, his appeal comes in part from a call to anyone who was a child in the 1960s," wrote Chris Savage King in the *New Statesman and Society.* While not a sportswriter, Hornby has also written movingly, wittily, and realistically, according to his critics, about soccer (known in England as football) and the obsessiveness with which its fans follow the game.

Becoming a Writer

Hornby was born April 17, 1957, to middle-class parents living just outside of London, England. When he was eleven years old, his parents divorced and he lived with his mother and his younger sister, Gill, who also became a writer. On weekends, Hornby would see his father, Sir Derek Hornby, an international businessman. Sir Hornby began taking his son to football matches (the sport known as soccer in the United States). Hornby grew up with an obsession for the game, and a devotion to his team, The Arsenal, in England's Premier League. In his book *Fever Pitch,* Hornby writes about his first football match with his father. "What impressed me most was just how much most of the men around me hated, really hated, being there. As far as I could tell, nobody seemed to enjoy, in the way that I understood the word, anything that happened during the entire afternoon."

Hornby graduated from Cambridge University in 1979 with a degree in English. He then worked for a year as a gas station attendant before attending two years at Kingston Polytechnic. He admits to having little ambition or direction. While in his twenties, he held jobs as a high school English teacher and an English-as-a-second-language teacher. "I started writing in 1983," Hornby told Tom DeMarchi in the *Writer's Chronicle.* "Funnily enough, I did start by writing plays. They were sort of screen-cum-radio-cum-TV plays, and they weren't very good. They got me an agent . . . but nothing much beyond that. I didn't think I could write prose. When I left the university and I tried to write, everything came out sounding like bad essays, so I thought I should stick to dialogue. I hadn't done

RIVERHEAD ESSENTIAL EDITIONS

HIGH FIDELITY

This 1995 novel centers on a record shop employee who wants to win back his girlfriend. (Riverhead, 1995. Used by permission of Penguin Group (USA) Inc.)

enough reading—not of the things I wanted to emulate—so it took me a while, a long while, to grapple with voice." Hornby later established himself as a freelance writer, contributing to the *New Republic, GQ, Elle, Time, Vogue,* and *Premiere.* He also landed a position as a columnist for the *Independent* in London, writing about pop culture. "Everything changed for me when I read Anne Tyler, Raymond Carver, Richard Ford, and Lorrie Moore," he told DeMarchi. "I'd never read short stories like Carver's and Moore's—her first collection, *Self-Help,* just seemed to be me in some way I couldn't have articulated at the time—so I started writing some, and sold a couple. But voice, tone, simplicity, humor, soul . . . all of these things seemed to be missing from the contemporary English fiction I'd looked at, and I knew then what I wanted to do."

In his first book-length publication, 1992's *Contemporary American Fiction,* Hornby collected essays on American fiction writers of the "dirty realist" school, as it was defined in two issues of the influential British literary journal *Granta.* The works of writers such as Ann Beattie, Raymond Carver, Richard Ford, and Tobias Wolff are discussed in terms of plot and Hornby's estimation of "what it is that makes each of the chosen authors interesting and worth reading," explained *Modern Language Review* contributor Deborah L. Madsen. Hornby's stated purpose is to give the British reader the basic aesthetic and cultural equipment needed to understand American writers. "This is a worthy critical project," Madsen remarked, "but it is dull; and the essays generally are a dull accumulation of plot summaries spiced with catalogue descriptions of narrative or fictional characteristics." Judie Newman stated in the *Journal of American Studies* that *Contemporary American Fiction* would have benefited from a preface or conclusion, which would serve to focus what is "more a serendipitous collection of loosely connected essays than a comprehensive survey." However, Newman added, despite the volume's limitations, it nonetheless "forms a lively, readable introduction to its chosen topic."

A Football Fanatic

First published in England in 1992, *Fever Pitch* is Hornby's memoir of growing up an ardent football fan. From age eleven, when Hornby's parents separated and his father began taking him to see the North London Premier League club Arsenal play football, to his adulthood, when he measures future possibilities with women by their reaction to the knowledge that he follows the sport, he depicts his life as revolving around England's working-class sport. Critics asserted that the work is more about obsession than about football. Laurence O'Toole, for instance, remarked in the *New Statesman and Society:* "*Fever Pitch* is the anatomy of a fixation exquisitely laid out and intelligently picked over."

Fever Pitch received praise from British critics for its wry humor, shrewd insight into human behavior, and moving tribute to North London in the 1960s. The book "is a sophisticated study of obsession, families, masculinity, class, identity, growing up, loyalty, depression and joy," wrote Brendan O'Keefe in the London *Observer.* "It's also a fine book about football." Although some American critics expressed the need for an occasional translation of the British slang terms Hornby employs, understanding of the author's themes was universal. "If [Hornby's] obsession sounds strange," observed Frederick C. Klein in the *Wall Street Journal,* "just substitute 'baseball' for 'soccer.'"

Jimmy Fallon and Drew Barrymore in a scene from the 2005 film *Fever Pitch.* (Screenplay by Nick Hornby. Courtesy of 20th Century Fox/The Kobal Collection/Michaels, Darren.)

Hornby also edited the anthology *My Favourite Year: A Collection of New Football Writing.* Critics noted that, as in *Fever Pitch,* there is a strong theme of "mental illness" in *My Favourite Year.* The book "isn't much about football at all," wrote David Horspool in the *Times Literary Supplement.* "What we have instead is a kind of group therapy for football dependents." Despite the absence of descriptions of actual play, Horspool concluded: "Football fans will like this book, [and] it will also help others to understand why football can be so addictive."

Pens Bestselling Novels

Hornby's novel *High Fidelity* centers on a character with an obsession equally as compulsive as that depicted in *Fever Pitch.* Rob, the novel's protagonist, has just been abandoned by Laura, his live-in girlfriend, and for solace he resorts to his penchant for drawing up "top five" lists: he decides that

Laura would fail to make his list of the top five most painful break-ups of his life. Rob runs a vintage record shop, and references to popular music and other elements of pop culture appear throughout the narration of his quest to get Laura back. "Sometimes this can pall," wrote the reviewer for *Publishers Weekly,* who maintained that the novel "is not quite as hip as it wishes to be." Others focused on Hornby's ability to make Rob a sympathetic character. "Mr. Hornby captures the loneliness and childishness of adult life with such precision and wit that you'll find yourself nodding and smiling," Mark Jolly remarked in the *New York Times Book Review.*

Critics expressed differing opinions about the merits of *High Fidelity.* In the *London Review of Books,* Jenny Turner wrote that the novel "is elegantly crafted, subtly plotted, and its first-party voice is a lively, charming offspring of [J.D.] Salinger and [Scottish writer James] Kelman and [Roddy Doyle's] young Paddy Clarke. And yet, the book still reads more like a superior piece of lifestyle journalism than like a work of art." Similarly, King concluded in his *New Statesman and Society* review: "This is a wonderful read, funny and moving. It's not a novel, exactly—but who cares?" Some critics offered praise for the book's emotional effect upon its readers. As Turner put it, "I have never seen my type of people so vividly rendered on the page before. And I have never before, since I was a grown-up, responded to a piece of writing so immediately either." Margaret Forster concluded in *Spectator*, "Such a relief actually to enjoy a novel and not worry about whether it is Great Literature. . . . I'll put *High Fidelity* on my own list of best five funny, light novels of contemporary times."

As it was for Rob in *High Fidelity*, music is an essential part of Hornby's life; he once served as the pop music critic for the *New Yorker*. In the collection *31 Songs*, Hornby blends criticism and personal experience, examining such wide-ranging topics as an adolescent's need for rebellious rock and roll, the virtues of privately-owned record stores, and his autistic son's love of music. According to *Spectator* contributor Marcus Berkmann, *31 Songs* is "an intelligent and highly distinctive overview of modern pop music, built around this pile of songs Hornby happens to adore. It's quite unlike most music criticism, and all the better for it." Hornby is also the author of "Stuff I've Been Reading," a monthly column about literature that appears in *McSweeney's Believer*. As Hornby told Dave Weich in an interview for Powells.com, he came up with the idea for the column when he realized there wasn't a forum "where people just write about what they read, where they let their own natural inclinations guide them. They're usually being paid to write about books, which obviously changes the relationship with the book a little bit." Hornby presents fourteen essays from "Stuff I've Been Reading" in *The Polysyllabic Spree*. "What makes this book of interest, Hornby fan or not, is not what he's read, but the books he didn't read and why—and how he found his way to other books instead," observed Stephanie Dickison in the *Writer*.

Todd Louiso, John Cusack, and Jack Black star in the 2000 film version of *High Fidelity*. (Screenplay by Nick Hornby. Courtesy of Touchstone/The Kobal Collection.)

Nicholas Hoult and Hugh Grant star in the 2002 film *About a Boy.* (Screenplay by Nick Hornby. Courtesy of Working Title/The Kobal Collection/ Sparham, Laurie.)

An awkward twelve-year-old forms an unusual bond with an scheming womanizer in *About a Boy*. Will Freeman, a confirmed bachelor, has coasted through life on royalties earned from a hit song his father wrote. Freeman has settled on the perfect way to meet woman—by pretending to be a single father—and so he joins a single-parent support group. When he needs to produce evidence of his parenthood, however, he "borrows" Marcus, an oddly endearing lad with a suicidal mother, and passes him off as his own. "The conceit of the novel is that both Marcus and Will need to grow up, and that both are able to help each other," noted a critic in the *Economist*. "Will is enough of an adolescent to give Marcus advice on appropriate haircuts and musical tastes; Marcus is sufficiently dogged and impervious to sarcasm to force Will to make an emotional commitment to him." Though critics found much to praise in *About a Boy*, some expressed some disappointment that it did not match the promise of *High Fidelity*. Cheech Marin, reviewing the work in *Newsweek*, observed that Hornby "puts more energy into Marcus than Will, who's something of a cipher," and *People* contributor Kyle Smith found the novel to be "well-observed but laden with too many hugs and tears."

Hornby's next title, *How to Be Good*, concerns the troubled marriage of Katie Carr, a doctor, and her husband, David, a surly newspaper columnist. Katie has cheated on David but breaks off the affair out of guilt, while David becomes a convert to religion at the hands of D.J. Goodnews. Becoming overzealous in his newfound beliefs, David invites Goodnews to move into their house and proceeds to start giving away the family's possessions. "Naturally Katie, who is bothered by her own moral shifts and slippages on the how-to-be-good scale (good doctor? good mother? good wife?), is brought up short by the fact that her sneering and cynical husband has turned into Mother Teresa of north London overnight," noted Vicki Woods in *Spectator*. Tom Deignan in the *World & I* concluded that *How to Be Good* is an "ultimately insightful and even wise novel."

Hornby's *A Long Way Down* has the unlikely premise of four suicidal characters meeting on a building's roof. Discovering that they are all there for the same reason, they become somewhat ashamed, and instead of killing themselves form a temporary pact to continue living—at least for a while. A darkly comic work, the novel earned mixed reviews. Jon Zobenica, writing in the *Atlantic Monthly*, felt that it was difficult to empathize with the characters, especially when the author allows them to lapse into "often irritating testimonials." *Time* critic Lev Grossman offered a different views, stating, "The pain feels real in *A Long Way Down*, although not at the price of Hornby's pleasantly bitter wit. But what makes the book work is Hornby's refusal to give an inch to sentimentality or cheap inspirational guff."

This 2005 novel tells of a group of would-be suicides who decide to stay alive. (Riverhead, 2005. Cover photos: Black sneakers copyright © Lomo/nonstock; Brown wingtips copyright © Jonathan Knowles/Getty Images; Tan shoes copyright © David Harriman/Getty Images. Used by permission of Penguin Group (USA) Inc.)

"Hornby's gift is never to leap over situations to draw lessons, never to jump to an analogy," remarked Philip Hensher in *Spectator*. "These lives, one is convinced, are just as they are, not constructed in order to draw general lessons."

If you enjoy the works of Nick Hornby, you may also want to check out the following books:

Amanda Eyre Ward, *How to Be Lost,* 2005.
Greil Marcus, *Like a Rolling Stone,* 2005.
David Sedaris, *Me Talk Pretty One Day,* 2001.

The popularity of Hornby's novels, according to Moseley, is that "they are, as he acknowledges, 'redemptive.' "They suggest the possibility of human improvement and offer love as a solvent for at least some of life's problems." According to Hensher, "The oddity of Hornby's career is that he has maintained his attachment to what he said, in *Fever Pitch,* was a crucial feature of a really enjoyable match—'some kind of disgraceful incident (aka "silliness," aka "nonsense," aka "unpleasantness")—we are entering doubtful moral territory here'—without in the slightest compromising his claim to be read, in the end, as the warmest and most committed of moralists."

■ **Biographical and Critical Sources**

BOOKS

Dictionary of Literary Biography, Volume 207: *British Novelists since 1960, Third Series,* Thomson Gale (Detroit, MI), 1999.

PERIODICALS

America's Intelligence Wire, May 12, 2006, Thomas Wagner, "Nick Hornby Never Takes Half Measures, Whether It's Fiction, Rock 'n' Roll or Soccer."

Atlantic Monthly, July-August, 2005, Jon Zobenica, "You Might as Well Live," review of *A Long Way Down,* p. 148.

Book, March, 2001, "Hornby Gets His Wings," article about *Speaking with the Angel* and TreeHouse charity.

Booklist, February 1, 2001, Danise Hoover, review of *Speaking with the Angel,* p. 1041; March 15, 2005, Joanne Wilkinson, review of *A Long Way Down,* p. 1246.

Entertainment Weekly, August 10, 2001, Troy Patterson, "'Good' Behavior," review of *How to Be Good,* p. 67; January 10, 2003, Brian M. Raftery, "Music, To His Ears," p. 74; June 17, 2005, Mark Harris, "Tangled Up in Blues," review of *A Long Way Down,* p. 84.

Journal of American Studies, December, 1993, Judie Newman, review of *Contemporary American Fiction,* pp. 432-433.

Kliatt, January, 2004, Daniel Levinson, review of *Songbook,* p. 37.

Library Journal, June 15, 2001, Heather McCormack, review of *How to Be Good,* p. 102; April 15, 2005, Heather McCormack, review of *A Long Way Down,* p. 73.

London Review of Books, May 11, 1995, Jenny Turner, review of *High Fidelity,* pp. 10-11.

Modern Language Review, Volume 89, number 4, 1994, Deborah L. Madsen, review of *Contemporary American Fiction,* pp. 991-992.

National Catholic Reporter, July 1, 2005, Jeff Severns Guntzel, "For Love of Books: Infectiously Entertaining Essays Reflect a Bibliophile's Passion."

New Leader, May-June, 2005, Mark Kamine, "The Leap Not Taken," review of *A Long Way Down,* pp. 43-45.

New Statesman and Society, October 2, 1992, Laurence O'Toole, review of *Fever Pitch,* pp. 40-41; April 14, 1995, Chris Savage King, review of *High Fidelity,* pp. 47-48; October 20, 2003, Nicholas Blincoe, "Rock and Read," pp. 38-39.

Newsweek, Nay 11, 1998, Cheech Marin, review of *About a Boy,* p. 84; July 16, 2001, Devin Gordon, "High Infidelity," review of *How to Be Good,* p. 61.

New York Times Book Review, September 3, 1995, Mark Jolly, review of *High Fidelity,* p. 6.

Observer (London, England), September 20, 1992, Brendan O'Keefe, review of *Fever Pitch,* p. 54.

People, June 1, 1998, Kyle Smith, review of *About a Boy,* p. 34; June 6, 2005, Kyle Smith, review of *A Long Way Down,* p. 49.

Publishers Weekly, July 24, 1995, review of *High Fidelity,* p. 46; June 21, 2005, review of *How to Be Good,* p. 45; April 4, 2005, Tom Perrotta, review of *A Long Way Down,* p. 41.

School Library Journal, November, 2005, Jamie Watson, review of *A Long Way Down,* p. 181.

Spectator, April 8, 1993, Margaret Forster, review of *High Fidelity,* p. 35; May 26, 2001, Vicki Woods, review of *How to Be Good,* p. 50; February 22, 2003, Marcus Berkmann, "One Man's Prime Numbers," review of *31 Songs,* p. 37; May 7, 2005, Philip Hensher, The Proximity of Death," review of *A Long Way Down,* p. 48.

Time, June 6, 2005, Lev Grossman, "Suicide's Light Side," review of *A Long Way Down,* p. 89.

Times Literary Supplement, December 17, 1993, David Horspool, review of *My Favourite Year: A Collection of New Football Writing,* p. 12.

Wall Street Journal, June 15, 1994, Frederick C. Klein, review of *Fever Pitch.*

World & I, December, 2001, Tom Deignan, "Beyond 'Good' and Evil: Commentary on Nick Hornby's *How to Be Good,* p. 219.

Writer, June, 2006, Stephanie Dickison, "Nick Hornby on Reading," review of *The Polysyllabic Spree,* p. 49.

Writer's Chronicle, February, 2003, Tom DeMarch, "An Interview with Nick Hornby."

ONLINE

Nick Hornby Home Page, http://www.nickhornby.co.uk (January 17, 2006).

McSweeney's, http://www.mcsweeneys.net/authorpages/ (September 1, 2006), "Nick Hornby."

Powells.com, http://www.powells.com/ (June 15, 2005), Dave Weich, "Nick Hornby's Funny Folk-Pop."

Salon.com, http://www.salon.com/ (October 14, 1996), Cynthia Joyce, "LitChat: Nick Hornby."*

Baz Luhrmann

(Photograph by Reed Saxon. AP Images.)

■ Personal

Original name, Mark Anthony Luhrmann; born September 17, 1962, in Sydney, New South Wales, Australia; son of Leonard (a farmer and gas station owner) Luhrmann and his wife (a dress shop owner and ballroom dance teacher); married Catherine Martin (a production designer and producer), January, 1997; children: two. *Education:* Attended National Institute of Dramatic Arts, Sydney, New South Wales, Australia, 1985.

■ Addresses

Agent—International Creative Management, 8942 Wilshire Blvd., Beverly Hills, CA 90211; Contact: c/o Hilary Linstead, 500 Oxford St., Bondi Junction NSW 2022, Australia.

■ Career

Director, screenwriter, producer, production designer, and actor. Six Years Old Company (theater troupe), founder and artistic director, 1985—. Ap-

peared in the films *Winter of Our Dreams,* 1981, *The Dark Room,* 1982, and *The Highest Honor—A True Story,* 1982; originated the opera, *The Pure Merino Fandango* with Felix Meagher; director of stage productions, including *Strictly Ballroom,* 1986; and *Crocodile Creek,* first produced at the New Moon Theatre (Australia), 1987; director of operas, including *La Bohème* and *Lake Lost,* both 1990; and *A Midsummer Night's Dream,* 1992; director of films, including *Strictly Ballroom,* Miramax, 1992; (and producer) *William Shakespeare's Romeo + Juliet,* Twentieth Century-Fox, 1996; and *Moulin Rouge,* Twentieth Century-Fox, 2001; director of televised production of *La Bohème* for "Great Performances" series, Public Broadcasting System (PBS), 1994.

■ Awards, Honors

World Youth Theater Festival awards for best production and best director, 1986, for *Strictly Ballroom;* Mo Award for operatic performance of the year, 1990, for *La Bohème;* Prix de Jeuness, Cannes Film Festival, Audience Prize, Sydney Film Festival, Audience Prize, Melbourne Film Festival, Calsberg People's Choice Award, Toronto Film Festival, Best First Feature Film Award, Golden Globe Award nomination, Australian Film Institute Award, and British Academy of Film and Television Arts (BAFTA) Award, all 1992, all for *Strictly Ballroom;* Critic's Prize, Edinburgh Festival, 1994, for *A Midsummer Night's Dream;* BAFTA Award, Alfred Bauer Award, Berlin International Film Festival, and

Five Continents Award nomination, European Film Award, all 1997, all for *William Shakespeare's Romeo + Juliet;* Victorian Green Room Award, for *Lake Lost.*

■ Writings

SCREENPLAYS

(With Craig Pearce) *Strictly Ballroom* (screenplay), Miramax, 1992.

(With Craig Pearce) *William Shakespeare's Romeo + Juliet* (screenplay), Twentieth Century-Fox, 1996.

(With Craig Pearce) *Moulin Rouge* (screenplay), Twentieth Century-Fox, 2000.

OTHER

Strictly Ballroom (stage play), National Institute of Dramatic Arts (Sydney, New South Wales, Australia), 1986.

(With Miro Bilbrough and Sue Adler) *Moulin Rouge: The Splendid Illustrated Book That Charts the Journey of Baz Luhrmann's Motion Picture,* Newmarket Press (New York, NY), 2001.

Also originator (with Felix Meagher) of the opera, *The Pure Merino Fandango.* Guest editor of premier issue of *Australian Vogue.*

■ Work in Progress

A feature film.

■ Sidelights

Cutting-edge film director Baz Luhrmann creates rich and visually stimulating worlds in his movies that are fast-paced, relentless, and dramatic. He started out in Australia on the stage, but is most known for his work on the big screen. Luhrmann made his debut with one of Australia's most commercially successful films, 1992's *Strictly Ballroom.* He followed that up with an updated version of *William Shakespeare's Romeo + Juliet*that made purists cringe, but appealed to younger, MTV audiences. The lush music-and-dance extravaganza *Moulin Rouge* came out in 2001, further polarizing audiences but creating a hype around Luhrmann

that made him one of Hollywood's hottest directors and screenwriters. Together the three films make up Luhrmann's "Red Curtain" trilogy, in which he attempted to reinvent the movie musical.

An Unusual Childhood

Luhrmann was born Mark Anthony Luhrmann in 1962, and was raised in a conservative family in the isolated town of Heron's Creek in New South Wales, deep in the Australia bush. His entrance into the world was as dramatic as any of his films; his mother, Barbara, gave birth to him in the backseat of a van as she was being rushed to the hospital. His father, Leonard, owned a gas station, and the young Luhrmann and his siblings used to entertain the customers who came to fill up their gas tanks with mock radio programs he'd make up on the spot. "My relationship with the audience is the same relationship that we had with our customers, that my father drummed into us," he told John Lahr in the New Yorker. "They were our guests. We had to perform. The audience came in every day. We were the Luhrmann Boys. We had to dress up, wear little ties, white shirts, and suits." Luhrmann's parents were intense and driven and, despite their humble surroundings, wanted nothing less than the best for their sons. Leonard taught the boys horseback riding, farming, and even military training. "He'd drop us in the middle of the bush and we had to find our way home," Luhrmann recalled to Lahr. By age ten, Luhrmann had learned to use his father's motion picture camera.

Leonard's demanding ways eventually proved too much, however. "If we ever just sat down, the sense from my father was that it was wrong," Luhrmann explained to Lahr. "We weren't allowed to eat until dinner. We had work to do. It was absolutely nonstop until we dropped at night. We got up early in the morning, and—bang!—you'd do it again." When Luhrmann was ten, his parents divorced, and he eventually ran away from home to live with his mother in Sydney. In high school he began growing his hair long, earning him the derogatory nickname Basil Brush, after a fuzzy puppet on television. He later changed his name to Bazmark. "Baz and Mark are the two sides of who I am," he told Lahr.

Luhrmann fell in love with acting while in high school, and he eventually took his love of stories and theater to the National Institute of Dramatic Arts (NIDA) in Sydney, Australia. His acting desires soon gave way to a yen to direct, and he began directing theater pieces at NIDA, though he appeared in front of the camera in the 1981 film *The*

Paul Mercurio and Tara Morice in the 1992 film *Strictly Ballroom*. (Directed by Baz Luhrmann. Courtesy of M and A Film Corp/The Kobal Collection.)

Winter of Our Dreams, opposite Judy Davis, and in the film *The Dark Room* a year later. In 1985, Luhrmann was chosen from a field of many eager applicants to assist on Peter Brook's epic play, *The Mahabarata.*

Producing Works on the Stage

In 1986, he conceived, co-wrote, staged, and directed the original stage version of *Strictly Ballroom,* which began as a thirty-minute student revue that Luhrmann produced for 50 dollars. He then expanded it into a full-scale musical which toured the world in 1986. The production marked his first effort with writer Craig Pearce, who would become his longtime collaborator. After its debut at NIDA, Luhrmann took *Strictly Ballroom* on the road to the World Youth Theater Festival in the former Czechoslovakia, where it won awards for Best Production and Best Director. Also in 1986, he directed *Crocodile Creek,* a musical-theater piece set and performed in the Australian outback, for the New Moon Theater Company. After graduating NIDA, Luhrmann formed an independent theater troupe called the Six

Years Old Company, and worked as artistic director for the group. He revived *Strictly Ballroom* with the Six Years Old Company, and enjoyed a successful season at the Wharf Theater in Sydney and toured with the show to the World Expo in Brisbane.

In addition to several productions of *Strictly Ballroom,* Luhrmann also staged several original operas. Among his original works for the stage, Luhrmann worked with composer Felix Meagher to create the opera *Lake Lost,* which earned Luhrmann the Victorian Green Room Award for Best Director. *Lake Lost* was Luhrmann's first production with production and costume designer Catherine Martin, who became his constant collaborator and, in 1997, his wife. He and Meagher also worked together to create *The Pure Merino Fandango.* The 1989 Sydney Festival featured a large-scale musical event called "Dance Hall" in which Luhrmann recreated a 1940s dance hall in which participants relived the night celebrating the end of World War II.

Luhrmann staged his highly acclaimed Australian Opera production of Puccini's classic *La Boheme* in 1990. While the original opera was set in Bohemian

Paris in the 1830s, Luhrmann updated his version to take place in the 1950s. The production's more contemporary feel and Martin's striking, monochromatic sets and costumes appealed to a wide audience—opera aficionados applauded, but so did younger theater goers who may have been less familiar with opera. Luhrmann's *La Boheme* won the Mo Award for Operatic Performance of the Year, and aired on the PBS series *Great Performances*. Luhrmann later won the Critic's Prize at the 1994 Edinburgh Festival for his direction of Benjamin Britten's operatic version of *A Midsummer's Night's Dream* for the Australian Opera. Luhrmann's production of Shakespeare's classic was set in 1923 colonial India, a concept that "worked well," according to *Opera News* critic John Cargher. The production was the "hit of the season" for the Australian Opera in 1994, Cargher concluded. "To

see Australian Opera's remarkable production of . . . *A Midsummer Night's Dream*," wrote Glenn Loney in *TCI*, "was to discover the delights of the fable all over again."

Makes Film Debut

Luhrmann released the film version of *Strictly Ballroom* in 1992. Though he had produced his work for the stage many times, this was his debut as a film director. The film premiered at the prestigious Cannes Film Festival, and came away with both the Prix de la Juenesse and a special mention for the Camera D'Or. *Strictly Ballroom* also garnered a collection of other international awards, including three BAFTA (British Academy of Film and Televi-

Claire Danes and Leonardo Di Caprio starred in the 1996 film adaptation of William Shakespeare's *Romeo and Juliet.*
(Directed by Baz Luhrmann. Courtesy of 20th Century Fox/The Kobal Collection/Morton, Merrick.)

Luhrmann and actress Nicole Kidman on the set of the 2001 film *Moulin Rouge.* (Courtesy of The Kobal Collection, 2001. Reproduced by permission.)

sion Arts) awards and eight AFI (Australian Film Institute) awards. *Strictly Ballroom* follows the development of one of Australia's best ballroom dancers, Scott Hastings, who takes a dramatic turn in his life when he becomes fed up with the rigid requirements of competitive dancing and decides in favor of his own, more creative steps. This change in his attitude toward ballroom dancing stupefies his partner, who decides she can no longer dance with him. In steps an amateur dancer, Fran, a quiet, unassuming woman who is attracted to Scott's creative energy. The film garnered comparisons to the Cinderella fairy tale and the films *Flashdance* and *Dirty Dancing,* and was considered "enormously entertaining" by critic Lawrence O'Toole in *Entertainment Weekly,* and "delirious camp—a kitschy parody of romantic ardor . . . absurd and sincere at the same time" by Owen Gleiberman in *Entertainment Weekly.* Though it was made on a relatively

low budget—$2.6 million—*Strictly Ballroom* became the most commercially successful Australian film since *Crocodile Dundee. Strictly Ballroom* "is a ball—a buoyant, crowd-pleasing musical with an irreverent wit," wrote *Maclean's* critic Brian D. Johnson.

In 1996, Johnson declared Luhrmann "Hollywood's hottest screenwriter" after the release of his second film, *William Shakespeare's Romeo + Juliet.* Starring Leonardo DiCaprio and Claire Danes, the popular Shakespearean love story was told in a more contemporary setting, but kept true to the original dialogue and became a hit with young moviegoers. His take on the classic dealt with murder, the Mafia and gang war, illicit romance, lethal drugs, and drag queens, and took place on a funky urban strip called Verona Beach. The feuding Capulet and Montague families are corporate dynasties in Luhrmann's version. The film "is a luscious, balletic, candy-colored spectacle," Johnson wrote. Luhrmann employed quick, frantic editing during the film's tense, violent scenes, and slowed the drama down for the tender love scenes between DiCaprio and Danes. Luhrmann also cut Shakespeare's text by almost half.

Purists and some critics took issue with Luhrmann's updates, but "Luhrmann contends that his *Romeo + Juliet* is just the kind of movie Shakespeare might have made if he were around today," Johnson wrote. *People* critic Leah Rozen called the film "loud, garish, violent, and determinedly in-your-face. . . . What's missing amid all this frantic activity and eye candy is the poetry." *Entertainment Weekly's* Gleiberman asked, "Who would have guessed that a modern-day *Romeo and Juliet* could be this preeningly outrageous—or that it would leave you this cold?" *Newsweek* critic David Ansen concurred. "For all the excitement this production supplies, there is finally something amiss in a *Romeo and Juliet* whose final scene doesn't tear your heart. Luhrmann pays a price for his relentless razzle-dazzle; by the time he needs to throw his knockout blow, he's punched himself out." In defense of the film, Luhrmann told Johnson: "What people forget is that Shakespeare was a relentless entertainer. . . . He was a rambunctious, sexy, violent, entertaining storyteller, and we've tried to be all those things." The film earned Luhrmann honors from across the globe, including two BAFTA awards.

Luhrmann first began his multi-media exploration in 1994, when he and Martin served as guest editors and produced a special, signature issue of the fashion magazine *Vogue Australia,* which featured actress Nicole Kidman and pop singer Kylie Minogue. After *Romeo + Juliet,* he set up his firm,

Nicole Kidman as the glamorous Satine in the 2001 film *Moulin Rouge.* (Directed by Baz Luhrmann. Courtesy of 20th Century Fox/The Kobal Collection.)

Bazmark Inq., in Sydney. He produced a concept album called *Something for Everybody,* which featured the hit single "Everybody's Free to Wear Sunscreen" and achieved platinum certification for sales in Australia. In 1998, Bazmark, under Martin's direction, produced an extravagant fashion show for Australian designer Collette Dinnigan's Autumn/ Winter 1998 line at the Louvre in Paris. The Bazmark team then designed the streetscape for Fox Studio's (Australia) backlot, and produced the show *Lights Camera Chaos.* Under the Bazmark name, Luhrmann has since signed a deal with News Corp. that allows him to develop projects in any medium, including film, music, and theater

Moulin Rouge

Five years after *Romeo + Juliet,* Luhrmann returned to theaters with *Moulin Rouge,* a brazen, big-production musical starring Kidman and Ewan McGregor. Luhrmann spent five years mulling over the text and musical concepts before shooting *Moulin Rouge,* which ran over budget and over schedule, and was plagued by reshoots and calamity. Kidman suffered a few injuries and had to shoot some of her scenes from a wheelchair after damaging her knee. "It was just an endless series of disasters," Luhrmann told the *Daily News'* Glenn Whipp.

Moulin Rouge is set in Paris in 1899, and centers on the famed Parisian cabaret of the same name. It features McGregor as Christian, a poor, innocent, heartsick poet, whose motto is "Truth, beauty, freedom, love!" Nicole Kidman is Satine, a glamorous entertainer and high-priced courtesan who is torn between her love for Christian and her desire for the security to be had with her wealthy male patron. Between comic bits and dramatic scenes, the film is bolstered by grand musical and dance productions. The music is a collection of inventive arrangements of twentieth-century pop songs, from Madonna's "Like a Virgin" and Nirvana's "Smells Like Teen Spirit" to a medley of Beatles' tunes. *Mou-*

Luhrmann's 2002 Broadway version of the Italian opera *La Boheme*. (Photograph by Sue Adler/AFP/Getty Images.)

lin Rouge" is an extension of Baz," actor John Leguizamo, who plays the dwarfish Toulouse-Lautrec in the film, told the *Daily News.* "It's fanciful, theatrical, melodramatic, excessive. Most directors say less is more. But, for Baz, there can never be enough 'more.'"

Critics' opinions of the work were decidedly mixed. "I've talked to people who loved it and people who hated it," Kidman told Whipp. "But I haven't yet talked to one person who said they were bored by it." *Variety* critic Todd McCarthy called the film "a tour de force of artifice, a dazzling pastiche of musical and visual elements at the service of a blatantly artificial story." McCarthy commended Luhrmann's "resourcefulness" at blending a wide variety of musical genres and film styles in *Moulin Rouge.* Many accused Luhrmann of "putting style ahead of substance," according to Whipp. *New York Times* critic Elvis Mitchell wrote that the film was full of "whirlwind excitement," loaded with "jump cuts and flamboyant camera moves" but displayed a lack of characterization on Luhrmann's part. "What Mr. Luhrmann has done is take the most thrilling moments in a movie musical . . . and made an entire picture of such pinnacles. . . . This movie is simultaneously stirring and dispiriting." He continued: "The film is undeniably rousing, but there is not a single moment of organic excitement because Mr. Luhrmann is so busy splicing bits from other films. . . . *Moulin Rouge* will be accused of having no heart. But . . . the movie has so much heart that the poor overworked organ explodes in every scene."

In an interview with Pam Grady of *Reel.com* Luhrmann mused about the themes that unite his "Red Curtain" trilogy. "I mean, to me, all stories, anyway, have some form of love in them." He added, "When it comes to storytelling, there's a reason why, 'Some people want to fill the world with silly love songs. What's wrong with that, I'd like to know, because here I go again,' to quote Paul McCartney . . . . The point is that artists—storytellers, painters, musicians—they deal with that subject, because it dominates us. I know the rich and the powerful and the groovy and the successful, and all they really care about is being loved—loving and being loved in return."

In December of 2002, Luhrmann brought a stylized, updated production of his award-winning *La Boheme* to New York City. The show became the hottest ticket on Broadway, and Luhrmann's audacious staging mesmerized audiences. As Peter Conrad noted in the *New Statesman,* "The highlight of the production is a scene change, carried out in full view: a chaotic mob disassembles the furniture, a grid of extra lights descends, scenic flats are repositioned and, suddenly, to everyone's gaping delight, the starveling attic has become a Left Bank street, bustling with hawkers and hookers, pimps and poets, shrieking children and a brass band on patriotic parade." Some critics, however, felt that the director again favored style over substance. "Luhrmann the showman seduces with downtown-style stagecraft (the stagehands are visible, manipulating snow and other Fantasticks-style effects), Moulin Rouge-rich mise-en-scenes, and a truncated libretto (sung in the original Italian, but translated into lusty modern idiom) timed for those who need to catch a train," observed *Entertainment Weekly* critic Lisa Schwarzbaum.

If you enjoy the works of Baz Luhrmann, you may also want to check out the following DVDs:

Chicago, 2003.
Cabaret, 2003.
All That Jazz, 2007.

Lurhmann then turned his attention to a project ten years in the making, an epic motion picture about Alexander the Great. He stopped production on the film, however, after Oliver Stone announced his own biopic of the great military leader, which was released in 2004. Luhrmann contented himself with other projects, including a multi-million dollar commercial for Chanel No. 5, which featured Kidman.

Asked by Grady if he considered himself a renaissance man or a showman, Luhrmann responded, "I think both. These titles can be dangerous, but I don't think of myself as a film director or as an opera director. We deal in story and ideas and culture. And what we try to do is—we're not for hire. We're not, like, looking for a job. We just try to decide, what would we like to do that will be creatively fulfilling and we go and do that. That's the discipline that we try to maintain. It's difficult, but it also is very fulfilling."

■ Biographical and Critical Sources

BOOKS

Contemporary Theatre, Film, and Television, Volume 43, Thomson Gale (Detroit, MI), 2002.

Cook, Pam, *Baz Luhrmann*, BFI Publishing (London, England), 2006.

PERIODICALS

Advocate, April 2, 2002, Dave White, "Moulin Rumba," p. 59.

American Spectator, May, 1993, p. 59.

Billboard, April 10, 1999, p. 11.

Commentary, February, 1997, Donald Lyons, review of *William Shakespeare's Romeo + Juliet*, pp. 57-58.

Daily News(Los Angeles), May 18, 2001, p. L5.

Entertainment Weekly, March 19, 1993, p. 44; February 18, 1994, Lawrence O'Toole, review of *Strictly Ballroom*, p. 118; November 8, 1996, p. 46; April 11, 1997, Ira Robbins, review of *William Shakespeare's Romeo + Juliet*, p. 90; May 25, 2001, Jeff Jensen, "First Tango in Paris: Suddenly Single Nicole Kidman Show Her Gams—and Takes a Big Gamble—with the Sexy *Moulin Rouge*," p. 30, and Owen Gleiberman, "Ballroom Blitz," review of *Moulin Rouge*, p. 48; January 3, 2003, Lisa Schwarzbaum, "Surface Aria," review of *La Boheme*, p. 71.

Film Comment, July/August, 2001, p. 8.

Guardian, September 7, 2001, Geoff Andrew, "Baz Luhrmann."

Knight-Ridder/Tribune News Service, May 30, 2001, Chris Hewitt, review of *Moulin Rouge*, p. K0150; May 30, 2001, Mary F. Pols, review of *Moulin Rouge*, p. K0136.

Maclean's, February 22, 1993, Brian D. Johnson, review of *Strictly Ballroom*, pp. 56-57; November 11, 1996, Brian D. Johnson, review of *William Shakespeare's Romeo + Juliet*, pp. 74-75.

New Stateman, March 17, 2003, Peter Conrad, "Bohemian Rhapsody," p. 42; October 27, 2003, Peter Conrad, "Indian summer," pp. 42-43.

Newsweek, November 4, 1996, David Ansen, review of *William Shakespeare's Romeo + Juliet*, pp. 73-74; May 28, 2001, John Horn, "The Land of Baz," p. 58, and David Ansen, "Yes, *Rouge* Can, Can, Can: Not since *Cabaret* Has a Musical Had Such a Kick," p. 61.

New Yorker, December 2, 2002, John Lahr, "The Ringmaster," p. 50.

New York Times, February 7, 1993, Peter Brunette, "More than Romance Colors *Strictly Ballroom*, p. H24; April 4, 1997, review of *William Shakespeare's Romeo + Juliet*, p. B36; May 18, 2001, p. E10; May 25, 2001, Peter M. Nichols, review of *Moulin Rouge*, p. B10; March 14, 2002, p. 1.

Opera News, October, 1994, p. 63; March, 2003, Eric Myers, "Strictly Bohemian: Eric Myers talks to Baz Luhrmann," p. 18, and "From around the World: New York City," review of *La Boheme*, p. 80.

People, Marcy 8, 1993, Leah Rozen, review of *Strictly Ballroom*, p. 14; November 11, 1996, p. 21; January 13, 2003, Samantha Miller, "All That Baz," review of *La Boheme*, p. 93.

Sight and Sound, March, 1997, José Arroyo, "Kiss Kiss Bang Bang, pp. 6-9.

TCI, January, 1995, p. 9.

Time, February 15, 1993, review of *Strictly Ballroom*, p. 67; May 14, 2001, Richard Corliss, "Face the Music: Hollywood at Last Awakes and Sings," p. 70.

Variety, April 2, 2001, p. 35; April 16, 2001, p. 7; May 14, 2001, Todd McCarthy, review of *Moulin Rouge*, p. 21; February 25-March 3, 2002, p. A4.

Vogue, October, 1992, Joan Julier Buck, review of *Strictly Ballroom*, p. 166.

ONLINE

About.com, http://movies.about.com/ (March 9, 2002), Rebecca Murray, "Baz Luhrmann Talks Awards and *Moulin Rouge*."

Baz Luhrmann Web site, http://www.bazmark.com/ (September 1, 2006).

Fox Searchlight Web site, http://www.foxsearchlight.com/lab/lectures/ (August, 2005), "Baz Luhrmann."

Reel.com, http://www.reel.com/reel.asp?node=features/interviews/archive (2002), Pam Grady, "Blame It on the Baz-a Nova."

OTHER

Additional information was provided by the Twentieth Century Fox publicity department, 2002.*

Barbara Mertz

■ Personal

Born September 29, 1927, in Canton, IL; daughter of Earl D. (a printer) and Grace (a teacher) Gross; married Richard R. Mertz (a professor of history), June 18, 1950 (divorced, 1968); children: Elizabeth Ellen, Peter William. *Education:* University of Chicago, Ph. B., 1947, M.A., 1950, Ph.D., 1952. *Hobbies and other interests:* Reading, needlework, cats, music, football, gardening, and "long conversations with fellow mystery writers."

■ Addresses

Home—Frederick, MD. *Office*—P.O. Box 57, Myersville, MD 21773. *Agent*—Dominick Abel Literary Agency, 146 West 82nd St., Ste.1B, New York, NY 10024.

■ Career

Historian and writer. Member of editorial advisory board, *KMT: Modern Journal of Ancient Egypt* and *The Writer;* member of board of governors of the American Research Center in Egypt.

■ Member

American Crime Writers League, Egypt Exploration Society, James Henry Breasted Circle of the Oriental Institute, Society for the Study of Egyptian Antiquities, National Organization for Women, Malice Domestic (mystery writers' convention; founding member).

■ Awards, Honors

Grand Master Award, Bouchercon, 1986; Agatha Award for best mystery novel of 1989, Malice Domestic Convention, for *Naked Once More;* D.H.L., Hood College, 1989; Grand Master, Mystery Writers of America, 1998; Malice Domestic Lifetime Achievement Award, 2003.

■ Writings

Temples, Tombs, and Hieroglyphs: The Story of Egyptology, Coward (New York, NY), 1964, revised edition, Peter Bedrick (New York, NY), 1990.
Red Land, Black Land: The World of the Ancient Egyptians, Coward (New York, NY), 1966, revised edition, Peter Bedrick (New York, NY), 1990.
(With husband, Richard R. Mertz) *Two Thousand Years in Rome,* Coward (New York, NY), 1968.

ROMANTIC SUSPENSE NOVELS; UNDER PSEUDONYM BARBARA MICHAELS

The Master of Blacktower, Appleton (New York, NY), 1966.

Sons of the Wolf, Meredith Press (New York, NY), 1967, published as *Mystery on the Moors,* Paperback Library (New York, NY), 1968.

Ammie, Come Home, Meredith Press (New York, NY), 1968.

Prince of Darkness, Meredith Press (New York, NY), 1969.

Dark on the Other Side, Dodd (New York, NY), 1970.

The Crying Child, Dodd (New York, NY), 1971.

Greygallows, Dodd (New York, NY), 1972.

Witch, Dodd (New York, NY), 1973.

House of Many Shadows, Dodd (New York, NY), 1974.

The Sea King's Daughter, Dodd (New York, NY), 1975.

Patriot's Dream, Dodd (New York, NY), 1976.

Wings of the Falcon, Dodd (New York, NY), 1977.

Wait for What Will Come, Dodd (New York, NY), 1978.

The Walker in the Shadows, Dodd (New York, NY), 1979.

The Wizard's Daughter, Dodd (New York, NY), 1980.

Someone in the House, Dodd (New York, NY), 1981.

Black Rainbow, Congdon & Weed (New York, NY), 1982.

Here I Stay, Congdon & Weed (New York, NY), 1983.

Dark Duet, Congdon & Weed (New York, NY), 1983.

The Grey Beginning, Congdon & Weed (New York, NY), 1984.

Be Buried in the Rain, Atheneum (New York, NY), 1985.

Shattered Silk, Atheneum (New York, NY), 1986.

Search the Shadows, Atheneum (New York, NY), 1987.

Smoke and Mirrors, Simon & Schuster (New York, NY), 1989.

Into the Darkness, Simon & Schuster (New York, NY), 1990.

Vanish with the Rose, Simon & Schuster (New York, NY), 1992.

Houses of Stone, Simon & Schuster (New York, NY), 1993.

Stitches in Time, HarperCollins (New York, NY), 1995.

The Dancing Floor, HarperCollins (New York, NY), 1997.

Other Worlds, HarperCollins (New York, NY), 1999.

"AMELIA PEABODY" MYSTERY NOVELS; UNDER PSEUDONYM ELIZABETH PETERS

Crocodile on the Sandbank, Dodd (New York, NY), 1975.

The Curse of the Pharaohs, Dodd (New York, NY), 1981.

The Mummy Case, Congdon & Weed (New York, NY), 1985.

Lion in the Valley, Atheneum (New York, NY), 1986.

Deeds of the Disturber, Atheneum (New York, NY), 1988.

The Last Camel Died at Noon, Warner Books (New York, NY), 1991.

The Snake, the Crocodile, and the Dog, Warner Books (New York, NY), 1992.

The Hippopotamus Pool, Warner Books (New York, NY), 1996.

Seeing a Large Cat, Warner Books (New York, NY), 1997.

The Ape Who Guards the Balance, Avon (New York, NY), 1998.

The Falcon at the Portal, Avon (New York, NY), 1999.

He Shall Thunder in the Sky, Avon (New York, NY), 2000.

Lord of the Silent, Morrow (New York, NY), 2001.

The Golden One, Morrow (New York, NY), 2002.

Children of the Storm, Morrow (New York, NY), 2003.

(Editor, with Kristen Whitbread) *Amelia Peabody's Egypt: A Compendium to Her Journals,* Morrow (New York, NY), 2003.

Guardian of the Horizon, Morrow (New York, NY), 2004.

The Serpent on the Crown, Morrow (New York, NY), 2005.

Tomb of the Golden Bird, Morrow (New York, NY), 2006.

"JACQUELINE KIRBY" MYSTERY NOVELS; UNDER PSEUDONYM ELIZABETH PETERS

The Seventh Sinner, Dodd (New York, NY), 1972.

The Murders of Richard III, Dodd (New York, NY), 1974.

Die for Love, Congdon & Weed (New York, NY), 1984.

Naked Once More, Warner Books (New York, NY), 1989.

"VICKY BLISS" MYSTERY NOVELS; UNDER PSEUDONYM ELIZABETH PETERS

The Camelot Caper, Meredith Press (New York, NY), 1969.

Borrower of the Night, Dodd (New York, NY), 1973.

Street of the Five Moons, Dodd (New York, NY), 1978.

Silhouette in Scarlet, Congdon & Weed (New York, NY), 1983.

Trojan Gold, Atheneum (New York, NY), 1987.

Night Train to Memphis, Warner Books (New York, NY), 1994.

OTHER MYSTERY NOVELS; UNDER PSEUDONYM ELIZABETH PETERS

The Jackal's Head, Meredith Press (New York, NY), 1968.

The Dead Sea Cipher, Dodd (New York, NY), 1970.

The Night of 400 Rabbits, Dodd (New York, NY), 1971, published as *Shadows in the Moonlight*, Coronet (London, England), 1975.

Legend in Green Velvet, Dodd (New York, NY), 1976, published as *Ghost in Green Velvet*, Cassell (London, England), 1977.

Devil-May-Care, Dodd (New York, NY), 1977.

Summer of the Dragon, Dodd (New York, NY), 1979.

The Love Talker, Dodd (New York, NY), 1980.

The Copenhagen Connection, Congdon & Lattes (New York, NY), 1982.

Elizabeth Peters Presents Malice Domestic: An Anthology of Original Traditional Mystery Stories, Pocket Books (New York, NY), 1992.

■ Sidelights

Through her alter egos Barbara Michaels and Elizabeth Peters, Barbara Mertz has been responsible for dozens of mystery and suspense novels and was acknowledged for the quality and quantity of her works by being named a Grand Master by the Mystery Writers of America. Although Barbara Michaels is known primarily for quasi-supernatural tales of romantic suspense and Elizabeth Peters for humorous, often historical mysteries, in both cases Mertz uses her skill in setting, factual research, and subversion of the genre's conventions. "Whatever her pseudonym," stated a contributor in *Contemporary Popular Writers*, "Mertz produces lucid prose, reliable and scholarly details, good humor, and lively, knowledgeable, and unpretentious heroines who are willing to defy conventional manners to pursue intellectual or personal challenges." As Dulcy Brainard similarly noted in *Publishers Weekly*, all of Mertz's books feature "female protagonists who survive danger and solve mysteries with wit, intelligence, good humor and, usually, good fortune in romance."

The characters in the Peters's books, for instance, are women who "burst forth their corsets of self-doubt and outside denigration, and learn to make it on their own or as equal partners with their lovers," Sarah Booth Conroy wrote in the *Washington Post*. "All are opinionated, independent, strong, brusque, suspicious, quick to take offense, slow to ask for help, and funny." Among Peters's recurring characters are Amelia Peabody, an Egyptologist; Jacqueline Kirby, a librarian; and Vicky Bliss, an art historian. "Peters's female protagonists," wrote Kay Mussell in the *St. James Guide to Crime and Mystery Writers*, "are intelligent, strong, and intrepid. Rarely overtly feminist, all are nevertheless independent women who relate to men from a position of equality and respect."

From Archeologist to Author

Mertz was born in Canton, Illinois, a town so small it had no public library. Fortunately, she came from a family of readers. "From my mother and a wonderful great-aunt I acquired most of the childhood classics and a few classic mysteries," the author stated on her Web site. "My father's tastes were somewhat more eclectic. By the time I was ten I had read (though I won't claim to have understood) Mark Twain, Shakespeare, Edgar Rice Burroughs, Dracula, and a variety of pulp magazines, to mention only a few. I can't emphasize too highly the importance of this early reading experience—its diversity as well as its extent." Her family eventually moved to Oak Park, a suburb of Chicago. Mertz discovered her talent in a creative writing class at Oak Park-River Forest High School. In fact, a teacher once called her out of the classroom and asked if she had copied a sonnet titled "To a Book," which she had turned in for an assignment. Eventually the teacher realized Mertz had not plagiarized her work, an event Mertz once recalled as "the first time anyone took my writing seriously." She did not return to writing for several years. Instead, she majored in Egyptology in college, then went on to earn a Ph.D. in the field, hoping to become an archeologist.

After Mertz was married, she settled into being a homemaker and mother—she and her husband, Richard R. Mertz, had two children. She found few opportunities to pursue a career in her highly specialized profession because her husband's work required the family to travel frequently. While they were living in Europe, however, Mertz became interested in history, architecture, and art. Once her children were in school, she used her research materials as the basis for three nonfiction books. The first two, *Temples, Tombs, and Hieroglyphs: The Story of Egyptology* and *Red Land, Black Land: The World of the Ancient Egyptians*, stemmed from her interest in Egypt. The third, which she coauthored with her husband, was *Two Thousand Years in Rome*. Recalling her unusual path to becoming a published author, Mertz wrote on her Web site: "Egyptology was an impractical career, especially for a young married woman forty years ago. Writing was, and

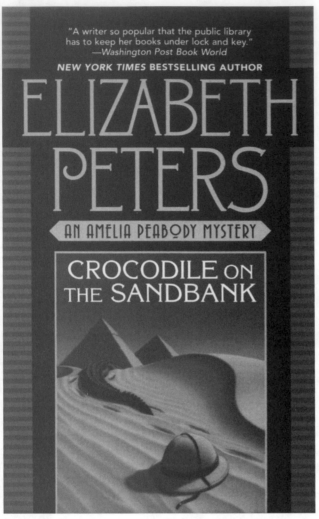

"A writer so popular that the public library has to keep her books under lock and key."
—*Washington Post Book World*

NEW YORK TIMES BESTSELLING AUTHOR

ELIZABETH PETERS

AN AMELIA PEABODY MYSTERY

CROCODILE ON THE SANDBANK

Amelia Peabody journeys to Egypt, where she encounters a strangely active mummy and mysterious goings-on in this 1975 novel. (Philip Singer, illustrator. Mysterious Press, 1988. Reproduced by permission.)

still is, an impractical career, because so few people succeed in earning a living that way. I was one of the lucky ones; and if I hadn't been so obsessed with ancient Egypt (as I still am) I might have noticed that I did enjoy writing, and that some people thought I was pretty good at it. But I've never regretted studying Egyptology even though I was unable to make it my career."

Mertz and her husband had also written several spy stories together in the 1950s, but none had ever been published. After completing the book on Rome, Mertz decided to try writing a romantic suspense novel, which was becoming a popular genre. The result was *The Master of Blacktower*, and it immediately found a publisher. Though Mertz

once described the book as "very derivative," she also noted that it was "very educational" because she "learned a lot about plotting and character development." Moreover, she discovered, "writing is hard work!"

Mertz and her husband were divorced in 1968, and she began writing full time to support her children. Since then she has published novels under the Barbara Michaels and Elizabeth Peters pen names. Both "authors" have faithful fans—young readers as well as adults—who look forward to each new Michaels or Peters novel. She gained early success as Barbara Michaels with *Ammie, Come Home*. The story opens with the heroine, Sara, coming to visit her Aunt Ruth, who is living in an old house in the Georgetown section of Washington, DC Briefly married years ago, Ruth rediscovers romance when Sara introduces her to Pat MacDougal, an anthropology professor. Sara also awakens ghosts in the house who were involved in tragic events during the 1780s. Sara and her boyfriend, along with Ruth and Pat, manage to lay the ghosts to rest. A reviewer for *Horn Book* praised the book for making "cries in the night, shadowy manifestations in the parlor, and possession by demons seem almost possible."

Works Feature Strong Female Protagonists

The Barbara Michaels novels feature independent women solving puzzles—often personal ones—and provide each heroine with a chance to discover romance. "In the Michaels books," wrote Conroy, "customarily the woman has just broken up with (or, notably in the delightful *Devil-May-Care*, is about to break up with) her current lover, or her husband has been removed from the cast before the book opens by divorce or death." Most Michaels books, however, differ from a Peters in tone, for they are more serious and contain more supernatural elements—a side that has led some to classify them as "modern Gothics." Mertz disputes this term as inaccurate, however: "Gothics are a type of fiction popular around the turn of the nineteenth century," she told Brainard. "They were supernatural horror stories with ghosts. The only things those novels and some of the things I've done have in common is setting—ruined castles off in the mists. Gothics have nothing to do with the moderns, which are suspense stories."

Search the Shadows, for instance, follows Haskell Maloney as she searches for the truth about her parentage. Her investigation leads her to the University of Chicago, where her mother studied Egyptology, and eventually to a spooky mansion-museum. "Michaels follows the form" of the genre, wrote *Washington Post* contributor Bruce Van Wyngarden, "but manages for the most part to transcend the formula," due in particular to her "strong characterizations."

Another Michaels novel, *Here I Stay,* also features a ghost in an old house. Andrea Torgeson and her brother Jim, who lost his leg in a car accident, have inherited a mansion in Maryland. They invest nearly all their money in turning the house into an inn. Their first guest is a writer named Martin Greenspan, who likes the place and decides to extend his stay. When Jim and Martin begin researching the history of the house, a ghost pays the level-headed Andrea a visit. Soon Andrea and Martin become romantically involved, and the novel culminates in a shocking tragedy. Priscilla Johnson noted in *School Library Journal* that the "themes explored in this fine story, as well as its fast-paced plot, make it especially suitable for YAs." A *Publishers Weekly* reviewer praised the characterization, calling *Here I Stay* "a very good ghost story" that goes "right to the heart of the dilemma of a woman who cannot help being overly possessive toward those she loves."

Michaels's novels *Shattered Silk* and *Into the Darkness* portray heroines who encounter terror in human form. In *Shattered Silk,* Georgetown is once again the setting as newly divorced Karen Nevitt moves back to her home in the city. After working for awhile in a vintage clothing shop, she makes plans to open her own store. By chance Karen meets a former boyfriend, Congressman Mark Brinckley. Then someone begins stalking her, and the story builds to an action-filled conclusion. Susan Penny predicted in *School Library Journal* that the book would keep young adult readers "engrossed until the final page." Similarly, a *Publishers Weekly* reviewer observed that Michaels "adroitly keeps the suspense mounting."

In the best-seller *Into the Darkness,* which Michaels wrote in 1990, Meg Venturi returns to her New England home. After unexpectedly inheriting a jewelry business from her recently deceased grandfather, she learns she has a co-owner named A.L. Riley. According to town rumors, Riley was responsible for her grandfather's death. As she readjusts to life in her hometown, Meg discovers shocking family secrets involving her father. In the process she comes to realize that her life is in danger, and she struggles to find the answers to mounting questions. Critics registered mixed responses to *Into the Darkness.* A *Publishers Weekly* reviewer, for instance, stated that "Memorable characters and complex mystery make this one of Michaels's best novels of romantic suspense." On the other hand, Denise Perry Donavin noted in *Booklist* that "Michaels has written far better suspense stories (such as *Shattered Silk*). . . ." During the 1990s Michaels continued her prolific output of romantic novels, including *Stitches in Time, The Dancing Floor,* and *Other Worlds.*

Mertz has been equally successful and prolific as Elizabeth Peters. (She created the pen name by using the first names of her daughter and son.) Early Peters novels include *The Jackal's Head* and *The Camelot Capers,* which were followed by *The Dead Sea Cipher.* A popular work, it features the adventures of Dinah Van der Lyn, a minister's daughter and opera singer. While touring the Middle East, Dinah spends some time in Beirut, Lebanon. Since a woman cannot venture out at night alone, she is confined to her hotel. One evening she overhears an argument in Arabic in the room next door. Thus begins a whirlwind of events caused by the discovery of an ancient scroll and involving spies and counterspies—all pursuing Dinah. A *Publishers Weekly* reviewer commended the book for its "fine, authentic background [and] lots of thrills and romance."

The Mysteries of Egypt

Mertz's most popular creation as Elizabeth Peters is Amelia Peabody-Emerson, a thoroughly modern Victorian who sets out on adventures with her archaeologist husband, precocious son, and shrewd cat companion. While combining the "comic detective story" with the "period whodunit" can be very challenging, as Kevin Moore asserted in a Chicago *Tribune Books* review of *Deeds of the Disturber,* "no one is better at juggling torches while dancing on a high wire than Elizabeth Peters." The Peabody novel *Lion in the Valley* is a "heady melange of excitement and merriment, enhanced by the Victorian locutions in the peppery archeologist's journal," *Publishers Weekly* critic Sybil Steinberg stated. And while the "superhuman" characters of *Lion in the Valley* are somewhat unbelievable, a Toronto *Globe and Mail* reviewer stated, nevertheless the author's "use of the setting and the archaeological information is first rate." As the Amelia Peabody series has developed, Peters has added to the humor and mystery of the books a thread that highlights the personal lives of her characters and their relationships—some intimate, some familial, some collegial, and some adversarial. A *Publishers Weekly* contributor said of the 1997 *Seeing a Large Cat,* "Peters's fans will relish this latest adventure that explores mysteries of the heart as well as murder."

In an interview with Jean Swanson in *Publishers Weekly,* Mertz explained that the "Peabody" series has changed over the course of it's lifetime: "It

NEW YORK TIMES BESTSELLER!

ELIZABETH PETERS

author of *Guardian of the Horizon*

THE SERPENT ON THE CROWN

"Packs a harrowing emotional wallop."
Winston-Salem Journal

An Egyptian statue may be cursed, putting Amelia Peabody and friends in great danger in this 2005 novel. (Avon Books, 2006. Copyright © 2005 by MPM Manor, Inc. Reproduced by permission of HarperCollins Publishers.)

started out being a rather giddy, frivolous sendup of various forms of genre fiction: the detective story, the gothic novel. . . . I had a very jolly time with it. Then, as time went on, not only did the characters change, but I thought I should introduce a new viewpoint. And then Amelia had a baby . . . Ramses the terror—he was described by someone as the most awful child in mystery fiction, which I thought was a huge compliment!"

Eventually, Ramses becomes a teen, and Mertz introduces what she calls a "second point of view."

She commented to Swanson: "I'd been giving his mother's view of him all these years, which is a little unfair. I thought it'd be fun to show what he thought of her, and what he was doing on the side." So, by the time Mertz wrote *He Shall Thunder in the Sky*—which finds the extended Peabody-Emerson family excavating an archeological site in Cairo as World War I begins and in which even Lawrence of Arabia makes an appearance—Ramses has been transformed into a "grown heartbreaker," according to a review by Deidre Donahue in *USA Today*. "Some big surprises are in store for readers while Peters deftly ties her subplots together," commented Jeff Zaleski in a *Publishers Weekly* review.

Lord of the Silent introduces Ramses's new wife, Nefret. Mertz's next work, *The Golden One*, concerns the efforts of Amelia and her husband, Radcliffe, to thwart tomb robbers in Luxor while Ramses pursues a master criminal in Gaza. Series fans will relish the underlying humor, which is particularly good here," noted *Booklist* critic Stephanie Zvirin. In *Children of the Storm*, the fifteenth Peabody novel, Amelia is a globetrotting grandmother caught up in political intrigue. "Readers who enjoy this series for its crisp repartee and interpersonal dynamics will be sufficiently entertained," Zvirin wrote. Mertz steps back in time for *Guardian of the Horizon*, setting the action in the remote Lost Oasis, a hidden city previously visited in an earlier title, *The Last Camel Died at Noon*. According to a reviewer in *Publishers Weekly*, the author's background in Egyptology and "early archeological attempts in the region allow her to dress her melodrama with authentic trappings that add greatly to the enjoyment." *The Serpent on the Crown* finds Amelia given a cursed Egyptian statuette by a strange woman dressed in black. The woman wants her to destroy the evil object. While Amelia does not believe the story of a curse, others soon hear of the valuable gold statuette and scheme to acquire it for themselves. According to a critic for *Publishers Weekly*, Peters "delivers another winner that you can't put down and yet don't want to see end." The Peabody-Emerson family is witness to the opening of King Tutankhamen's tomb in *Tomb of the Golden Bird*. Mertz "delivers an irresistible mix of archeology, action, humor and a mystery that only the redoubtable Amelia can solve," wrote a *Publishers Weekly* critic.

In the Peters books that feature librarian-turned-romance novelist Jacqueline Kirby, the author makes effective use of her various backdrops. The early Kirby novel *The Murders of Richard III*, for instance, takes place during a role-playing conference conducted by aficionados of the fifteenth-century English king. The mystery includes a debate over Richard's actual historical role—as well as a murder—and "Peters has researched her material carefully and rearranged the implausible into the likely," a *New Republic* critic remarked. The result is that the book has "sustained her well-earned superior reputation." And *Die for Love* is set in a romance writers' convention. Nevertheless, it is the protagonist that gives the series its style and humor; Jacqueline's "hilarious habit of lapsing into exquisitely crafted romance cliche" is particularly commendable, Carolyn Banks noted in a *Washington Post* review of *Naked Once More*. And although some critics, such as *New York Times Book Review* contributor Joanne Kaufman, find the satire in the Kirby books "not consistent enough in style to work as parody," "nonetheless Elizabeth Peters manages to pull this . . . out," Florence King wrote in another *New York Times Book Review* article. In the course of the mystery, the author "makes some valid points about the importance of being selfish for women in the creative arts, delivers some hilariously cynical reflections on book tours and literary fans and wisely avoids the gratuitous sex scenes that spoil so many mysteries," the critic concluded.

Vicky Bliss, Peters's third series character, faces a world where it is a curse to be tall, blonde, and smart. But this American art historian—who works for the Munich National Museum in Germany, and who travels to exotic locations in search of art, mystery, and love—manages because of her strong self-reliance. In *Night Train to Memphis*, Vicky voyages up the Nile to help the Munich police foil a plot by art thieves. A reviewer for *Publishers Weekly* observed that this "quirky, lighthearted novel sports some harrowing moments . . . but with its emphasis on Vicky's love life, the story remains essentially a spirited soap opera interspersed with guidebook descriptions."

well in maintaining a consistent level of quality and reader interest in a body of works written over a period of three decades. Yet, perhaps the main reason she has been able to keep her writing fresh is due to her strong, compelling characters. Writing about the Michaels book *Vanish with the Rose*—a novel that involves Diana Reed, a lawyer-turned-amateur detective trying to find her missing brother—a *Publishers Weekly* reviewer commented: "Michaels once again offers a witty, intricate and ultimately surprising story, with strong characterizations that keep the sparks flying."

No matter which pseudonym, series character, or subject Mertz uses, "the suspense is the most important element," the author said in *Love's Leading Ladies*. While the romantic and humorous elements are important, especially in pacing, she added, "the part I enjoy is the mystery; I read books like this long before I started to write them." As a result, a *USA Today* critic concluded, "In the skilled hands of Barbara Mertz, murder can be terrifying. Or it can be laugh-aloud hilarious, particularly when one of Mertz's wonderful heroines takes control."

Of her life as an author of nonfiction on Egyptology, mysteries, and romantic suspense novels, Mertz commented on her Web site: "The craft of writing delights me. It is impossible to attain perfection; there is always something more to be learned—figuring out new techniques of plotting or characterization, struggling with recalcitrant sentences until I force them to approximate my meaning. And nothing is ever wasted. Everything one sees and hears, everything one learns, can be used."

If you enjoy the works of Barbara Mertz, you may also want to check out the following books:

Agatha Christie, *Death on the Nile*, 1937.
Anne Perry, *Dark Assassin*, 2006.
C.J. Sansom, *Sovereign*, 2007.

The Author Reflects

Mertz's comfort with the formal aspects of the romantic suspense genre, her feel for the power of setting, and her command of style have served her

■ **Biographical and Critical Sources**

BOOKS

Contemporary Novelists, 7th edition, St. James Press (Detroit, MI), 2001.
Contemporary Popular Writers, St. James Press (Detroit, MI), 1997.
Falk, Kathryn, *Love's Leading Ladies*, Pinnacle Books (New York, NY), 1982.
Grape, Jan, and other editors, *Deadly Women*, Carroll & Graf (New York, NY), 1998.
Malling, Susan, editor, *A-Z Murder Goes . . . Artful*, Poisoned Pen Press (Scottsdale, AZ), 1998.
Nicholas, Victoria, and Susan Thompson, *Silk Stalkings: When Women Write of Murder*, Black Lizard Books (Berkeley, CA), 1988.

St. James Guide to Crime and Mystery Writers, 4th edition, St. James Press (Detroit, MI), 1996.

Twentieth Century Romance and Historical Writers, 3rd edition, St. James Press (Detroit, MI), 1994.

PERIODICALS

Armchair Detective, summer, 1996, Elizabeth Foxwell, "Novels of Many Shadows: The Messages of Barbara Michaels," pp. 330-333.

Atlantic Monthly, May, 1964, review of *Temples, Tombs, and Hieroglyphs: The Story of Egyptology,* p. 142.

Book, March-April, 2003, Lee Smith, "The Jewel of the Nile," pp. 30-31.

Booklist, May 1, 1975, review of *Crocodile on the Sandbank,* p. 908; March 15, 1984, review of *Die for Love,* p. 1009; April 1, 1990, Denise Perry Donavin, review of *Into the Darkness,* p. 1506; June 1, 1992, p. 1733; October 15, 1993, p. 418; May 1, 1995, p. 1531; January 1, 1997, p. 779; April 15, 1999, Ilene Cooper, review of *The Falcon at the Portal,* p. 1484; February 15, 2002, Stephanie Zvirin, review of *The Golden One,* p. 971; February 1, 2003, Stephanie Zvirin, review of *Children of the Storm,* p. 956; March 1, 2004, Stephanie Zvirin, review of *Guardian of the Horizon,* pp. 1101-1102; March 1, 2005, Stephanie Zvirin, review of *The Serpent on the Crown,* p. 1102; February 15, 2006, Stephanie Zvirin, review of *Tomb of the Golden Bird,* p. 6.

Book Week, April 12, 1964, William Albright, review of *Temples, Tombs, and Hieroglyphs: The Story of Egyptology,* p. 8.

Boston Globe, May 13, 2002, Clea Simon, "Serial Mysteries Meet Domestic Bliss," p. D14.

Chicago Tribune, December 27, 1987; September 7, 1989.

Clues: A Journal of Detection, fall-winter, 2001, Amy Hauser, "Digging beneath the Surface: Victorian Archaeologist Amelia Peabody," pp. 125-140.

Crime, April 20, 2003, Marilyn Stasio, review of *Children of the Storm,* p. 22.

Denver Post May 7, 2000, Tom and Enid Schantz, review of *He Shall Thunder in the Sky,* p. F-02.

Economist, December 2, 1967, review of *Red Land, Black Land: The World of the Ancient Egyptians,* p. 18.

Entertainment Weekly, June 1, 2001, Rachel Orvino, review of *Lord of the Silent,* p. 84.

Guardian (London, England), September 29, 2001, Maxim Jakubowski, review of *Lord of the Silent,* p. 12.

Globe and Mail (Toronto, Ontario, Canada), August 30, 1986, review of *Lion in the Valley.*

Horn Book, February, 1969, review of *Ammie, Come Home,* p. 79.

Kirkus Reviews, July 1, 1989, review of *Naked Once More,* p. 957; February 15, 2005, review of *The Serpent on the Crown,* p. 202.

Library Journal, May 1, 1970, Mary Kent Grant, review of *The Dead Sea Cipher,* p. 1763; March 15, 2003, Barbara Rhodes, review of *The Golden One* (audiobook), p. 131.

Locus, November, 1991, Scott Winnett, review of *The Last Camel Died at Noon,* p. 35.

Los Angeles Times, June 2, 1999, Margo Kaufman, review of *The Falcon at the Portal,* p. 12.

Mystery Scene, Number 71, 2001, special Elizabeth Peters issue.

Natural History, April, 1967, A.R. Shulman, review of *Red Land, Black Land,* p. 76.

New Republic, September 14, 1974, review of *The Murders of Richard III..*

New York Times Book Review, October 4, 1970; June 24, 1984, Joanne Kaufman, review of *Die for Love,* p. 22; November 9, 1986; October 15, 1989, Florence King, review of *Naked Once More,* p. 46; October 20, 1991, Peter Theroux, review of *The Last Camel Died at Noon,* p. 34.

Paradoxa: Studies in World Literary Genres, Volume 3, numbers 1-2, 1997, Kay Mussell, "Paradoxa Interview with Barbara G. Mertz," pp. 180-183.

Publishers Weekly, March 9, 1970, review of *The Dead Sea Cipher,* p. 82; February 17, 1975, review of *Crocodile on the Sandbank,* p. 72; April 3, 1981, review of *Curse of the Pharaohs,* p. 71; July 29, 1983, review of *Here I Stay,* pp. 64-65; March 16, 1984, review of *Die for Love,* p. 70; March 7, 1986, Sybil Steinberg, review of *Lion in the Valley,* p. 85; August 1, 1986, review of *Shattered Silk,* p. 70; October 23, 1987, Dulcy Brainard, "Barbara Michaels—Elizabeth Peters; Writing Romantic Suspense Fiction under One Pseudonym, and Mysteries under Another, She Often Uses Her Knowledge of Archeology in Both Genres" (interview), p. 39; July 14, 1989, review of *Naked Once More,* p. 61; April 27, 1990, review of *Into the Darkness,* p. 52; June 1, 1992, review of *Vanish with the Rose,* p. 54; September 20, 1993, p. 62; August 15, 1994, review of *Night Train to Memphis,* p. 89; January 13, 1997, p. 53; May 5, 1997, review of *Seeing a Large Cat,* p. 201; May 1, 2000, Jeff Zaleski, review of *He Shall Thunder in the Sky,* pp. 43, 46; April 23, 2001, Jean Swanson, "Elizabeth Peters" (interview), p. 53; April 23, 2001, Peter Cannon, review of *Lord of the Silent,* p. 52; March 11, 2002, Peter Cannon, review of *The Golden One,* pp. 54-55; March 3, 2003, review of *Children of the Storm,* p. 57; March 1, 2004, review of *Guardian of the Horizon,* p. 54; March 7, 2005, review of *The Serpent on the Crown,* p. 53; February 13, 2006, review of *Tomb of the Golden Bird,* pp. 64-65.

School Library Journal, August 8, 1981, Cathy Clancy, review of *Curse of the Pharaohs, School Library*

Journal, p. 82; February, 1984, Priscilla Johnson, review of *Here I Stay,* p. 87; February, 1987, Susan Penny, review of *Shattered Silk,* p. 99; December, 1988, Annette DeMeritt, review of *The Deeds of the Disturber,* pp. 131-32; November, 1995, p. 139.

Thalia: Studies in Literary Humor, Volume 20, numbers 1-2, 2000, Jacqueline Tavernier-Courbin, "Sleuthing and Excavating in Egypt: Elizabeth Peters's Humor," pp. 24-54.

Time, June 2, 2003, Andrea Sachs, "Mystery Tours: Barbara Mertz," p. A8.

Tribune Books (Chicago, IL), April 24, 1988, Kevin Moore, "Whodunits with a Sprinkle of Laughter," review of *The Deeds of the Disturber,* p. 7; July 8, 1990.

USA Today, July 27, 1987; May 18, 2000, Deirdre Donahue, review of *He Shall Thunder in the Sky,* p. 6D.

Victoria, July, 2002, Michelle Slung, "Sleuthing the Sahara," p. 7.

Washington Post, April 28, 1984; November 27, 1987, Bruce Van Wyngarden, "The High-Grade Heroine," p. G04; June 11, 1989, Sarah Booth Conroy, "The Triple-Threat Mystery," p. F1; October 10, 1989, Carolyn Banks, "Mystery Most Mirthful," p. C2; June 17, 2001, "Barbara Mertz: A Writer of Many Parts," p. WBK3.

Washington Post Book World, January 6, 1980; March 16, 1980; September 4, 1983; January 5, 1986.

Wilson Library Bulletin, September, 1973, Jon L. Breen, review of *Crocodile on the Sandbank,* p. 35.

ONLINE

Barbara Mertz Home Page, http://www.mpmbooks.com (December 2, 2003).

Amelia Peabody.com, http://www.ameliapeabody.com/ (January 26, 2005).*

(Photograph by John Atwell, copyright © 2005.)

Gary Spencer Millidge

■ **Personal**

Born 1961, in London, England. *Education:* Attended Southend Art School, London, England.

■ **Addresses**

Home—Leigh-on-Sea, England. *Office*—Abiogenesis Press, P.O. Box 2065, Leigh-on-Sea SS9 2WH, England. *Agent*—c/o Chris Staros, Top Shelf Productions, P.O. Box 1282, Marietta, GA 30061. *E-mail*—gary@millidge.com.

■ **Career**

Former musician, comic-book store owner, and shoe salesman; Abiogenesis Press, Leigh-on-Sea, England, founder and publisher.

■ **Awards, Honors**

National Comic Award for Best Self-Published Comic, 1997, for *Strangehaven;* Eagle Award nomination, 2004, for *Strangehaven;* Bram Stoker Award nomination, Horror Writers Association, 2004, for *Alan Moore: Portrait of an Extraordinary Gentleman; Comic Book Galaxy* named *Insomnia* best mini-comic, 2004; Comics Creators Guild Best Ongoing Title nomination; Ignatz Outstanding Series Award nomination; two Eisner Award nominations.

■ **Writings**

"STRANGEHAVEN" SERIES

Strangehaven: Arcadia (contains issues 1-6 of *Strangehaven* comic book), Abiogenesis Press (Leigh-on-Sea, England), 1998.

Strangehaven: Brotherhood (contains issues 7-12 of *Strangehaven* comic book), introduction by Brian Talbot, Abiogenesis Press (Leigh-on-Sea, England), 2000.

Strangehaven: Conspiracies (contains issues 13-18 of *Strangehaven* comic book), Abiogenesis Press (Leigh-on-Sea, England), 2005.

Author and illustrator of *Strangehaven* comic book series, Abiogenesis Press (Leigh-on-Sea, England), 1995—.

OTHER

(Editor with "smoky man") *Alan Moore: Portrait of an Extraordinary Gentleman,* Abiogenesis Press (Leigh-on-Sea, England), 2003.

Insomnia (mini-comic), Abiogenesis Press (Leigh-on-Sea, England), 2004.

Contributor to *Bart Simpson's Treehouse of Horror* and *Negative Burn*.

■ Adaptations

David Lancaster Productions have optioned the television rights to the *Strangehaven* series.

■ Sidelights

Writer and artist Gary Spencer Millidge is best known as the creator of the comic book series *Strangehaven*, set in an English village populated with eccentric characters whose relationships form an ongoing saga. The village, explained Alan David Doane in *Comic Book Galaxy*, is "filled with respectable people leading respectable lives, until the veil is drawn back by Millidge and we see the strange bedfellows, the mixed motives, the hidden agendas." The story begins when Alex Hunter has a car accident one night and finds himself stranded in Strangehaven, an eccentric village from which he cannot leave. His efforts to learn more about the town, and to escape from it, lead him into ever more puzzling and potentially dangerous situations. "Awash with references to folklore, mythology and the supernatural," Nick Brownlow wrote in *NinthArt.com*, "Millidge creates and maintains a powerful sense of otherworldliness that somehow manages to be perfectly in tune with the mundane setting." Speaking with Joel Meadows in *Tripwire*, Millidge noted: "I never wanted *Strangehaven* to follow the format of a regular comic book, or adhere to any storytelling conventions in general. It was my original intention to create as realistic an environment as possible, with believable characters, but to portray the mystery and wonder of real life, and to examine the different ways in which different people interpret the world around us." Millidge has built his self-published series (he owns the Abiogenesis Press which issues the *Strangehaven* books) into an international phenomena, with editions of his books sold in England and America, and translations appearing in Spain, France, Italy, Brazil, and Portugal.

Millidge became interested in comic books at a young age. He credits his parents with keeping him supplied with the monthly issues he read as a child,

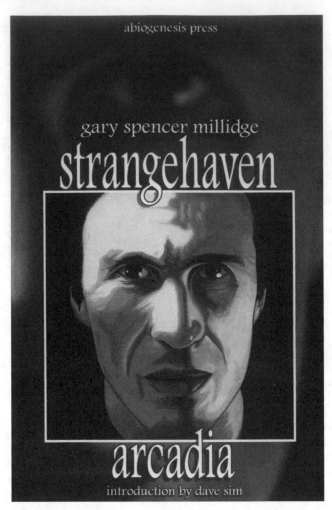

This 1998 collection gathers issues 1 through 6 of Millidge's mysterious Strangehaven comic book series. (Courtesy of Abiogenesis Press, 1998. Copyright © 1995, 1996, 1997, 1998, 2003 Abiogenesis Press/Gary Spencer Millidge. Reproduced by permission.)

and encouraging him in his attempts to copy both the art and the stories, as well as for passing on an entrepreneurial spirit. In an interview with Brownlow for the *Village Voice*, Milledge stated that "it always seemed to me that the combination of words and pictures in comics were an equal, if not superior form of entertainment/communication than art, literature, or film. It saddens me that most 'adults' appear to have an unshakeable prejudice against comics." After completing his primary education, Millidge attended Southend Art School, at the Southend College of Technology, where he studied art. While he was encouraged to attempt new forms and techniques, comic-book art was not part of his education, and a few of his lecturers even attempted to dissuade him from following his interests.

Millidge continued to pursue his passion for comics outside of his formal education. He banded together with several art school friends and started a comic-strip fanzine that led to his first venture in self-publishing. The first production, *Amon*Spek* was issued as photocopies, followed by lithograph copies for the second issue. Millidge spent five years on the venture before he became discouraged with the amount of time he was spending on administrative duties versus drawing. He told Ben Graham in the *Heckler* that "all my time was spent getting in contact with writers and artists. The fifth issue was the last one I did and I had a one-page illustration in it, all the rest was other people's stuff. And that just wasn't why I was doing it. After that I put all the comics stuff aside and I started playing in bands."

Runs a Comic-Book Store

Millidge divided his time after he left college between comics and the music industry, running a comic-book store by day and playing bass guitar for the band Sorcerer by night. His next publications were *Comics News Monthly* and the benefit comic *Food for Thought*, which included the work of Alan Moore, Grant Morrison, Bryan Talbot, and Warren Ellis and was meant to be a comic-book equivalent of the Band-Aid song recorded to aid the famine victims in Ethiopia. However, Millidge's divided career eventually landed him in debt, and he was forced to close his comic-book business. He briefly focused on his music career, setting up his own record company in order to maintain control of his royalties. He also played in several rock bands, including the Watchmen and Rebel. That experience eventually led him back to comics, with an eye toward self-publishing his own long-term project.

Strangehaven grew out of a comic book that Millidge created while still concentrating on his music career. The idea was to center an open-ended series around a common place, so that each arc is linked through the setting, but not necessarily in any other way. Millidge believed this would enable him to work on the project indefinitely without getting bored. As the concept evolved, the setting itself took on its own identity, becoming a character unto itself. Milledge told Brownlow: "I wanted a vehicle that would enable me to tell all kinds of stories without relying on a single plot-driven narrative. I was getting more interested in personal relationships and the way in which people perceive reality in different ways." He founded Abiogenesis Press in order to produce the comic books and has continued to self-publish the entire series, despite offers from other presses to take over the production.

Creates a Strange Village

The village of Strangehaven is outwardly reminiscent of any small village in England, complete with pub, grocery, tea shop, and church, but the inhabitants tend to be a bit more unusual than one would expect from such a setting. The series follows the lives of such individuals as Adam, who wears X-ray glasses and claims that he is from another planet; Alberto, an Italian mechanic whose ability to fix damaged cars borders on the superhuman; and a secret order, the Masonic Knights of the Golden Light, who hold nocturnal meetings that involve chanting in white robes and hats. Alex Hunter, newly arrived from London, has an accident on the outskirts of the village and wakes to find himself involved in a series of strange adventures, while also recognizing his mysterious inability to leave town. Millidge told a writer for *Wizard* that the story

The surreal story of Strangehaven continues in this 2000 collection. (Courtesy of Abiogenesis Press, 2000. Copyright © 1997, 1998, 1999, 2000, 2001 Abiogenesis Press/Gary Spencer Millidge. Reproduced by permission.)

is based on a real road trip experience involving he and some friends: "We kept going around and around, coming back to the same crossroads and going past the same places. Eventually we came over this hill and came face to face with this beautiful little secluded village. I modelled Strangehaven after it, I've put some landmarks from the village in, as well as a few of my favourite shops and buildings, so I've got the best of both worlds." Millidge's drawings for the series are realistic. In fact, he bases his work on photographs. "My natural tendency is to put a lot of detail into stuff, and I like to get my facts right, whether it's in the illustration or the story," Millidge told a critic for *Wizard*. "When I actually sat down to start it, I naturally drew realistically when I got all the reference together. I just did a complete about-turn and decided to go whole-hog and base it on lots of reference photographs and made sure I got everything right."

In 1998 Millidge gathered the first six issues of the series and published them as the graphic novel *Strangehaven: Arcadia*. A contributor to *Publishers Weekly* commented that the volume "offers a serious jolt of unsettling elements that give readers an unswerving and looming sense of uneasiness." In the second Strangehaven collection, *Strangehaven: Brotherhood*, Hunter tries to unravel the mysteries of the village, including the beautiful ghostly woman who haunts him, why the locals celebrate Christmas in the summer, and the truth behind the village's Amazonian shaman. *Strangehaven: Conspiracies* finds Hunter drawn into a battle between the secretive Knights of the Golden Light and a witches' coven while local police investigate a string of unsolved murders. Craig Taylor in the *Guardian* found that "Millidge puts together a good-looking book. His black and white panels are never showy, but tell the tale in an uncluttered fashion." Ray Olson in *Booklist* noted that Millidge employs "a gratifyingly kitchen-sinkish realism that he periodically disrupts with something outre . . . that restores a spooky ambience." Stephen Holland in *Silver Bullet Comics* explained: "In all honestly I should perhaps warn you that if you do start reading this, you will—just like Alex Hunter, the guy who crashed his car— never, ever be able to leave Strangehaven again."

Barry Lyga, reviewing for the *Diamond Comics Web site*, remarked of the fictional village that "you feel as though you're in the town itself. Millidge's artwork is crisp and realistic . . . his dialogue rings true, with characters speaking in their own voices. . . . You don't read *Strangehaven*; you move there." According to Nisha Gopalan in *Entertainment Weekly*: "In a medium rife with pows and bams and booms, *Strangehaven* is something of an anomaly: It ambles; it stalls; it digresses. Yet remarkably, it works. Be this a function of his deft pen or a

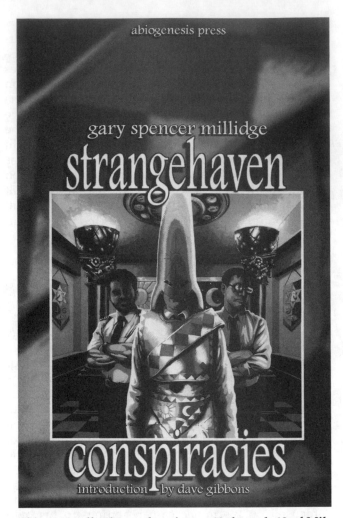

This 2005 collection gathers issues 13 through 18 of Millidge's comic book series. (Courtesy of Abiogenesis Press, 2005. Copyright © 2001, 2002, 2003, 2004, 2005 Abiogenesis Press/Gary Spencer Millidge. Reproduced by permission.)

disdain for deadlines, Millidge flirts just enough with our sense of curiosity to keep us glued to each mesmerizing page, rarely compromising his work's air of impending doom." "If you love mysteries set in the British countryside, populated with characters who feel and sound real, have exotic backstories that ramp up the suspense and intrigue and do things you never expect," a reviewer for *IllustratedFiction.com* concluded, "*Strangehaven* is a must-read."

Speaking to Rich Watson in *Comic World News*, Millidge stated: "I have to say *Strangehaven* has exceeded all my expectations in every way (except probably financially). I'm proud (if that's the right word) of my Eisner Award nominations in particular, but being part of the comic industry has enabled me to travel to places I would never have visited

An illustration from the 2005 collection *Strangehaven: Conspiracies.* (Courtesy of Abiogenesis Press, 2005. © 2001, 2002, 2003, 2004, 2005 Abiogenesis Press/Gary Spencer Millidge. Reproduced by permission.)

otherwise . . . and the best thing has been the friendships that I've made."

If you enjoy the works of Gary Spencer Millidge, you may also want to check out the following books:

Alan Moore, *Watchmen*, 1995.
Chris Ware, *Jimmy Corrigan: The Smartest Kid on Earth*, 2000.
Charles Burns, *Black Hole*, 2005.

In addition to his own comics, Millidge's Abiogenesis Press has produced *Alan Moore: Portrait of an Extraordinary Gentleman*, a collection of work from 145 film and comic-book-industry writers and artists, including Terry Gilliam, Neil Gaiman, Will Eisner, and Bill Sienkiewicz. The volume was presented to renowned comics creator Moore as a fiftieth birthday gift. In an interview with Daniel Robert Epstein posted at Underground Online, Millidge gave his opinion of Moore: "If there has ever been a genius working in the comics industry, he is it. . . . He strikes me as a highly intelligent, exceedingly knowledgeable, down-to-earth, unpretentious and amazingly friendly man."

■ Biographical and Critical Sources

PERIODICALS

Big Planet Orbit, November, 1997, Joel Pollack, "Strangehaven's Magical Realism."

Booklist, December 1, 2005, Ray Olson, review of *Strangehaven: Conspiracies*, p. 33.

Comics International, April, 1999, review of *Strangehaven Eleven*; December, 1999, review of *Strangehaven Twelve*.

Dream Factory, December, 1998, "Stranger from a Strange Land."

Entertainment Weekly, April 17, 2006, Nisha Gopalan, "'Strange' Brew."

Evening Echo, January 15, 1997, Nicola Taylor, "Comic Book Gary's Award Hope"; August 26, 1998, Nicola Taylor, "Hit for Comic Author."

Guardian (London, England), July 29, 2006, Craig Taylor, review of *Strangehaven: Conspiracies*, p. 17.

Heckler, March, 1999, Ben Graham, "Self Publishing: A Haven for the Strange?"

Illuminations, July-August, 1997, Steve Pay, review of *Strangehaven*; December, 1997, Marin Averre, review of *Strangehaven Seven*.

Independent, November 7, 1996, Paul Slade, "Flying Solo" (interview).

In the Village, autumn, 1998, Chris Goodrich, review of *Strangehaven*.

Publishers Weekly, August 11, 2003, review of *Strangehaven: Arcadia*, p. 259.

Southend Mail, June 3, 1999, Matt Adams, "Seeking a Strangehaven."

Strands, January, 1997, Ceri Jordan, review of *Strangehaven*.

Tripwire, October-November, 1997, Joel Meadows, review of *Strangehaven: Arcadia*; spring, 2000, Joel Meadows, "10 Questions with . . . Gary Spencer Millidge."

Village Voice, July 15, 2002, Nick Brownlow, interview with Millidge.

Washington Post Book World, February 14, 1999, Mike Musgrove, review of *Strangehaven: Arcadia*, p. X10.

Wizard, July, 1997, "A Strange Story of Secrets."

Yellow Advertiser, March 7, 1997, Matt Adams, "Comic and Weird with a Touch of Essex" (interview); April 3, 1998, Matt Adams, "Strange Fiction"; September 11, 1998, Matt Adams, "Gary's Comic Success"; November 29, 2000, Matt Adams, "Comic Book Creator Set for Move to Big Time."

ONLINE

Comic Book Galaxy, http://www.comicbookgalaxy.com/ (August 29, 2006), Alan David Doane, reviews of *Insomnia* and *Strangehaven #15*.

Comic World News, http://cwn.comicraft.com/ (August 25, 2006), Rich Watson, "People Are Strange: The Gary Spencer Millidge Q & A."

Diamond Comics Web site, http://www.diamondcomics.com/ (February 9, 2005), "Gary Spencer Millidge."

Gary Spencer Millidge Home Page, http://www.millidge.com (August 28, 2006).

IllustratedFiction.com, http://illustratedfiction.com/ (April 12, 2006), "The Classics: *Strangehaven* by Gary Spencer Millidge."

Lambiek.net, http:// www.lambiek.net/ (February 9, 2005), "Gary Spencer Millidge."

NinthArt.com, http:// www.ninthart.com/ (June 7, 2002), Nick Brownlow, review of *Strangehaven* comic book series; (February 9, 2005), "Gary Spencer Millidge."

Silver Bullet Comics, http://www.silver bullet comicbooks.com/ (August 25, 2006), Stephen Holland, review of *Strangehaven: Conspiracies*.

Underground Online, http://www.ugo.com/ (August 25, 2006), Daniel Robert Epstein, interview with Gary Spencer Millidge.*

Katsuhiro Otomo

■ Personal

Born April 14, 1954, in Tome-gun, Miyagi Prefecture, Japan; married; wife's name, Yoko.

■ Addresses

Home—Tokyo, Japan. *Agent*—c/o Author Mail, Dark Horse Comics, 10956 South East Main St., Milwaukie, OR 97222.

■ Career

Writer, graphic artist, comic book creator, film animator and director. Creator of commercial print and television advertising for clients that include Honda and Canon. Animator for films, including *Roujin Z*, 1991, *Labyrinth Stories*, *Robot Carnival*, and *Memories*, 1995. Director of live-action film, *World Apartment Horror*, 1991.

■ Awards, Honors

Science Fiction grand prize, Japan, 1983, for *Domu*; Kondansha Comic Strip Award, 1984, for *Akira*; the Dark Horse Comics black and white edition of *Akira* was the winner of two Eisner Awards, for best archival collection/project, and for best U.S. edition of foreign material, both 2002.

■ Writings

WRITER; EXCEPT AS NOTED

Domu, [Japan], 1981, published as *Domu: A Child's Dream*, Dark Horse Comics (Milwaukie, OR), 1996, 2nd edition, 2001.
Akira (colorized version), Epic Comics (New York, NY), 1988, (black and white version) Volumes 1-6, Dark Horse Comics (Milwaukie, OR), 2000–04.
(And director) *Akira* (film), Streamline (Japan), 1988.
Legend of Mother Sarah: Tunnel Down (collection), Dark Horse Comics (Milwaukie, OR), 1996.
(Animator) *Spriggan* (animated film), ADV Films, 1998.
Metropolis (animated film), TriStar Pictures, 2001.
(With Sadayuki Murai; and director) *Steamboy* (film), Triumph, 2004.

Creator of comic book series, including *Jyu-sei* (title means "Gun Report", *Nippon Sayonara, Fireball, Katsuhiro's Memories, Katsuhiro Otomo's Farewell to Weapons, Akira, Domu: A Child's Dream, The Legend of Mother Sarah, the Legend of Mother Sarah: City of the Children, The Legend of Mother Sarah: City of the Angels,* and *Hipira.*

■ Adaptations

Akira was adapted for a film in Japan, 1988, in DVD format, Pioneer, 1988, and again in 2001; production of a live-action, English-language feature film of *Akira* was by Warner Bros., 2002; *Steamboy*, the film, was adapted for a graphic novel, Viz Media, 2005.

■ Sidelights

Considered a master of *manga*, or Japanese comic books, and of *anime*, or animated films, in his native country, Katsuhiro Otomo surged onto the international scene in 1988 with the film version of his comic *Akira*. That film "almost single-handedly launched anime fandom in the West," according to Jake Forbes, writing in the *Los Angeles Times*, and "started an animation revolution." Writing for *Big in Japan*, John Paul Catton noted that upon the release of *Akira* in the United States, "audiences were shocked by its hyper-realism, and hailed the series and its creator . . . as the emergence of a new cultural phenomenon." Known for his realistic style as an animator and writer of both comics and films, Otomo is, by Japanese standards, a slow worker, having produced only about three thousand pages of manga in a twenty-year career (before he turned to filmmaking), whereas other artists might churn out that many pages in three years. His intense attention to detail is the reason for this relatively small output. His second major film release, *Steamboy*, is a further example of Otomo's patience and attention to detail. The 2005 movie was ten years in the making and cost $22 million, making it the most expensive anime film ever produced, and the most expensive animation film outside of the United States. In addition to these major productions, Otomo is also known for his award-winning manga series, *Domu*, and as the creator and writer of *The Legend of Mother Sarah*.

Early Successes

Otomo was born in 1954, in a small town in the agricultural Miyagi Prefecture about 300 miles from Tokyo. As a youth he fell in love with film and would travel three hours by train to see the newest releases from America and Europe. Some of his favorite movies of the period were violent action films including *Bonnie and Clyde* and *Easy Rider*. His fascination with film later became apparent in his early manga work. Graduation from Sanuma High School, he decided to forego formal art training, and instead simply moved to Tokyo to try and find work in the manga industry. As Forbes noted, Otomo's "early works didn't feature the science fiction themes he would become known for but were about jazzmen, car nuts and college students." He first found work writing short strips for *Action* comics, which began publishing in 1973.

His first work, *Jyu-sei*, (title means "Gun Report"), was published in 1973. An adaptation of Prosper Merimee's *Mateo Falcone*, the work featured many of the odd assortment of characters who lived in the same apartment building as Otomo. Thereafter, Otomo experimented with a wide assortment of tales for *Action* comics, some of which looked at the bleak urban reality of Tokyo with its drug abuse and sexual perversion. With the 1977 *Nippon Sayonara*, Otomo tells the story of a martial arts expert who lives in Manhattan. It was his longest series to date. Two years later, Otomo ventured into science fiction, with the unfinished *Fireball*, a precursor to Otomo's later successes with a story of humans against a supercomputer. Otomo also introduces the theme of a post-nuclear totalitarian state for the first time with this work, a subject he would return to several more times.

From 1980 to 1982 Otomo serialized his first major success, *Domu* (published in the United States as *Domu: A Child's Dream*), and in 1983, the collected edition was awarded Japan's Science Fiction grand prize, the first time the literary prize was awarded to a comic book. This honor established Otomo as a master artist and comics writer. Catton described this work as a "stunning tale of a suburban community manipulated by a mysterious resident, with the power to telepathically control others." Similarly, Matt Fraction, writing in *ArtBomb.net*, called *Domu* a "riveting and chilling story about what happens when the devil himself comes to play in hell." The graphic novel sold over half a million copies in Japan. During this same time, Otomo was working on several other manga projects and also completed his first full-length film, *Give Us Guns*.

Akira

In 1982 Otomo began his epic masterpiece, *Akira*, which was serialized for a decade and contained two thousand pages. The series was later reprinted in the United States, first in a colorized version by Marvel Comics's adult imprint, Epic, and then in its original black and white version by Dark Horse Comics. According to a contributor for *ArtBomb.net*, *Akira* is an "epic of staggering illustrative virtuosity and gut-wrenching thematic power." Also writing

A scene from the 1988 animated feature *Akira*. (Courtesy of Akira/The Kobal Collection.)

in *ArtBomb.net*, Peter Aaron Rose noted that the saga was set in "the world of Neo-Tokyo, a post-Third World War city dominated by hi-tech street gangs and shadowy government organizations." Two young friends, Tetsuo and Kaneda, discover the existence of the top-secret project, Akira, set up to research the psychic powers of a youth by the same name. Kaneda and his biker gang battle the powers of this malignant project in a work that Rose called "pure adrenaline somehow distilled into comic book pages." A *Publishers Weekly* contributor who reviewed the first volume wrote that it "is all action, nonstop car chases and gun fights strung together with exaggerated speed lines and lots of gigantic machinery." Another *Publishers Weekly* contributor found the work "one of the most compelling science fiction tales of recent years, full of remarkable imagery, . . . and real human pathos." Reviewing the second volume of *Akira* in *ArtBomb.net*, Adi Tantimedh commented that it was "the pinnacle of apocalyptic science fiction comics," and that "its genius is in linking the apocalypse with the rage of

disaffected teenagers." For a contributor to *U.S. News & World Report*, the entire six-volume collection was an "epic sci-fi fable about the dangers of militarism."

In 1988, with the comic book series not yet completed, Otomo adapted *Akira* for a feature length animated film. Otomo commented on *BlueBlade* about the development of the comic book and of its ultimate translation to film: "As I originally developed the comic, I used each issue to build more depth and size to this mammoth city. I kept trying to achieve this by creating a variety of situations to state the graphic story telling, but with film you get to combine this all into one. I think it's more convincing on film than in a serialized comic. A comic is just a picture, with animation you get to add colour, sound and motion; this way I felt I could really create the type of environment I wanted to depict in Neo Tokyo." The film was made at Akira Production Studio in Mitaka, Japan, with Otomo personally creating all the storyboards for the 783 scenes in the movie. Seventy other staff members were employed to do the artwork and coloring, and 327 different colors were used on 160,000 animation cels to achieve effects. Running more than two hours, *Akira* became a cult hit, both in Japan and the United States, where it continued to be a popular late-night feature on the movie circuit. The story begins in 1988 and flashes forward to 2019, when Tokyo, destroyed in World War III, has been rebuilt, but the city is now corrupt, immoral, and overrun with gangs. *Time* magazine critic Jay Cocks wrote that "Tokyo is imagined down to the last noodle shop and intersection, a place of deep night and lurid neon that looks like *Blade Runner* on spoiled mushrooms." Cocks further called the film a "visual dazzler." Writing in the *New York Times*, Janet Maslin had similar praise for the film, describing it as "a phenomenal work of animation with all the hallmarks of an instant cult classic." Maslin went on to observe that Otomo "invests this dark flowering of post-nuclear civilization with a clean, mean beauty."

Akira was also released on CAV, an early version of DVD. Reviewing that version, *Entertainment Weekly* contributor Steve Daly observed that it depicted a "thug-infested, post-apocalyptic Tokyo in staggering architectural detail." In 2001, the film was re-released on two DVD discs. The first disc contains the digitally restored images along with new sound, and both the original Japanese-language film, with subtitles, and an English dub. The second disc contains a documentary on the film's production and restoration, storyboards, trailers, a glossary, and an interview with Otomo. Reviewing the 2001 release, *Entertainment Weekly* critic Marc Bernardin called *Akira* a "violent, brooding, mature, quasi-intellectual tale," and further noted that "parts of *Akira* are as well-directed as anything you'll ever see." Steven Aoun also reviewed the DVD version for *Metro*, commenting that "the digital restoration and transfer bears witness to its original cinematic achievements. That's just a polite way of saying, of course, that Akira doesn't let credible characters or a focused storyline get in the way of the spectacular action and elaborate set pieces. . . . Themes and characters visually coalesce in a hallucinogenic revelatory encounter."

Turns Full Time to Cinema

Since the success of the film *Akira*, Otomo has increasingly turned to that medium, leaving manga behind. He has, however, contributed stories to the series *The Legend of Mother Sara*, with artwork by Takumi Nagayasu. The first eight issues were collected by Dark Horse Comics in the United States as *The Legend of Mother Sara: Tunnel Town*. The story is less violent and more of a girl's story than his

A scene from Otomo's 2004 film *Steamboy.* (Studio 4 Degrees/Sunrise/The Kobal Collection.)

previous comics. Survivors of a nuclear holocaust on earth have established colonies in space. Two factions, Epoch and Mother Earth, are at odds over a proposal to use a bomb to alter the earth's axis so that the changed climate would cover over the irradiated northern hemisphere. Sarah is separated from her children during the ensuing conflict and seeks them for years on earth, leading her to Tunnel Town, where a corrupt military has taken prisoners and uses them as slaves. Katharine Kan reviewed the work in *Voice of Youth Advocates*, saying that "while the story contains violence, it is more upbeat with a strong heroine commitment to justice and to helping others even as [Sarah] continues her own quest."

Among Otomo's film work is *Spriggan*, which he oversaw and produced. The film focuses on Noah's Ark, a powerful, hi-tech alien machine that has the potential for controlling life on earth. Then, in 2001, Otomo wrote, and Rintaro directed, *Metropolis*, a 1940s comic by pioneer manga artist Osamu Tezuka. The main character is Tina, a robotic girl who lives in a world of futuristic modes of travel, superweapons, evil scientists, and a Japanese detective. Writing in the *Hollywood Reporter*, David Hunter called the film "both beautiful and distant," and "a bleak, sometimes overly familiar cautionary tale of technology run amok." Similarly, A.O Scott, writing in the *New York Times*, found the film a "hallucinatory tour de force, perspective and scale, [that] virtually encapsulates the history of Japanese animation." For Scott, "the story is nearly as intricate as the animation."

If you enjoy the works of Katsuhiro Otomo, you may also want to check out the following books:

Akira Toriyama, *Dragon Ball*, 2000.
Nobuhiro Watsuki, *Rurouni Kenshin*, 2003.
Hiromu Arakawa, *Full Metal Alchemist*, 2005.

Meanwhile, Otomo was also at work, for over a decade, on his second major feature film, *Steamboy*, the tale of the son of a British inventor who comes into possession of a miraculous steam ball that could change the world in post-industrial Britain. Part of the reason for the lengthy production time was Otomo's need for detail and accuracy. He and

his crew spent a great deal of time in England getting the feel of the Victorian world that he recreates in animation, blending computer-generated graphics and hand-drawn cels. Another reason for the delay was his difficulty in finding funding for this hugely expensive project. Reviewing the finished work in *Entertainment Weekly*, Owen Gleiberman noted that the film is set in a "Jules Verne fantasy of Victorian London, a formal gray kingdom of bowler hats, muttonchop sideburns, and magic industrial inventions." For *Film Journal International* contributor Rex Roberts, *Steamboy* "is a curious work that thrives on incongruity." Roberts further thought that the film was "inspired" and that Otomo is the "master of anime." Kevin Crust, writing in the *Los Angeles Times*, however, voiced an opinion held by several reviewers. While finding *Steamboy* a "visual treat" and a "stunning-to-look-at film," Crust also felt it was "marred by a less than searing pace and some narrative incoherence." But for Jeff Jensen, writing in *Entertainment Weekly*, the same film was a "whimsical adventure steeped in retro sci-fi," and was, "at the very least, . . . a showcase for Otomo's artistry."

Otomo has been encouraged by his fans around the world to return to manga. However, as he told Jensen, "I have not set my mind as to which direction I am going." There was one thing, though, that Otomo was sure of after the long battle to get *Steamboy* into the theaters: "I don't want to wait another ten years to make a movie."

■ Biographical and Critical Sources

PERIODICALS

Entertainment Weekly, December 4, 1992, Steve Daly, review of *Akira*, p. 74; July 27, 2001, Marc Bernardin, review of *Akira* (DVD), p. 51; April 26, 2002, Marc Bernardin, review of *Spriggan*, p. 125; April 1, 2005, Owen Gleiberman, review of *Steamboy*, p. 50, and Jeff Jensen, "Head of 'Steam'," p. 50.
Film Journal International, April, 2005, Rex Roberts, review of *Steamboy*, p. 119
Hollywood Reporter, January 29, 2002, David Hunter, review of *Metropolis*, p. 20.
Los Angeles Times, March 14, 1990, Charles Solomon, review of *Akira*, p. F3; May 15, 1991, Charles Solomon, review of *Robot Carnival*, p. F3; March 17, 2005, Jake Forbes, "He's a Kubrik of Anime," p. E6; March 18, 2005, Kevin Crust, review of *Steamboy*, p. E4.
Metro (Australia), winter, 2003, Steven Aoun, review of *Akira* (DVD), p. 266.

New York Times, October 19, 1990, Janet Maslin, review of *Akira,* p. C12; January 25, 2002, A.O. Scott, review of *Metropolis,* p. E1.

Publishers Weekly, May 7, 2001, review of *Akira: Book One,* p. 227; May 5, 2003, review of *Akira: Volume 1,* p. 201; November 28, 2005, review of *Steamboy,* p. 30.

Time, February 1, 1993, Jay Cocks, review of *Akira* (DVD), p. 66; August 8, 2005, Richard Corliss, "5 Top Anime Movies on DVD," p. 70.

Time International, August 23, 1999, Richard Corliss, "From Asia's Film Factories, 10 Golden Greats," p. 115.

U.S. News & World Report, January 8, 2001, review of *Akira,* p. 54.

Variety, September 3, 2001, Derek Elley, review of *Metropolis,* p. 45; November 15, 2004, Leslie Felperin, review of *Steamboy,* p. 56.

Voice of Youth Advocates, February, 1997, Katherine Kan, review of *The Legend of Mother Sarah: Tunnel Town,* p. 324.

Washington Post, February 25, 1991, review of *Robot Carnival,* p. C4; March 25, 2005, Stephen Hunter, review of *Steamboy,* p. C1.

ONLINE

Anime News Network, http://www.animenewsnetwork.com/ (September 5, 2006), "Katsuhiro Otomo."

ArtBomb.net, http://www.artbomb.net/ (September 5, 2006), Peter Aaron Rose, review of *Akira* (Volume 1), and Adi Tantimedh, *Akira* (Volume 2).

Big in Japan, http://www.metropolis.co.jp/ (September 9, 2006), John Paul Catton, "Otomo, Katsuhrio."

BlueBlade, http://www.bbakira.co.uk/ (September 9, 2006), "Akira."

Midnight Eye, http://www.midnighteye.com/ (September 23, 2004), Tom Mes, review of *Steamboy.*

Internet Movie Database, http://www.imdb.com/ (September 5, 2006), "Katsuhiro Otomo."

Lambiek.net, http://www.lambiek.net/ (September 5, 2006), "Katsuhiro Otomo."

Ninth Art, http://www.ninthart.com/ (September 5, 2006), Nick Brownlow, "Thumbnail: Katsuhiro Otomo."*

Amada Irma Perez

■ Personal

Born c. 1951, in Mexico; married; children: two. *Education:* California State Polytechnic University, B.A.; California Lutheran University, M.A.

■ Addresses

Home—Ventura, CA. *Office*—Mar Vista Elementary School, 2382 Etting Rd., Oxnard, CA 93033. *E-mail*—ramadaz@aol.com.

■ Career

Writer, teacher. Mar Vista Elementary School, Oxnard, CA, third-grade teacher.

■ Awards, Honors

Tomas Rivera Award, Americas Honor Award, Outstanding Achievement in Books, 2000, Parent's Guide to Children's Media, all for *My Very Own Room*; Americas Award Commended Title, 2002, Pura Belpre Honor Book Narrative Award, 2004, both for *My Diary from Here to There.*

■ Writings

CHILDREN'S BOOKS

My Very Own Room/Mi propio cuartito, illustrated by Maya Christina Gonzalez, Children's Book Press (San Francisco, CA), 2000.

My Diary from Here to There/Mi diario de aqui hasta alla, illustrated by Maya Christina Gonzalez, Children's Book Press (San Francisco, CA), 2002.

Nana's Big Surprise!/Nana, Que Sorpresa!, illustrated by Maya Christina Gonzalez, Children's Book Press (San Francisco, CA), 2007.

■ Work in Progress

Nana's Chicken Coop Surprise, picture book, for Children's Book Press.

■ Sidelights

Writer and teacher Amada Irma Perez is the author of two award-winning bilingual children's books, *My Very Own Room/Mi propio cuartito,* and *My Diary from Here to There/Mi diario de aqui hasta alla.* Both titles are autobiographical sketches featuring a young girl who immigrates to the United States from Mexico as a child and must make her way in the alien culture. Perez teamed up with painter and illustrator Maya Christina Gonzalez for both titles. An advocate of multicultural understanding, Perez took inspiration from the children in her classroom and their love of storytelling to tell her own stories. As she noted on the *Project FRESA* Web site: "I believe that education can be used to transform lives in a positive way. Through building community and encouraging dialogue I have come to know that a classroom is filled with teachers and learners. . . . I believe that we all have stories to tell and are empowered when we share them orally and in writing."

Growing Up in Two Worlds

Perez, like most of the students she teaches in her bilingual third grade class in Oxnard, California, was born in Mexico. The oldest of six children, she was only five years old when her family left Mexico to find work in the United States. Their new home was the primitive housing of a labor camp in El Monte, California. Her father worked in an aluminum foundry while her mother took care of the large family. As Fred Alvarez noted in an author profile in the *Los Angeles Times*, "They all squeezed into a two-bedroom house, a place weathered and worn, with faded lime green floor tiles and a kitchen sink to match." There Perez and her family spent the next seven years, with the children sharing a crowded bedroom. Finally, when she was twelve, they were able to move to a better home. Perez was fortunate enough to be able to attend school, and graduating from high school, she went on to study English at California State Polytechnic University at Pomona, and then gained a master's degree in educational administration from California Lutheran University.

Despite a degree in administration, Perez has spent most of her education career in the classroom, and much of that time working with migrant children. Her elementary school is set amidst the strawberry fields around Oxnard, California, and her student's parents and siblings often work in those very fields. In fact, Perez has developed a writing program to honor the hard work of those relatives, sending the children out to interview the workers and creating poems and essays with the resulting information. With so much of her career spent attempting to get children to write their stories, Perez ultimately found herself wishing to do so, as well. In 1998, she took a writing workshop at the University of

A small girl imagines having her own bedroom in the family's tiny house in this 2000 title. (Children's Book Press, 2000. Illustrations copyright © 2000 by Maya Christina Gonzalez. Reproduced by permission.)

California Santa Barbara, and wrote the text for her first children's book there in her journal over the course of just five days.

From Teacher to Writer

Perez recalled an incident from her childhood in the El Monte labor camp for this first book, but it was not until the following year that she finally worked up the courage to actually try and sell it. Attending a bilingual education conference, she approached a representative of the San Francisco-based nonprofit publisher, Children's Book Press, and eagerly described her project. The executive editor, Harriet Rohmer, liked what she saw and brought painter Maya Christina Gonzalez on board as illustrator. The result was the 2000 publication of *My Very Own Room*, with text in English and Spanish. It is the tale of a young Mexican American girl who feels cramped in her tiny house with five little brothers, two parents, and numerous visiting relatives. A sensitive child, she longs for a little space of her own, where she could read her books, write in her journal, and dream of her future life. Her understanding family works together to convert a small storage closet into her own room. In so doing, the entire family takes pride in working toward this common goal to fulfill the dreams of the nine-year-old protagonist. A bed is donated by an uncle headed back to Mexico, a lamp is bought with Blue Chip trading stamps patiently saved up, and a wooden crate found by one of her brothers serves as a bookcase for the books she borrows from the library.

Perez's first book drew critical praise from many quarters. Writing in *Skipping Stones*, Mary Drew called it a "lovely, empowering story." Similarly, *Booklist* contributor Gillian Engberg felt "this book will resonate with all young ones growing up with limited space and resources." Likewise, a *Publishers Weekly* critic concluded that *My Very Own Room* was an "inspiring tale [that] will resonate with anyone who's ever wished for a room of one's own or worked hard to achieve an important goal," while writing in *School Library Journal*, Denise E. Agosto observed that the book demonstrates "that a child's need for privacy doesn't preclude being a loving

This 2002 story tells of a young Mexican girl who records her thoughts in a dairy as her family prepares to move to America. (Children's Book Press, 2002. Illustrations copyright © 2002 by Maya Christina Gonzalez. Reproduced by permission.)

family member." And Kathleen T. Horning, reviewing the same work in *Horn Book*, praised the "first-person narrative [which] realistically portrays a child who can take charge and make changes, luckily with the enthusiastic support of her entire family."

Everyone Has a Story

Perez's second children's book, *My Diary from Here to There*, also borrows from the author's own youthful experiences when her family decided to leave Mexico and come to the United States. The narrator of this story is young Amada, who overhears her parents talking one night about moving to the other side of the border, to Los Angeles, where economic opportunities are greater. Amada is fearful of leaving her home, her hometown, and her friends, and of coming to a new country and culture. How, for example, will she ever be able to learn English? Her father leaves first, to find work in the United States and get green cards for his family. Meanwhile, Amada and her brothers and mother leave Juarez to live with relatives in Mexicali until the father sends for them. Amada confides her fears, as well as her hopes and dreams for a new life, in a diary given to her by her grandmother as the family makes the trip northward to Mexicali, Tijuana, and finally to Los Angeles and a reunion with the father. Amada finally learns that through the love of her family and her own self-confidence, she will be able to adapt to any changes in her life.

This second book, once again illustrated by Gonzalez, was also warmly welcome by the critics. *Booklist* contributor Isabel Schon felt *My Diary from Here to There* "touchingly describes Amada's concerns, which will resonate with immigrant children who have left their own family, friends, and belongings behind." For Ann Welton, writing in the *School Library Journal*, the entries in Amada's diary "resonate with the tensions of the experience." Welton additional thought the problems of such a dislocation "are delineated with feeling." Further praise came from a *Publishers Weekly* contributor, who felt "Perez sensitively explores her protagonist's emotional journey, peppering the narrative with details of specific moments." *Horn Book* writer Nell D. Beram found the narrative "affecting," while a *Kirkus Reviews* critic wrote, "Perez captures the essence of the trauma of moving to a new place that is universal to all children, but here it is expanded by the facts of her [own] immigrant experience." The same critic concluded, "Very nicely done."

If you enjoy the works of Amada Irma Perez, you may also want to check out the following books:

R. Friedman, *How My Parents Learned to Eat*, 1987.
Lyn Littlefield Hoopes, *The Unbeatable Bread*, 1996.
Preston McLear, *The Boy under the Bed*,1998.

Perez has spoken widely about the immigrant experience as well as about working with migrant children in a bilingual classroom. She has joined a select group of authors providing works for young readers in bilingual editions. "Children need books they can relate to," Perez told Alvarez, "where they can see themselves in the characters."

■ Biographical and Critical Sources

BOOKS

Perez, Amada, Irma *My Very Own Room/Mi propio cuartito*, illustrated by Maya Christina Gonzalez, Children's Book Press (San Francisco, CA), 2000.
Perez, Amada Irma, *My Diary from Here to There/Mi diario de aqui hasta alla*, illustrated by Maya Christina Gonzalez, Children's Book Press (San Francisco, CA), 2002.

PERIODICALS

Book Links, January, 2004, review of *My Diary from Here to There/Mi diario de aqui hasta alla*, p. 45.

Booklist, July, 2000, Gillian Engberg, review of *My Very Own Room/Mi propio cuartito*, p. 2042; November 1, 2002, Isabel Schon, "Books in Spanish Published in the U.S.," review of *My Diary from Here to There*, p. 506.
Criticas, January-February, 2004, "Children's Book Press Wins 2004 Pura Belpre," p. 7.
Horn Book, November-December, 2000, Kathleen T. Horning, review of *My Very Own Room*, p. 749; September-October, 2002, Nell D. Beram, review of *My Diary form Here to There*, p. 556.
Instructor (1990), January, 2001, Judy Freeman, "All You Need Is Love," review of *My Very Own Room*, p. 19; October, 2001, review of *My Very Own Room*, p. 17;
Kirkus Reviews, August 1, 2002, review of *My Diary from Here to There*, p. 1139.
Los Angeles Times, August 21, 2000, Fred Alvarez, "A Teacher Tells Her Story in 2 Languages," p. 10.
Publishers Weekly July 3, 2000, review of *My Very Own Room*, p. 71; September 23, 2002, review of *My Diary from Here to There*, p. 73.
School Library Journal, August, 2000, Denise E. Agosto, review of *My Very Own Room*, p. 163; November, 2002, Ann Welton, review of *My Very Own Room*, p. 153.
Skipping Stones, May-August, 2001, Mary Drew, review of *My Very Own Room*, p. 8.

ONLINE

California Association for Bilingual Education Web site, http://www.bilingualeducation.org/ (May 13, 2005), "A Literary Evening: Amada Irma Perez."
Children's Book Press Web site, http://www.childrensbookpress.org/ (September 12, 2006), "Amada Irma Perez."
Project FRESA Web site, http://www.eden.elmer.csulb.edu/ (September 13, 2006), "All about Amada Irma H. Perez."*

Hal Roach

(Photograph by Nancy R. Shiff. Archive Photos/Getty Images.)

■ Personal

Born January 14, 1892, in Elmira, NY; died of pneumonia, November 2, 1992, in Los Angeles, CA; son of Charles H. (an insurance and real estate broker) and Mabel (maiden name, Bailey; a landlady); married Margaret Nichols (died, 1940); married Lucille Prin, 1942 (died, 1981); children: (first marriage) Hal, Jr., Margaret; (second marriage) Maria, Jeanne, Bridget.

■ Career

Producer, director, screenwriter. Worked as mule-skinner and gold miner, Alaska, 1910; Universal Studios, Hollywood, CA, stuntman and actor, 1912-14; Rolin Film Company, founder, 1914; Hal Roach Studios, founder, producer, director, 1920-62. Produced over one thousand short films and features, and directed 150 short films. Films include "Willie Work" and "Lonesome Luke" comedy series, starring Harold Lloyd; the "Our Gang" series; and hundreds of other short films starring Laurel and Hardy, Harry Pollard, Will Rogers, Charlie Chase, Edgar Kennedy, Thelma Todd, and ZaSu Pitts. Also producer of feature films, including *Topper*, 1937;

Topper Takes a Trip, 1938; *Of Mice and Men*, 1939; *One Million Years, B.C.*, 1940 and 1966; *Topper Returns*, 1941; and *Of Mice and Men*. Executive producer of television series, including *Racket Squad*, 1950; *The Stu Erwin Show*, 1950; *The Three Musketeers*, 1950; *My Little Margie*, 1952; *Passport to Danger*, 1954; *The Little Rascals*, 1955; *Screen Directors Playhouse*, 1955; *The Charles Farrell Show*, 1956; *The Gale Storm Show*, 1956; *Code 3*, 1957; *Blondie*, 1957; *The Lone Ranger; Amos 'n' Andy; The Life of Riley; The All New Mickey Mouse Club*, 1989; *The Little Kidnappers*, 1990; *Lantern Hill*, 1990. *Military service:* U.S. Army Signal Corps, 1942-45, stationed in England; became major.

■ Awards, Honors

Academy Award, Best Comedy Short Subject, 1931-32, for *Music Box*; Academy Award, Best One-Reel Live Action Short, 1936, for *Bored of Education*; Special Academy Award, 1983; James Smithson Bicentennial Medal, Smithsonian Institution, 1992.

■ Writings

SCREENPLAYS

(And producer) *A Sailor-Made Man*, Hal Roach Studios, 1921.

(And producer) *Doctor Jack,* Hal Roach Studios, 1922.

(And producer) *Grandma's Boy,* Hal Roach Studios, 1922.

(And producer) *Our Gang,* Hal Roach Studios, 1922.

(And producer) *One Terrible Day,* Hal Roach Studios, 1922.

(And producer) *Fire Fighters,* Hal Roach Studios, 1922.

(And producer) *Young Sherlocks,* Hal Roach Studios, 1922.

(And producer) *Saturday Morning,* Hal Roach Studios, 1922.

(And producer) *A Quiet Street,* Hal Roach Studios, 1922.

(And producer) *The Cobbler,* Hal Roach Studios, 1923.

(And producer) *Big Show,* Hal Roach Studios, 1923.

(And producer) *The Champeen,* Hal Roach Studios, 1923.

(And producer) *Boys to Board,* Hal Roach Studios, 1923.

(And producer) *Safety Last,* Hal Roach Studios, 1923.

Uncensored Movies, 1923.

Hustlin' Hank, 1923.

Gee Whiz, Genevieve, 1924.

The Cake Eater, Hal Roach Studios, 1924.

The Cowboy Sheik, 1924.

(And producer) *The Nickel Hopper,* Hal Roach Studios, 1926.

(And producer, director) *Flying Elephants,* Hal Roach Studios, 1927.

(And producer) *The Battle of the Century,* Hal Roach Studios, 1927.

(And producer) *Leave 'Em Laughing,* Hal Roach Studios, 1927.

(And producer) *Boxing Gloves,* Hal Roach Studios, 1929.

(And producer) *Brats,* Hal Roach Studios, 1930.

Contributor of over one hundred stories to short films; writer for *Little Rascals* television series, 1955.

■ Sidelights

Upon his death in 1992 at one hundred years of age, Hal Roach was declared a "founding father of American motion picture comedy," by *Washington Post* contributor Bart Barnes. Indeed, Roach's career spanned the era of silent, one-reel films to television situation comedies; he was older than the movies, the last living pioneer of the film industry. President Ronald Reagan, who had made propaganda films at

Roach on the set with the comedy team of Stan Laurel and Oliver Hardy. (Photograph courtesy of John Kobal Foundation/Getty Images.)

the Roach Studios during World War II, was quoted in Roach's *Los Angeles Times* obituary as saying, "Hal was one of the founding fathers of the motion picture industry, the original . . . producer, director, writer, and studio head." Roach discovered and developed such early film stars as the comedians Harold Lloyd and the unlikely comedic pair, Stan Laurel and Oliver Hardy. His "Our Gang" series, about the humorous adventures of a group of young children, lasted for sixteen years before Roach sold it to MGM; it later also became popular television fare. "Our Gang" was, as Charles Champlin noted in the *Los Angeles Times*, "one of film history's most famous series of shorts." According to Scott Eyman, writing for the *Washington Post*, Roach was the inventor of "the character-based situation comedy—a genre that flourishes today, in slightly cruder form, in . . . TV shows." At his Hal Roach Studios, Roach produced over fifty comedies a year for two decades, leaving behind a huge legacy of laughter.

It is additionally one of Roach's enduring legacies that he took the "film industry into the television production business," as a contributor for *International Dictionary of Films and Filmmakers* observed.

By 1951, his Hal Roach Studios, "one of the great comedy factories of all time" according to the same contributor, was already producing 1,500 hours of television shows per year. Roach also eventually moved from short subjects, the typical one-or two-reel films that accompanied feature films in the 1930s, to the production of numerous feature films of his own, including the popular *Topper* films, starring Cary Grant and Constance Bennett, and *Of Mice and Men,* the 1939 film adaptation of the John Steinbeck novel, starring Burgess Meredith and Lon Chaney. As a *Time* magazine critic commented at the time, with the production of the latter movie "Hollywood sat up and admitted that Hal Roach had widened his horizons in a hurry." But it is for his situation comedies that Roach is best known and remembered. Roach had a simple formula for his comedies, as quoted by Dennis McLellan in the *Los Angeles Times:* "It's portraying things a child does. . . . But it takes a great artist to do it—like Stan Laurel crying or scratching his head, or Oliver Hardy playing with his tie. They were adults playing children. The reverse was the Our Gang series with children playing grown-ups."

An Accidental Humorist

Born in Elmira, New York, in 1892, Roach was early on impressed by the power of humor, when the American writer Mark Twain gave a presentation at his grade school. However, the youthful Roach grew up with no plans to become a great comedic producer. He left home at seventeen to pursue an adventurous life in the West. He became a mule-skinner and prospector for gold in Alaska, drove trucks in Seattle, Washington, and worked construction in California. There he saw an ad for extras for

Comedian Harold Lloyd in the 1920 Roach film *From Hand to Mouth.* (Directed by Hal Roach. Courtesy of W and I Films/The Kobal Collection.)

a movie; it paid 5 dollars a day, and that was a good deal of money in 1912. That he was an expert horse rider and had also taken to dressing in cowboy clothing, with a Stetson hat, cowboy boots, and a bandana, made him a perfect choice as an extra in Western films of the day. He left construction for good, and for the next two years played bit parts at Universal Pictures.

Soon, however, Roach left acting behind and took on the role of assistant director, and then worked his way to director. In 1914, on the strength of a small inheritance, he formed the Rolin Film Company, with his friend, Dan Linthicum. But after a disastrous first year (his company lacked any distributor), Linthicum dropped out of the partnership. On his own, Roach found a distributor that was interested only in short comedies. The fledgling producer happened to have a number of such comedies, starring his friend Harold Lloyd, who was making a name for himself as a versatile comedian. Roach thus found himself specializing in such short comedies, and his studio, renamed in 1920 the Hal Roach Studios when he moved to Culver City, became famous for such humorous productions. Throughout the second decade of the century, Roach churned out vehicles for Lloyd, who had taken to wearing glasses to create his sincere if naive persona. As Barnes noted, Lloyd's "character had a bedrock foundation of honor and decency that made him the quintessential boy-next-door." Lloyd became more popular than even Charlie Chaplin in the 1920s.

Even at this early stage in his career, Roach always thought about his film business in the long term. "Roach was in the movie business to make a profit," John Brennan wrote in an article posted at the *Silents Are Golden* Web site, "and if a short film was going well but had strayed beyond the standard length of two reels, Roach was not adverse to allowing the film to go longer, as long as he felt the additional footage made for a better film. He did this knowing he would still only be able to sell a longer film at a two-reel price, essentially giving away extra reels for free. But for Roach, the long-term investment was more important—each successful Roach film made the Hal Roach name more valuable in the long run."

With the success of the Harold Lloyd films, including the "Lonesome Luke" series, Roach became financially secure. He brought his parents out to California, and his father became secretary-treasurer of the Hal Roach Studios. In 1921, Lloyd started to star in feature-length films, but with his 1923 *Safety*

Last, written by Roach and the height of the Roach Studios silent era productions, the hapless comedian performed in his last picture for Roach. Thereafter, he established his own independent production business. Roach turned to other comedic shorts, starring personalities such as Will Rogers and the seldom-remembered comedian, Charley Chase. In 1922, however, he stuck gold with another series.

From "Our Gang" to Laurel and Hardy

One day, while gazing out his window in Culver City, Roach watched the antics of a gang of kids playing in a lumber yard across the street. Playing with scraps of wood, two of the children began an altercation over who was the owner of a certain stick. Before he realized it, Roach had spent a quarter of an hour watching the argument and suddenly realized this was natural entertainment, watching children do what children normally do. If he could be taken out of his busy day for fifteen minutes, then he figured that audiences would enjoy it, too. Thus was born the idea for the "Our Gang" comedy shorts. He initially planned on calling the pictures the Hal Roach Rascals, but the title of the first film in the series, *Our Gang,* stuck instead. The gang included a youthful, working-class, multi-gender, and multi-ethnic blend of characters such as Sunshine Sammy, Farina, Spanky, Alfalfa, Buckweat, and Stymie. Child actors were rotated into these roles every three or four years as the children matured. Such a mix of races and of boys and girls, all on an equal footing, had not been done before in motion pictures. After the success of the "Our Gang" series, such a concept, however, became commonplace. Roach and his director, Robert F. McGowan, also attempted to show the child actors in natural situations and without affected acting techniques. Moreover, Roach was concerned about the well-being of his child actors, and insisted that the filming be scheduled around their school and recreational activities. An immensely popular series, "Our Gang" began in 1922 as a silent short, then received wider distribution in 1927 when the Roach Studios teamed with MGM for distribution, and went to sound in 1929. Roach sold the ever-popular series to MGM in 1938, and that company continued production of the comedies until 1944. Altogether, 220 short films and one feature were produced starring the gang of kids, and forty-one different child actors assumed the various roles, including Jackie Cooper. Eventually, the eighty episodes of "Our Gang" which Roach produced with sound were adapted for television as *The Little Rascals.*

Another Roach invention was the pairing of British comedian Stan Laurel, a veteran vaudevillian, with American heavy Oliver Hardy, who had begun his

The Our Gang kids included Carl Switzer as "Alfalfa" and George McFarland as "Spanky." (Directed by Hal Roach. Courtesy of The Kobal Collection.)

career as a bit player and singer. Roach realized that both were good actors and comedians who could play without benefit of a straight man. According to Roach's mathematics, this doubled or even tripled the laughs from one gag, as the camera cut from one to the other and back again for reactions. Barnes described a typical Laurel and Hardy short movie: "Their films followed a story line in which a single incident would escalate to a level of catastrophic dimensions, invariably with the help of the stupidity, vengefulness and pig-headedness of the two comedians." From 1927 to 1929, the pair made twenty-seven silent shorts, and then transitioned to sound, ultimately making over one hundred movies together. For Champlin, writing in the *Los Angeles Times*, Laurel and Hardy were "the most successful comedy team in film history." They gave rise to a host of other such comedy pairs, including Bud Ab-

bott and Lou Costello, Bob Hope and Bing Crosby, and Jerry Lewis and Dean Martin. Roach earned his two Academy Awards for short films from his two most popular series. In 1932, he won for the Laurel and Hardy film short, *The Music Box*, and in 1936 he won again for the "Our Gang" series title, *Bored of Education*.

The Last Half Century

Roach is perhaps best remembered for his work as producer, director, and writer of the short comedies that appeared in the 1920s and 1930s. With changing tastes in the later 1930s, he ventured into feature-length films, but with less success, especially in comedies, for he felt that ninety minutes was too long to sustain humor. Despite the success of such feature films as *Topper*, Roach's primary focus and bid for fame was with comedic film shorts. His career was put on hold during World War II, when his production studio was turned over to the military for the creation of training and propaganda films. Roach at fifty, served as a major in the U.S. Army Signal Corps, assigned to England.

Returning to Hollywood, Roach continued to oversee production at his studio, but increasingly he moved away from motion pictures to the new medium of television. He produced a number of successes for television, including *My Little Margie, Amos 'n' Andy, The Life of Riley, Racket Squad,* and *Topper,* the last-named adapted from his own movies. Roach sold the Hal Roach Studios to his son in 1955, when its television production aspects were quite successful. However, soon the other major Hollywood studios also began producing for television, and the Roach Studios could not compete

against the big budgets these others had at their disposal. Bankruptcy was declared in 1959 and the studio liquidated its assets the following year. It was demolished in 1963.

If you enjoy the works of Hal Roach, you may also want to check out the following:

The works of directors Preston Sturges, Billy Wilder, and D.W. Griffith.

Roach, however, still had a long life ahead of him, outliving both his son and daughter by his first marriage. He served as an associate producer on

Stan Laurel and Oliver Hardy in the 1933 comedy *The Devil's Brother.* (Directed by Hal Roach. Courtesy of MGM/The Kobal Collection.)

The 1940 prehistoric thriller *One Million B.C.* **starred Victor Mature and Carole Landis.** (Directed by Hal Roach. Courtesy of United Artists/The Kobal Collection.)

the 1966 remake of his *One Million Years B.C.*, starring Raquel Welch, and remained active in his private life, playing polo, hunting, and swimming. Into his last decade he was brimming with new ideas for television game shows, for situation comedies, and for movies. Shortly before his death in 1992, he was honored on the occasion of his hundredth birthday. Roach died of pneumonia on November 2, 1992. His legacy is manifold. He introduced a plethora of stars to the American public, including Lloyd and the Laurel and Hardy team. Additionally he was the first to give roles to future stars such as Jean Harlow and Paulette Goddard, and directors such as Leo McCarey and George Stevens apprenticed under him. He also developed a style of comedy that moved beyond

mere slapstick and was more character-driven. This in turn led to the development of television's situation comedies, or sit-coms. He was also the first of the studio heads to see the importance of the new medium of television, producing some of the finest early shows in that industry.

■ **Biographical and Critical Sources**

BOOKS

Everson, William K., *The Films of Hal Roach*, Museum of Modern Art (New York, NY), 1971.

International Dictionary of Films and Filmmakers, Volume 4: Writers and Production Artists, 4th edition, St. James Press (Detroit, MI), 2000.

Rohauer, Raymond, *A Tribute to Hal Roach,* Gallery of Modern Art (New York, NY), 1965.

Ward, Richard Lewis, *A History of the Hal Roach Studios,* Southern Illinois University Press (Carbondale, IL), 2005.

PERIODICALS

Los Angeles Times, January 12, 1992, Charles Champlin, "Hollywood's Oldest Storyteller Soon to Be 100," p.24; January 13, 1992, Aaron Curtiss, "A Celebrity's Celebrity: Hall Roach Honored on his 100th Birthday—Almost," p. B1; January 16, 1992, Bernice Hirabayashi, "He Made a Fine Mess of Things Film," p. J1; November 4, 1992, Charles Champlin, "An Appreciation: Hal Roach—Last Link to a Glorious Entertainment Era," p. F1.

New York Times, January 23, 1992, William Grimes, "Hal Roach Recalls His First Century," p. C15.

Smithsonian, April, 1992, Edwards Park, "Around the Mall and Beyond," p. 28.

Time, October 4, 1937, "Mussolini's Roach."

Washington Post, January 24, 1992, David Mills, "100 Years of Hal Roach," p. C1; November 8, 1992, Scott Eyman, "Laughing All the Way," p. G1.

ONLINE

Film Reference, http://www.filmreference.com/ (September 19, 2006), "Hal Roach."

Hal Roach Studios, http://www.halroachstudios.com/ (September 19, 2006).

Internet Movie Database, http://www.imdb.com/ (September 19, 2006), "Hal Roach."

New York Times Online, http://movies2.nytimes.com/ (September 19, 2006), "Movies: Hal Roach."

Silents Are Golden, http://www.silentsaregolden.com/ (September 19, 2006), John Brennan, "Hal Roach: A Man and His Studio."

OBITUARIES

PERIODICALS

Los Angeles Times, November 3, 1992, Dennis McLellan, "Film Pioneer Hal Roach, Comedy King, Dies at 100," p. A1.

New York Times, November 3, 1992, Peter B. Flint, "Hal Roach Is Dead at 100," p. B8.

Washington Post, November 3, 1992, Bart Barnes, "Movie Great Hal Roach Dies," p. B7.*

(Photograph by Evan Agostini/Getty Images.)

John Patrick Shanley

■ Personal

Born October 13, 1950, in New York, NY; father worked as a meat-packer and mother worked as a telephone operator; married Jayne Haynes, an actress (divorced); children: Frank, Nick. *Education:* New York University, B.S., 1977.

■ Addresses

Home—New York, NY. *Agent*—Creative Artists Agency, 9830 Wilshire Blvd., Beverly Hills, CA 90212-1815. *E-mail*—shanleysmoney@aol.com.

■ Career

Playwright, screenwriter, and director. Also worked as a bartender and house painter. *Military service:* U.S. Marines.

■ Member

Writers Guild of America.

■ Awards, Honors

Writers Guild of America Award and Academy Award (Oscar) from Academy of Motion Picture Arts and Sciences, both for best original screenplay, 1987, for *Moonstruck;* Los Angeles Drama Critics Circle award, 1987; special-jury prize at the Barcelona Film Festival for *Five Corners;* Pulitzer Prize for drama, Tony Award for best play, Obie Award from the *Village Voice,* New York's Drama Desk Award, four prizes at the Lucille Lortel Awards in New York (best play, best director, outstanding leading actress, and outstanding feature actress), and an Outer Critics Circle Award for best Broadway play, all 2005, all for *Doubt: A Parable;* Academy Award in Literature, American Academy of Arts and Letters, 2006; inducted onto the Playwrights' Sidewalk, 2006.

■ Writings

PLAYS

Saturday Night at the War, produced in New York, NY, 1978.

George and the Dragon, produced in New York, NY, 1979.

Rockaway, produced in New York, NY, at Vineyard Theater, 1982.

Welcome to the Moon (produced in New York, NY, 1982), published in *Welcome to the Moon and Other Plays,* Dramatists Play Service (New York, NY), 1985.

Savage in Limbo (produced in New York, NY, at 47th Street Theater, 1985), Dramatists Play Service (New York, NY), 1986.

the dreamer examines his pillow: A Heterosexual Homily (produced as a staged reading at the O'Neill Playwrights Conference, 1985, produced in New York, NY, at Double Image Theater, 1986), Dramatists Play Service (New York, NY), 1987.

Danny and the Deep Blue Sea (produced in Los Angeles, CA, at the Back Alley Theatre, 1986), published as *Danny and the Deep Blue Sea: An Apache Dance*, Dramatists Play Service (New York, NY), 1984.

Women of Manhattan, produced in New York, NY, at City Center Theater, 1986.

All For Charity, produced in New York, NY, at Ensemble Studio Theater, 1987.

Italian American Reconciliation, produced Off-Broadway, 1988.

The Big Funk: A Casual Play, Dramatists Play Service (New York, NY), 1991.

Beggars in the House of Plenty, Dramatists Play Service (New York, NY), 1992.

13 by Shanley, Applause Books (New York, NY), 1992.

What Is This Everything?, produced in New York, NY, 1992.

Four Dogs and a Bone; and, The Wild Goose, Dramatists Play Service (New York, NY), 1995.

Missing/Kissing: Missing Marisa, Kissing Christine, Dramatists Play Service (New York, NY), 1997.

Psychopathia Sexualis, (produced in New York, NY, 1997), Dramatists Play Service (New York, NY), 1998.

Where's My Money?, produced in New York, NY, 2001.

Cellini, produced in New York, NY, 2001), Dramatists Play Service (New York, NY), 2002.

Dirty Story (produced in New York, NY, at the Harold Clurman Theater, 2003), Dramatists Play Service (New York, NY), 2003.

Sailor's Song: A Watercolor, produced in New York, NY, at the Public Theater, 2004.

Doubt: A Parable (produced in New York, NY, at the Manhattan Theater Club, 2004), Theatre Communications Group (New York, NY), 2005.

Defiance, produced in New York, NY, at the Manhattan Theater Club, 2006.

SCREENPLAYS

Moonstruck, Metro Goldwyn-Mayer, 1987.

Five Corners, Handmade Films, 1988.

The January Man, Metro Goldwyn-Mayer, 1989.

(And director) *Joe versus the Volcano*, Warner Bros., 1990.

Alive (based on the novel by Piers Paul Read), Paramount, 1993.

We're Back! A Dinosaur's Story, Disney, 1993.

Congo (based on the novel by Michael Crichton), Paramount, 1995.

Moonstruck, Joe Versus The Volcano, and Five Corners, Grove Press (New York, NY), 1996.

(With Robert Wiener, Richard Chapman, and Timothy J. Sexton) *Live from Baghdad*, HBO Films, 2002.

Also author of television scripts.

■ Adaptations

Several of Shanley's screenplays have been adapted into storybooks and novelizations.

■ Sidelights

A popular playwright and screenwriter, John Patrick Shanley first gained national attention with the 1987 film *Moonstruck*, a highly emotional comedy about love, passion, and the relationships of an Italian family. To Charles Champlin of *Los Angeles Times*, *Moonstruck* "seems as nearly perfect as a script ever gets." Shanley began his career writing for the theater, however; his dramas, commonly set in Shanley's native New York City, feature eccentric, working-class characters and explosive dialogue. Shanley made an impressive Broadway debut in 2005 with *Doubt: A Parable*, which went on to win the Pulitzer Prize in drama as well as the Best Play honors at the season-ending Tony Awards. "Though he has specialized in characters who struggle with limited options, Shanley himself seems unencumbered by boundaries," observed Danile Vilmure in *American Writers*.

Born in 1950, Shanley grew up the youngest of five children in an Irish-Catholic family whose home was in the Bronx neighborhood of East Tremont. His father, a meatpacker, was an Irish immigrant, while Shanley's mother was herself the daughter of Irish immigrants. The East Tremont streets were home to similar working-class Irish and Italian families. "It was extremely anti-intellectual and extremely racist and none of this fit me," the playwright revealed in an interview with Alex Witchel in the *New York Times Magazine*. He recalled being "in constant fistfights from the time I was six," though he asserted he rarely picked the fight

Shanley won an Academy Award for the film *Moonstruck.*
(Photograph by Lennox Mclendon. AP Images.)

Works See the Stage

Shanley had already started writing plays by then. In his early twenties, he later recalled, "I tried the dialogue form, and it was instantaneous," he told *American Theatre*'s Robert Coe. "I wrote a full-length play the first time I ever wrote in dialogue, and it was produced a few weeks later." By the early 1980s, he had written a half-dozen works, and some of the one-act plays were staged together in a late 1982 production titled *Welcome to the Moon.* Its collective themes centered around love and the absence of it, and were filled with rather fanciful characters and props, such as a mermaid and a magical coat. Critics were less than kind.

Shanley had somewhat better fortune with *Danny and the Deep Blue Sea,* first produced in Waterford, Connecticut, in 1983. It went on to the New York stage the following year and then a London production as well that same year when it was included as part of the traveling arm of the Louisville Festival, a relatively new event at the time that showcased the best new American plays in the Kentucky city first. The play's action focused on two star-crossed lovers who meet in a seedy Bronx bar. John Turturro, who later went on to fame in films by Spike Lee and the Coen brothers, was the original Danny.

Shanley's rising star gave him access to a generous National Endowment for the Arts (NEA) grant, which freed him from the long series of jobs he usually held in order to make ends meet, including elevator operator, apartment painter, and bartender. When the NEA funds began running low, he thought that if he wrote a screenplay instead of a play, he might earn enough from selling it to Hollywood to get by for another year or so. He mined the familiar territory of the outer New York City boroughs and voluble Italian-American families for a script he originally titled "The Bride and the Beast." The title used instead, after a moderately well-known Hollywood director Norman Jewison filmed the story, was *Moonstruck.*

Big Screen Debut

Shanley's first produced screenplay, *Moonstruck* was a surprise hit and won an Academy Award for best original screenplay. Set in Brooklyn, the film relates the romantic entanglements and relationships of the Castorini family. A *Newsweek* reviewer declared that almost immediately, *Moonstruck* "lets you know it knows it's going to revel in—and tease—every Italian-American stereotype in the book." Loretta Castorini, a widow in her late thirties, accepts an

himself. "People would look at me and become enraged at the sight of me," he explained. "I believe that the reason was they could see that I saw them."

Shanley spent the first eight years of his formal education at St. Anthony's, a Roman Catholic school run by the Sisters of Charity religious order. He went on the all-boys Cardinal Spellman High School, where he rebelled against the strict, no-nonsense priests who taught at the school. During his two years there, Shanley spent every single week in after-school detention, until he was asked to leave. Instead of a public high school in the Bronx, he opted to attend a private school in New Hampshire that was affiliated with the Catholic church.

At the Thomas Moore school, away from the Bronx, Shanley began to thrive. His teachers encouraged his writing talents, which started around the age of eleven, and as a teen he wrote reams of poetry. When he graduated, he went on to New York University, but left after a semester of poor grades. He enlisted in the Marine Corps which, somewhat perversely, he liked for its Catholic-school style of discipline. He returned to New York University after his Vietnam War service ended, and in 1977, he graduated as the valedictorian of his class.

Cher and Nicolas Cage starred in the 1987 romantic comedy *Moonstruck.* (Written by John Patrick Shanley. Courtesy of MGM/The Kobal Collection.)

offer of marriage from timid, dull, but steady Johnny, although she does not love him. Her main concern is planning a traditional, by-the-book wedding to avoid the bad luck that she believes caused her first husband's death. Johnny leaves for Palermo to see his allegedly dying mother, instructing his fiance to invite his estranged younger brother, Ronny, to their wedding. Violent and passionate Ronny unfairly blames Johnny for the machinery accident that claimed his hand. Quickly infatuated, Loretta and Ronny begin an affair, which Loretta soon regrets and attempts to end. As excerpted in *American Film,* Ronny persuades Loretta to give up her plans with Johnny by explaining his views on love: "Love don't make things nice, it ruins everything, it breaks your heart, it makes things a mess. We're not here to make things perfect. Snowflakes are perfect. The stars are perfect. Not us. Not us! We are here to ruin ourselves and break our hearts and love the wrong people and die!"

Johnny unexpectedly arrives in town after his mother miraculously recovers. Ronny decides that

that morning would be a good time to meet Loretta's family, and he and Loretta—with the rest of the family gathered around the breakfast table—wait tensely for Johnny's arrival. As Loretta readies to cancel the wedding, Johnny surprises everyone by announcing that he will not marry her; apparently he breaks the engagement to appease his dying mother. In the final scene, the family toasts themselves and the engagement of Ronny and Loretta.

Shanley populated *Moonstruck* with interesting minor characters, including Loretta's dog-loving grandfather and a middle-aged professor whose disastrous dinner dates with younger women at a neighborhood restaurant lead to what *People* contributor Peter Travers called "a jewel of a scene" with Mrs. Castorini. Having guessed her husband's infidelity, Mrs. Castorini questions the professor about why men are driven to affairs. "When you see that the whole cast of family members are involved in libidinal confusions," remarked Pauline Kael in *New Yorker,* "the operatic structure can make you feel close to deliriously happy."

Many other critics responded enthusiastically to the film's characters, humor, and emotional mood. Travers found the characters "full of mischievous surprise" and felt the screenplay had "a real comic edge." Praising the script as "inventively written," a reviewer for *Newsweek* described it as "a very knowing piece of comic artifice." Champlin contended that *Moonstruck* "proved beyond argument. . . that Shanley has a rare gift for dialogue. I'm not sure that an *ear* for dialogue is the way to say it. Real speech rarely has the economy, the timing, the polish that Shanley gives his talk." Summing up the film's appeal, Kael called *Moonstruck* "a giddy homage to our desire for grand passion. With its own special lushness, it's a rose-tinted black comedy."

Shanley's next two films, *Five Corners* and *The January Man,* did not receive the popular and critical acclaim awarded *Moonstruck.* Like many of Shanley's plays, *Five Corners* was considered off-beat. Set in the Bronx, the 1988 film concerns a violent and disturbed delinquent's behavior when released from jail. David Ansen of *Newsweek* described *Five Corners* as "a seriocomic meditation on American violence seen through the prism of a half-dozen blue-collar kids in the dawning era of the civil-rights movement." Ansen added that the ending is disappointing, as Shanley "feels compelled to bring events to a rip-roaring melodramatic conclusion, and the climax gets out of hand."

Released in 1989, *The January Man* is a thriller about an ex-cop who, wrongly accused of corruption, responds to a plea that he return to police work to apprehend a maniacal killer. Critics felt that film's downfall was a confusing plot. "There are moments when watching *January Man* is like trying to follow the third episode of a miniseries mystery after you've missed the first two," asserted Champlin. Yet the critic stated that the film confirmed Shanley's talents for creating interesting dialogue and characters who are "poised somewhere between the abnormal and the bizarre."

The 1993 film *Alive* concerns the desperate survivors of a plane crash in the Andes Mountains. (Adapted by John Patrick Shanley from the book written by Piers Paul Read. Courtesy of Paramount/The Kobal Collection.)

Joe versus the Volcano marked Shanley's film directing debut. Upon reading the script, filmmaker Steven Spielberg called and offered to produce the film, leaving the directing duties to Shanley. In this 1990 film Joe Banks, a hypochondriac working in a remarkably bleak plant that manufactures medical devices, discovers that he has a fatal "brain cloud." When his doctor informs him of this symptomless time bomb, Joe decides to live what life he has left to the fullest. Into the picture comes a billionaire who proposes a free trip to the South Seas if Joe will sacrifice himself afterwards by throwing himself into a volcano. The billionaire believes that this act will pacify the gods and ensure the success of a business deal concerning a mineral on the island. Joe agrees to the plan, begins to enjoy life, and falls in love with his benefactor's daughters—Angelica, an artistic flower-child, and Patricia, the brave skipper of her father's yacht.

Though critics appreciated the film, they faulted it for having a weak ending. Sheila Benson declared in *Los Angeles Times* that "there's a quickly-tied-together feeling to it blessedly missing from the rest of the movie. . . . If you wish for more depth at the ending. . . you're not alone; the trick is to savor the trip along the way and to hope that Shanley keeps his style and deepens his substance with his next film." Some critics note sentimentality and overstatement in *Joe versus the Volcano* and Shanley's other works, but Dave Kehr remarked in *Chicago Tribune:* "Shanley's charm is in the obviousness of his imagery, the naive insistence of his symbols. . . . Yet that insistence," Kehr added, "loses all its charm once it is transformed into. . . windy, philosophical speeches." Benson, however, strongly affirmed Shanley's first directing venture: "Witty, disarming and beautiful, *Joe* is the tip-off that John Patrick Shanley is at least as distinctive a director as he has already been a playwright and screenwriter."

Shanley went on to write a few more Hollywood projects, such as *Alive,* the adaptation of a popular book from the 1970s based on a true story about an Uruguayan rugby team whose plane crashed in the Andes Mountains of South America in 1972; the survivors resorted to cannibalism to stay alive. Shanley also wrote the screenplay for the 1995 film *Congo,* a reworking of a Michael Crichton bestseller about apes and genetic mutation.

Shanley was still active in the New York theater world during these years. His plays included *Italian American Reconciliation,* from 1988, and *Beggars in the House of Plenty,* which was first produced in New York in 1991 and featured the typically dysfunctional characters who had become the hallmark of Shanley's work. In it, a Bronx butcher terrorizes his meek wife and adult children, one of whom turns to writing as a solace after finding little satisfaction in starting fires. Two more plays, *Kissing Christine* and *Missing Marisa,* debuted at the Louisville Festival in the 1990s, but Shanley found a more permanent home for his work finally in 2001 when he became involved with New York's LAByrinth Theater Company. His first play to be staged there was *Where's My Money?,* a drama about several jaded New Yorkers whose adulterous lives intersect. It contains one of Shanley's most-quoted lines of dialogue, as one of the play's lawyer-characters asserts, "Monogamy is like a 40-watt bulb. It works, but it's not enough."

Shanley wrote a few more plays, including 2003's *Dirty Story,* set in a post-9/11 world and dramatizing the Israeli-Palestinian conflict through its main characters, and *Sailor's Song,* a romantic fairy tale set to the waltzes of nineteenth-century German composer Johann Strauss. "This is not Mr. Shanley at his best," remarked Charles Isherwood in a *New York Times* review.

Award-winning Broadway Drama

By contrast, *Doubt: A Parable* earned outstanding praise from critics, as well as the most impressive honors for which a playwright could ever hope: the Pulitzer Prize for drama and the 2005 Tony Award for best play of the 2004-05 season. *Doubt* began its off-Broadway run in November of 2004, and went on to Broadway's Walter Kerr Theatre the following March. The story is set on familiar territory for Shanley: a Roman Catholic school in the Bronx in 1964. The original leads were Cherry Jones as the school principal Sister Aloysius and Brian F. O'Byrne as Father Flynn, one of the parish priests whom the Sister suspects of molesting the school's first African-American student.

Again, Shanley's intense dialogue served to anchor the drama, while the conclusion failed to answer any of the questions the play raised. Writing in the *New York Times,* Ben Brantley claimed that as the play's author, "Shanley is on no one's side. It seems safe to say the playwright agrees with Father Flynn when he explains his preference for parables over reality: 'The truth makes for a bad sermon. It tends to be confusing and have no clear conclusion.' But *Doubt* presents each point of view with reasonableness and an eloquence that never seem out of sync with the characters' Bronx accents and ecumenical backgrounds."

Part of the reason that *Doubt* resonated with theater audiences was the timeliness of its subject matter, with new revelations of past sexual abuse by Roman Catholic priests—and the ensuing legal proceedings—a frequent media topic over the past two years. As Shanley said in the *American Theatre* interview with Coe, those news stories prompted him to think about the nuns who taught him during his formative years at St. Anthony's. "I realized later on when the Church scandals were breaking that the way a lot of these priests were getting busted had to be by nuns. . . . But the chain of command in the Catholic Church was such that they had to report it not to the police but to their superior within the Church, who then covered up for the guy. This had to create very powerful frustrations and moral dilemmas for these women."

If you enjoy the works of John Patrick Shanley, you may also want to check out the following:

Raising Arizona, a comedy starring Nicolas Cage, 1987, and *Mermaids*, starring Cher, 1990.

Shanley' next play, *Defiance*, premiered in 2006. The second work in a projected trilogy, *Defiance* is set at Camp Lejeune, a Marine Corps base in North Carolina, in 1971. In an attempt to stem racial tensions at the camp, Lieutenant Colonel Morgan Littlefield promotes Captain Lee King, an African American, to executive officer, despite King's desire to finish his tour quietly and uneventfully. The men's strained relationship comes to a head when King learns that Littlefield has abused his power. As in *Doubt*, observed *Variety* critic David Rooney, Shanley asks "complex moral questions arising from inappropriate sexual conduct—this time confessed, not just suspected. But while *Defiance* is an absorbing work, thoughtful and intelligent, it lacks the clean lines and penetrating insights of its predecessor . . . ." Offering a more positive assessment was *CurtainUp* reviewer Elyse Sommer, who stated, "While Defiance is not quite as flawless as *Doubt*, it is nevertheless a stimulating, beautifully written drama. As such, it stands on its own, yet gains strength and richness when viewed as part of Shanley's cyclic master plan."

Shanley lives in New York City's Brooklyn Heights neighborhood and is parent to two teenagers, whom he and his former wife adopted within months of each other. The couple now share joint custody of the children. Shanley is uninterested in returning to Hollywood. The lucrative screenwriting work he once did seemed to satisfy his desire for fame and fortune for good. Asked by Coe how his work as a screenwriter influenced his dramas, Shanley responded, "Actually, the influence is very much the other way around. Playwriting has continued to make my screenwriting possible. Without that constant feedback from the audience, writing can become ungrounded. Audiences show up too late in cinema; you don't get a chance to fix it after they get there. So you better have a very strong sense of what you've got, of what the music is between you and the audience. The theatre gives so much back in that way. I feel genetically born to be a playwright."

■ Biographical and Critical Sources

BOOKS

American Writers, Supplement XIV, Scribner's (New York, NY), 2004.
Contemporary Dramatists, 6th edition, St. James Press (Detroit, MI), 1999.
Contemporary Literary Criticism, Volume 75, Thomson Gale (Detroit, MI), 1993.
Contemporary Theatre, Film, and Television, Volume 49, Thomson Gale (Detroit, MI), 2003.
Drama for Students, Volume 23, Thomson Gale (Detroit, MI), 2006.

PERIODICALS

American Film, September, 1989.
American Theatre, November, 2004, Robert Coe, "The Evolution of John Patrick Shanley," p. 22.
Bomb, summer, 1988, Craig Gholson, "John Patrick Shanley," pp. 21-25.
Chicago Tribune, March 9, 1990.
Christian Science Monitor, September 10, 1984, Hilary DeVries, "John Patrick Shanley, Playwright," p. 23.
Commonweal, April 22, 2005, Grant Gallicho, "The Cost of Justice: John Patrick Shanley's *Doubt*,"p. 21.
Entertainment Weekly, January 22, 1993, p. 40; April 1, 2005, Mary Kaye Schilling, "Leap of Faith," 78.
Gentleman's Quarterly, July, 1990, Eliot Kaplan, "A Couple of White Guys Sitting around Talking," pp. 137.
Harper's Bazaar, February, 1988, Polly Roberts, "Bard of the Bronx," pp. 110, 112, 206.

Interview, February, 1987, Fayette Hickox, "John Patrick Shanley," pp. 84.

Los Angeles Magazine, March, 1988, Dick Lochte, "Stardomstruck," p. 53.

Los Angeles Times, February 5, 1986; March 5, 1988; February 9, 1989; March 9, 1990.

Maclean's, April 4, 1988; January 23, 1989, p. 45.

Nation, May 19, 1997.

National Review, March 4, 1988, p. 53.

New Leader, January 17, 1994.

New Stateman, October 16, 1987.

Newsweek, December 21, 1987; January 25, 1988.

New York, October 20, 1986; November 14, 1988; December 6, 2004, John Smith, "Faith-based Initiative" April 11, 2005, John Simon, "Sure Thing"; April 18, 2005, Boris Kachka, "Influences: Pulitzer Winner John Patrick Shanley."

New Yorker, June 18, 1984; October 7, 1985; January 25, 1988.

New York Observer, February 26, 2001, 17; March 24, 2003, p. 19; December 13, 2004, p. 25.

New York Times, October 14, 1982; November 24, 1982; June 8, 1984, p. C3; September 26, 1985; May 5, 1986; December 27, 1987, Sonia Taitz, "John Shanley: Screenwriting in His Own Way," p. H23; April 10, 1988; January 13, 1989; October 24, 1991; February 27, 1997, Ben Brantley, "Well, You See, Doctor, Someone's Stolen Dad's Argyle Socks," review of *Psychopathia Sexualis,* p. C13; November 12, 2001, p. E5; November 8, 2004; November 24, 2004; April 1, 2005, p. E3.

New York Times Magazine, November 7, 2004, Alex Witchel, "The Confessions of John Patrick Shanley," p. 31.

People, January 18, 1988.

Time, November 7, 1988; January 23, 1989.

Times (London, England), March 29, 1984, p. 8.

Times Educational Supplement, May 20, 2005, Stephen Phillips, "Faith, Hope, and Doubt," p. 6.

Variety, December 17, 1990, p. 63; February 19-25, 2001, p. 49; March 1, 2006, David Rooney, review of *Defiance,* p. 5.

ONLINE

CurtainUp, http://www.curtainup.com/ (March 1, 2006), Elyse Sommer, review of *Defiance.*

(Photograph by Suzanne Plunkett. AP Images.)

Susan Stroman

■ Personal

Born October 17, 1954, in Wilmington, DE; daughter of Charles (a salesperson) and Frances Stroman; married Mike Ockrent (a director), December, 1995 (died 1999). *Education:* Graduated from University of Delaware.

■ Addresses

Agent—Flora Roberts, Inc., 157 West 57th St., New York, NY 10019.

■ Career

Dancer until mid-1980s; choreographer, 1980—, director, 1999—. Dancer in stage productions, including *Chicago,* 1977-78, *Whoopee,* 1979, *Richard III,* 1980, *Peter Pan,* 1983, and regional and stock theater. Assistant choreographer and assistant director, *Musical Chairs* (Off-Broadway), 1980; co-conceiver, *Trading Places,* Equity Library Theatre Informals, 1983; director and co-conceiver, *Living Color* (Off-Broadway), 1986. Choreographer, *Broadway Babylon* (Off-Broadway), 1984; *Sayonara,* 1987; *Flora, the Red Menace,* 1987; *Shenandoah,* 1988; *Slasher,* 1988; *Rhythm Ranch,* 1989; *Don Giovanni,* 1989; *A Little Night Music,* 1990; *The Roar of the Greasepaint—The Smell of the Crowd,* 1990; *Gypsy,* 1991; *And the World Goes 'Round,* 1991; *Liza Minnelli: Stepping out at Radio City Music Hall,* 1991; *Crazy for You,* 1992; *110 in the Shade,* 1992; *Picnic,* 1993; *Show Boat,* 1994; *A Christmas Carol,* 1994, 1997; *Big,* 1996; *Steel Pier,* 1997; *Oklahoma!,* 1998; *Contact: A Dance Play* (also director and coauthor), 1999-2000; *The Music Man* (and director), 2000; *The Producers* (and director), 2001; and *Thou Shalt Not* (and director), 2001; *Double Feature* (and director), 2004; *The Frogs* (and director), 2004-05. Television and film work includes director, *An Evening with the Boston Pops: A Tribute to Leonard Bernstein,* 1989; choreographer and co-conceiver, *Sondheim—A Celebration at Carnegie Hall,* 1992; *Liza Minnelli Live from Radio City Music Hall,* 1993; and *Center Stage,* 2000; director, *The Producers* feature film, Universal Pictures, 2005.

■ Awards, Honors

Outer Critics Circle Award, 1991, for *And the World Goes 'Round;* Tony Award, Drama Desk Award, and Outer Critics Circle Award, 1992, and Laurence Olivier Award, 1993, all for *Crazy for You;* nominated for an Emmy Award, 1993, for Outstanding Achievement in Choreography, for *Liza Minnelli Live from Radio City Music Hall;* Astaire Award, 1994, and

Tony Award, 1995, both for *Show Boat;* Astaire Award, and Outer Critics Circle Award, both 2000, both for *Contact* and *The Music Man;* Tony Awards for choreography and for best new musical, 2000, for *Contact;* Astaire Award, and Tony Awards for choreography and directing, both 2001, both for *The Producers;* Mr. Abbott Award, Stage Directors and Choreographers Foundation, 2001; *Dance Magazine* Award, 2001; Elan Award, 2005. Honorary doctorate, University of Delaware, 2005.

■ Writings

(With John Weidman) *Contact: A Dance Play,* produced in New York at Lincoln Center, 1999.

■ Sidelights

Susan Stroman is a versatile and prolific former dancer, choreographer, and stage and film director. The winner of five Tony Awards, two Olivier Awards, and numerous other prestigious honors in the musical theater, Stroman has been likened to dancer/choreographers such as Gene Kelly and George Balanchine. Moving seamlessly from Broadway to the big screen, Stroman made her film director debut with the 2005 *The Producers,* an adaptation of the stage hit revival of the same title.

In 2001, when she was called the "hottest thing on Broadway" by a writer for the online *CNN/TIME* online, Stroman had three hits on Broadway simultaneously. Praised for her choreographic work in Broadway musicals, Stroman is famous for a style that recalls dance eras of old. Her first big hit, *Crazy for You,* in the early 1990s, was quickly followed by further work on *Show Boat* and *Big.* With her 1999 work, *Contact: A Dance Play,* she turned to directing as well as choreography, and has continued this dual role in the 2000 revival of *The Music Man,* and the stage adaptation of *The Producers,* as well as the original musical *Thou Shalt Not* and the 2004 adaptation of the Stephen Sondheim musical, *The Frogs.* "I feel that I am a writer of dance," Stroman told the correspondent for *CNN/TIME.* "When I am dancing and choreographing, I am telling a story. So therefore, every dance step I do is plot-oriented, and it's always about pushing the plot forward."

From Child Dancer to Professional

A native of Wilmington, Delaware, Stroman once told Hilary Ostlere in *Dance Magazine,* "I always wanted to be a choreographer even when I was so

Stroman based her choreography for the 1992 stage hit on dances from George and Ira Gershwin' play *Girl Crazy.* (From a cover of Playbill™. All Rights reserved. Used by permission.)

little I hardly knew what the word meant." Her father sold instruments and appliances by day, and was also a self-taught musician at home, building in his daughter a love of show tunes. Early on, Stroman's parents recognized her musical ability and her dancing talent. When she was five, they sent their daughter to a dance studio in Wilmington, and every Saturday they would encourage her by turning on *American Bandstand.* Another and vital encouragement came from old films featuring dancers Fred Astaire and Ginger Rogers, films that would influence Stroman's style later in her life. While Stroman went on to study ballet at James Jamieson's Academy of the Dance, she continued to love jazz and tap. In high school she choreographed the halftime shows at football games. Stroman went on to major in theater at the University of Delaware while continuing to study dance at the Delaware Center for Tap and Jazz.

After graduating from college, Stroman first earned parts around the Wilmington area, and then toured with the original cast of Bob Fosse's *Chicago* in the late 1970s. Subsequently, Stroman landed small dancing roles in regional troupes, and then in 1987 she entered the world of New York dance when director Scott Ellis hired her to choreograph an Off-Broadway revival of *Flora, the Red Menace.* She quickly became friends with John Kander and Fred Ebb, who wrote the play, and would work with them again in 1991 on their successful Off-Broadway revue *And the World Goes 'Round,* which ran for over a year. *Flora* also attracted to the audience producer Hal Prince and entertainer Liza Minnelli, the latter who had been in the original. Later, when Minnelli needed a choreographer who could tap dance, she recruited Stroman for her show *Liza—Stepping out at Radio City Music Hall.*

Breaks into Broadway as Choreographer

Meanwhile, in 1989 Prince hired Stroman to choreograph *Don Giovanni* for the New York City Opera. She then ventured into directing with the PBS special *An Evening with the Boston Pops—A Tribute to Leonard Bernstein.* In addition, she choreographed New York City Opera's *Little Night Music,* which was broadcast on PBS in 1990.

It took a few more years before critics began to look at Stroman as the next big thing in the dance world. In 1992 she choreographed the smash Broadway hit *Crazy for You,* with dances based on those from George and Ira Gershwin's 1930 work *Girl Crazy.* Reaction was overwhelmingly positive, with some reviewers likening Stroman to choreographic greats such as Bob Fosse, Tommy Tune, and even George Balanchine. Stefan Kanfer, reviewing the musical in *New Leader,* called it a "smash." Dick Lochte, writing in *Los Angeles Magazine,* remarked that Stroman's choreography for *Crazy for You* "is as dazzlingly inventive and witty as any I've seen." And writing in *Dance Magazine,* Sylviane Gold noted that Stroman "came out of nowhere to dazzle Broadway with her inventive routines for *Crazy for You.*"

In 1995 Stroman teamed up with Prince again for a revival of *Show Boat.* a show which "grabs the mind and, at its best, the heart," wrote *Dance Magazine* contributor Robert Sandla, who further called the musical "a magnificent production." Stroman's next Broadway hit came in 1996 with the blockbuster

Big, a stage adaptation of the popular 1988 film starring Tom Hanks. Stroman incorporated hip-hop, "signal" dancing including handshakes, finger snaps, and waves and other moves from the world of adolescents. The result was a box office and critical success. Jess Cagle, writing in *Entertainment Weekly,* praised the "engaging music and Susan Stroman's hip choreography." Reviewing the show in *Back Stage,* David Sheward wrote that "Stroman's as-always innovative choreography provides an eloquent vocabulary of movement for the characters."

In 1997, Stroman teamed again with Kander and Ebb on *Steel Pier,* a musical about marathon dancing. Her choreography on this project earned high praise from *Newsweek* reviewer Jack Kroll, who dubbed her "the most creative of the younger choreographers." The following year, Stroman worked on an updated

This 1999 play tells three stories through dance. (From a cover of Playbill™. All Rights reserved. Used by permission.)

PLAYBILL®

NEIL SIMON THEATRE

THE MUSIC MAN

WWW.PLAYBILL.COM

Stroman created new dances for the 2000 production of the perennial favorite. (From a cover of Playbill™. All Rights reserved. Used by permission.)

version of the workhorse musical *Oklahoma!* at London, England's National Theatre. Kate Kellaway wrote in *New Statesman & Society*, "Stroman's choreography is tremendous, with cowboys flying through the air as if they were human lassos."

Turns to Directing

Further success came Stroman's way in 1999 and 2000 with two projects, the original *Contact* and a revival of the 1957 blockbuster *The Music Man*. As with *Oklahoma!*, Stroman received permission from the respective estates in order to tinker with the dance arrangements in *The Music Man*. A box office success, Stroman's *The Music Man* also earned critical praise. Jennie Schulman applauded Stroman's

debut as both director and choreographer in a *Back Stage* review: "Her directorial action scintillates, in the foreground and overall—never asign of a slight lag ever." Kroll also praised her in *Newsweek*: "Director-choreographer Susan Stroman's rousing revival does brilliant justice to this all-American classic."

For *Contact,* not only did Stroman handle the choreography and direction, but she was also listed, along with John Weidman, as its author, due to the fact that the dancing was such an integral part of the storylines. She and Weidman joined forces to come up with a creative new form in which three "short stories" are depicted primarily by dancers trained in acting. Stroman worked on these numbers through the final illness of her husband, director Mike Ockrent, with whom she had collaborated on many other shows. Ockrent died of leukemia in 1999, yet Stroman did not let this personal tragedy keep the show from going on. The entire show was danced to prerecorded music rather than a new score. Terry Teachout wrote in *Time,* "All this may sound implausible on paper—how can you have a musical without singers?—but the results are magical." Other critics also commended the production. Matt Dobkin, writing in *Harper's Bazaar,* called it a "soaring dance-theater fantasia" and "this season's break-out hit." *Dance Magazine* reviewer Ostlere described *Contact* as "a dance work with a persuasive story to tell, a great score, and marvelous dancers." And Charles Isherwood, reviewing the show in *Variety,* called it "an intoxicating adornment to the young theater season."

The ever-busy Stroman next collaborated with writer-producer Mel Brooks in an adaptation of his 1968 movie, *The Producers,* for the stage. This tale of a down-and-out Broadway producer and an accountant who scheme to over-finance a sure-to-lose play, was one of Brooks's early hits, and Stroman was wildly successful in her adaptation. *The Producers* "throws its arms around you and squeezes until you cry 'Uncle,'" wrote David A. Rosenberg in a *Back Stage* review. The "smash hit musical . . . wraps all of showbiz in a big, fat, hilarious package that defies an audience not to love it," Rosenberg further commented. In *Entertainment Weekly* Ty Burr dubbed Stroman's show a "paralyzingly funny musical" and "unstoppably entertaining." Starring Matthew Broderick and Nathan Lane, *The Producers* won twelve Tonys at the 2001 awards, including two for Stroman, for direction and for choreography.

Again acting as director and choreographer, Stroman worked on the 2001 production of *Thou Shalt Not,* an adaptation of the 1867 novel, *Therese Raquin,* by Emile Zola, a morality tale about a woman and

In her debut as a film director, Stroman brought her stage production of *The Producers* **to the big screen.** (Directed by Susan Stroman. Courtesy of Universal/Columbia/The Kobal Collection/Schwartz, Andrew.)

her lover who kill the woman's sickly husband. Adapted for the stage with book by David Thompson and music and lyrics by Harry Connick, Jr., *Thou Shalt Not,* is set in New Orleans in 1946. This time out, however, the results were not so positive. *Entertainment Weekly* contributor Burr ironically referred to *Thou Shalt Not* as a "happy-go-lucky jazz musical about adultery, murder, vengeful ghosts, and suicide," while Frank Scheck, writing in *Hollywood Reporter,* remarked that the show "is a disappointing affair that defeats the efforts of all concerned." Scheck went on to note that "Stroman attempts to enliven the proceedings with a great deal of choreography, but her inventiveness gets the better of her."

Into the New Millennium

Stroman has continued her energetic schedule into the new millennium, working as both choreographer and director of stage plays, and directing her first feature film. As a choreographer, she developed "an

homage to silent film as much as to the spirit of [famed choreographer George] Balanchine," as Barbara Isenberg noted in the *Los Angeles Times,* describing Stroman's 2004 production for the New York City Ballet, *Double Feature.* A salute to Balanchine, *Double Feature* was Stroman's first full-length ballet. Dubbed the "queen of pastiche" by *New York Times* critic Anna Kisselgoff, Stroman "delivers a surefire hit [with *Double Feature*], channeling silent-film clichés into a style of her own." Kisselgoff further called the ballet "playful, entertaining, often hilarious and superb in its theatrical timing and its musical irony."

Less well-received was Stroman's choreography and direction of the 2004 production, *The Frogs.* Based both on the original Greek comedy of the same title by Aristophanes, as well as on a 1974 adaptation, the 2004 production was reworked by and starred Nathan Lane, whom Stroman had worked with on *The Producers.* As Dionysus, Lane ventures into the underworld to retrieve a famed playwright who will restore order in a troubled world. Writing in the *New York Times,* Ben Brantley felt that Stroman's "choreography shows little of the wit and individuality she brought to *The Producers* and *Contact*." Instead, Brantley noted, "Featuring cleavage-flashing Caesar's Palace-style beauties and a Cirque de Soleilesque corps of dancers, the show suggests a Las Vegas revue tailored to a convention of dirty old academics." Peter Marks, reviewing the same musical in the *Washington Post*, felt that Stroman "has only spotty success with the material." More positive in her assessment was *Variety* contributor, Marilyn Stasio, who felt that Stroman and company "concoct a brash and breezy style covering everything from burlesque and vaudeville to Broadway extravaganza."

With the 2005 film version of *The Producers*, Stroman debuted as a cinema director. She essentially kept the same cast from the Broadway production, adding, however, such film names as Will Ferrel as the Nazi playwright Franz Liebkind, and Uma Thurman as the luscious secretary to the aging producer. Speaking with *Dance Magazine* contributor Barbara Isenberg, Stroman noted some of the differences between choreographing and directing for the stage and for film: "When we were shooting the dance numbers, the camera essentially became another dancer. The camera has to move on the exact same counts and keep a spatial relationship as if it were a dance partner."

The resulting film drew mostly positive reviews. While *Washington Post* critic Stephen Hunter felt the movie is "too long to be grant and it's too square to be great and it's too loud to be great," he also could not "imagine anyone coming out sadder than they went in." David Ansen, writing in *Newsweek*, called it a "stubbornly faithful movie of the musical." Kevin Crust of the *Los Angeles Times*, thought *The Producers* was a "grand, old-school movie musical." Crust went on to note, however, that the film was also "bloated and self-satisfied." *Hollywood Reporter* writer Kirk Honeycutt was more direct in his criticism, commenting that it was a "mistake" to use Stroman as director of the film, for it "needed fresh eyes and an experienced filmmaker to reconceptualize *The Producers* for the screen." For Honeycutt, the film was a "missed opportunity." Likewise, *New York Times* critic A.O. Scott, found that the "loud, lavish crudeness" of the film "reduces its one interesting idea to incoherence." Scott further felt that Stroman "does not have the filmmaking instincts to matcher her deft, emphatic choreography." A more positive assessment was offered by Richard Corliss and Richard Schickel in a *Time* magazine review: "A good time is had be all, and the spirit is infectious." And *Variety* contributor Todd McCarthy, despite reservations about the film being "determinedly old-fashioned," also found it an "exuberant, sometimes hilarious picture."

Tony Award-winning director Stroman. (Photograph by Steve Granitz/WireImagecom.)

If you enjoy the works of Susan Stroman, you may also want to check out the following:

The Music Man, 1962.
Anchorman: The Legend of Ron Burgundy, 2004.
Strangers with Candy, 2005.

After her first successful outing as a film director, Stroman set to work on a film adaptation for her stage piece, *Contact*. Speaking with Isenberg in *Dance Magazine*, she recalled the positive experience of filming *The Producers* on the lavish scale of the old movie musicals she had watched as a child: "All of us in musical theater grew up watching those MGM musicals, and that's where many of our dreams about being on Broadway began. Making a movie like this was an opportunity that most of us felt we would never have."

■ Biographical and Critical Sources

BOOKS

Newsmakers 2000, Issue 4, Thomson Gale (Detroit, MI), 2000.

PERIODICALS

Back Stage, December 9, 1994, p. 40; May 3, 1996, David Sheward, review of *Big,* p. 23; October 29, 1999, Jennie Schulman, "*Contact:* Versatility Galore," p. 11; May 12, 2000, Jennie Schulman, "Stroman's Masterful *Music Man,*" p. 11; May 4, 2001, David A. Rosenberg, review of *The Producers,* p. 48.

Daily Variety, December 12, 2005, Todd McCarthy, review of *The Producers,* p. 4.

Dance Magazine, May, 1992, Hilary Ostlere, "Susan Stroman's Dream Season," pp. 36-39; December, 1994, Robert Sandla, review of *Show Boat,* pp. 76-77; April, 1996, Hilary Ostlere, "Susan Stroman: It's Her 'Big' Year," pp. 63-64; December, 1999, Hilary Ostlere, "Making Contact," p. 64; February, 2000, Sylviane Gold, "Choreographer Stroman Makes Contact with a Vision in Yellow," p. 64; April, 2001, Sylviane Gold, "Master Class at Stroman U.," p. 20; December, 2005, Barbara Isenberg, "Screen Test," p. 34.

Entertainment Weekly, June 14, 1996, Jess Cagle, review of *Big,* p. 37; November 2, 2001, Ty Burr, "Le Jazz 'Not,'" p. 67; December 21, 2001, Ty Bur, "3 The Producers," p. 30; November 18, 2005, Melissa Rose Bernardo, "The Producer." p. 47.

Film Journal International, January, 2006, Kevin Lally, review of *The Producers,* p. 36.

Forbes, September 18, 2000, Deborah Grace Winer, "Stroman's Moment," p. 270.

Harper's Bazaar, January, 2000, Matt Dobkin, "Flight of Fancy," p. 76.

Hollywood Reporter, October 26, 2001, Frank Scheck, review of *Thou Shalt Not,* pp. 11-12; December 15, 2005, Kirk Honeycutt, review of *The Producers,* p. 10.

Los Angeles Magazine, July, 1993, Dick Lochte, review of *Crazy for You,* p. 94.

Los Angeles Times, January 14, 2004, Barbara Isenberg, "Celebrating Mr. B," p. E3; November 6, 2005, Patrick Goldstein, "'The Producers'; Why a Movie?," p. E25; December 16, 2005, Kevin Crust, "Not the Same Old Song and Dance," review of *The Producers,* p. E. 1.

New Leader, March 9, 1992, Stefan Kanfer, review of *Crazy for You,* p. 22.

New Statesman & Society, July 24, 1998, Kate Kellaway, review of *Oklahoma!,* pp. 41-42.

Newsweek, May 5, 1997, Jack Kroll, review of *Steel Pier,* p. 70; May 8, 2000, Jack Kroll, "Ruckus in River City," p. 79; December 19, 2005, David Ansen, review of *The Producers,* p. 69.

New York Times, October 8, 1999, Ben Brantley, review of *Contact;* January 26, 2004, Anna Kisselgoff, "Plenty of Pastiche and Pizazz, but, Sorry, No Popcorn," p. E1; July 23, 2004, Ben Brantley, "Gods, Greeks and Ancient Shtick," review of *The Frogs,* p. E1; September 11, 2005, Charles Isherwood, "And Five, Six, Seven, Eight, Action!," p. 2; November 6, 2005, Jessie McKinley, "A Broadway Blockbuster Does the Hollywood Math," p. 2; December 16, 2005, A.O. Scott, review of *The Producers,* p. 10.

New York Times Magazine, May 7, 2006, "Susan Stroman, Director of the 2005 Film, 'The Producers,'" p. 69.

O, The Oprah Magazine, January, 2006, Aaron Gell, "Springtime for Stroman," p. 36.

Time, October 18, 1999, Terry Teachout, review of *Contact,* p. 104; July 9, 2001, p. 73; December 19, 2005, Richard Corliss and Richard Schickel, review of *The Producers,* p. 138.

Variety, December 22, 1997, Robert L. Daniels, review of *A Christmas Carol,* p. 72; October 11, 1999, Charles Isherwood, review of *Contact,* p. 162; July 26, 2004, Marilyn Stasio, review of *The Frogs,* p. 68.

Wall Street Journal, December 15, 2005, Joe Morgenstern, review of *The Producers,* p. W1.

Washington Post, February 1, 2004, Terry Teachout, review of *Double Feature,* p. N2; July 23, 2004, Peter Marks, review of *The Frogs,* p. C1; December 24, 2005, Stephen Hunger, review of *The Producers,* p. C1.

ONLINE

Broadway.com, http://www.broadway.com/ (September 24, 2006), "Susan Stroman.".

CNN/TIME, http://www.cnn.com/ (September 24, 2006), "All the Right Moves: Director/Choreographer Stroman Steps out as Broadway's Brightest."

Dark Horizons, http://www.darkhorizons.com/ (December 9, 2005), "Exclusive Interview: Susan Stroman."

Hollywood.com, http://www.hollywood.com/ (September 24, 2006), "Susan Stroman.".

Internet Broadway Database, http://www.ibdb.com/ (September 24, 2006), "Susan Stroman."

Internet Movie Database, http://www.imdb.com/ (September 24, 2006), "Susan Stroman."

Playbill, http://www.playbill.com/ (September 24, 2006), "Celebrity Buzz: Susan Stroman."

Susan Stroman Biography, http://www.geocities. com/jorgeplace/people_SusanStromanBiography. htm (January 2, 2002).*

University of Delaware Daily Online, http://www. udel.edu/ (October 31, 2005), Jerry Rhodes, "Susan Stroman Wins Honorary Doctorate."*

(Photograph by Richard Drew. AP Images.)

Julie Taymor

■ Personal

Born December 15, 1952, in Boston, MA; daughter of Melvin Lester (a gynecologist) and Elizabeth (a political science teacher; maiden name, Bernstein) Taymor; companion of Elliot Goldenthal (a composer). *Education:* Oberlin College, B.A., 1974; studied anthropology at Columbia University.

■ Addresses

Agent—International Creative Management, 40 West 57th St., New York, NY 10019.

■ Career

Film and stage director, set and costume designer, producer, puppeteer, playwright, actress, and writer. British Theatre Group, Paris, France, creator of puppetry, masks, set, and costumes, 1970; Bread and Puppet Theatre, VT, 1971; Robin Wood, Boston, MA, theatre director, 1972; Ohio Arts Council, teacher of workshop in puppet construction, 1974; conducted lectures and theatre workshops in Tokyo, Bangkok, Singapore, Manila, Sumatra, and Java for U.S. Information Service, 1977, and for Baltimore International Theatre Festival, 1979; New School for Social Research, New York, NY, teacher, 1981-82.

Creator of puppets, costumes, production design, masks, and sets for stage productions, including *The Elephant Calf,* Oberlin College, OH, 1973; *Seeds of Atreus,* Oberlin Group, 1974; *Way of Snow,* Treatr Loh, Java, Bali, 1976, Ark Theatre, New York, NY, 1980, and World Puppet Festival, Washington, DC, 1980; *Tirai,* Teatr Loh, Java, Bali, 1978, La MaMa Theatre, New York, NY, 1980; *The Odyssey,* Center Stage, Baltimore, MD, 1979; *Sea Rhythms,* Smithsonian Institution, Washington, DC, 1980; *The Haggadah,* New York Shakespeare Festival, New York, NY, 1980-82; *Black Elk Lives,* Entermedia, NY, 1981; *La Gioconda and Si-u,* Dance Theatre Workshop, TalkingBand, La MaMa Theatre, and European cities, 1982; *Savages,* Center Stage, Baltimore, MD, 1982; *Do Lord Remember Me,* American Place Theatre, New York, NY, 1982; *This Chameleon Love,* Theatre for a New Audience, New York, NY, 1982-83; *Transposed Heads,* Lincoln Center Theatre, New York, NY, 1984; *The King Stag,* Loeb Theatre, American Repertory Theatre, Cambridge, MA, 1984, Royce Hall, UCLA, Los Angeles, CA, 2001; *Juan Darién: A Carnival Mass,* St. Clement's Church, New York, NY, and in international cities, 1988, Vivian Beaumont Theatre, New York, NY, 1996-97; *The Green Bird,* Theatre for a New Audience, then La Jolla Playhouse, San Diego, CA, 1996; *The Lion King,* New Amsterdam Theatre, New York, NY, 1997-98.

Director of stage works, including *The Haggadah*, New York Shakespeare Festival, New York, NY, 1980-82; *Transposed Heads*, Lincoln Center Theatre, New York, NY, 1984; *Liberty Taken*, Castle Hill Festival, 1985; *The Tempest*, Theatre for a New Audience, San Diego, CA, 1986, CSC Repertory Theatre, New York, NY, and American Shakespeare Festival, Hartford, CT; *The Taming of the Shrew*, Theatre for a New Audience, San Diego, CA, 1988; *Oedipus Rex* (opera), Saito Kinen Festival, Matsumo, Japan, 1992; *The Magic Flute*, Teatre della Pergola, Florence, Italy, 1993, Piccolo Teatro del Communale, Florence, Italy, 1997; *Titus Andronicus*, Theatre for a New Audience, then La Jolla Playhouse, San Diego, CA, 1996; *Juan Darién: A Carnival Mass*, Vivian Beaumont Theatre, 1996-97; *The Lion King*, New Amsterdam Theatre, New York, NY, 1997-98. Director of *Salome*, Kirov Opera, St. Petersburg, Russia, and *The Flying Dutchman*, Los Angeles Opera, Los Angeles, CA; *Die Zauberfloete*, Metropolitan Opera, New York, NY, 2004; *Grendel* (opera; and cowriter), Los Angeles Opera, Los Angeles, CA, 2006; also director of *Way of Snow* and *Perjuangan Suku Naga*.

Producer, director, and creator of puppets, costumes, and set designs for television productions, including "Fool's Fire," *American Playhouse*, PBS, 1992; "Oedipus Rex," *Great Performances*, PBS, 1993. Appeared in television productions, including *The Music Center 25th Anniversary*, PBS, 1990; *Broadway '97: Launching the Tonys*, PBS, 1997; and *Behind the Scenes*, PBS, 1992.

Director of films, including *Titus*, Fox Searchlight, 1999, *Frida*, Miramax, 2002; and *All You Need Is Love*, Revolutions Studios, 2006. *Exhibitions:* "Julie Taymor: Playing with Fire," National Museum of Women in the Arts, Washington, DC, 2000.

■ **Member**

Phi Beta Kappa.

■ **Awards, Honors**

Ohio Arts Council grant, 1974; Watson fellow in Eastern Europe, Indonesia, and Japan, 1974; Ford Foundation grant, 1977-78; U.S. State Department grant, 1978; Villager Theatre Award, distinguished prop and set design and puppets, and Maharam Theatre Design Award, both 1979-80, both for *The Haggadah*; International Communications Agency, Ford Foundation, and Asian Cultural Council, special funding to direct Asian and American Theatre Workshop sponsored by La MaMa Third World Institute of Theatre Art Studies, 1980; Villager Theatre Award, art of play direction, 1980-81, for *Way of Snow*; Citation of Excellence in the Art of Puppetry, American Center of the Union Internationale de la Marionette, 1980-81, for *Way of Snow* and *The Haggadah*; Maharam Theatre Design Citations for *Way of Snow* and in costumes for *Tirai*; Peg Santvoord Foundation grant, script development, 1981; National Endowment for the Arts (NEA) Opera-Musical production grant for *Revolutionary*; Creative Arts Public Service (CAPS) Award, 1982, for development of a mixed media theatre piece; NEA grant, Artistic Association to the American Place Theatre, 1982-83; OBIE Award, special citation, 1984-85, for *Transposed Heads*; OBIE award, best direction, 1988, for *Juan Darién*; Guggenheim fellowship, 1990; Dorothy B. Chandler Performing Arts Award, 1990; Brandeis Creative Arts Award, 1990; MacArthur Foundation fellowship, 1992; Emmy Award, outstanding individual achievement in costume design for a variety or music program, 1992, for "Oedipus Rex," *Great Performances*; International Classical Music Award, best production, 1994; Tony Award, best director of a musical and best costume designer, Outer Critics Circle Awards, outstanding director of a musical and outstanding costume design, and New York Drama Critics Circle award, best musical, all 1998, all for *The Lion King*; Norton Prize for Sustained Excellence, Boston Theatre Critics Association, 1998; Mimmo Rotella Foundation Award, Venice Film Festival, 2002, for *Frida*.

■ **Writings**

PLAYS

Liberty's Taken, produced at Castle Hill Festival, 1985.
Juan Darién: A Carnival Mass, St. Clement's Church, New York, 1988.
Fool's Fire (based on Edgar Allan Poe's short story, "Hop-Frog"), 1992.
(Author of libretto, with J.D. McClatchy) *Grendel* (opera), score by Elliot Goldenthal, produced at Los Angeles Opera, 2006.

OTHER

(With Eileen Blumenthal) *Julie Taymor, Playing with Fire: Theater, Opera, Film*, Henry M. Abrams Books (New York, NY), 1995, revised edition, 1999.

(With Alexis Greene) *The Lion King: Pride Rock on Broadway*, Hyperion Books (New York, NY), 1997.

Titus: The Illustrated Screenplay, Newmarket Press (New York, NY), 2000.

(Author of introduction, with Salma Hayek) *Frida: Bringing Frida Kahlo's Life and Art to Film*, foreword by Hayden Herrera, screenplay by Gregory Nava and Anna Thomas, Diane Lake, and Clancy Sigal, Newmarket Pictorial Moviebooks (New York, NY), 2002.

Contributor of music and lyrics, *The Lion King*, New Amsterdam Theatre, 1997-98.

■ Sidelights

Julie Taymor is, in the words of *Time* magazine critic Richard Corliss, a "magician." Other reviewers and critics have called this American theater and film director's work innovative and sometimes revolutionary. As David Cote noted in *Opera News:* "The celebrated designer and mastermind behind Disney's long-running Broadway hit *The Lion King* and the critically acclaimed movies *Titus* and *Frida* refuses to separate dance, drama, music and spectacle the way many other directors do." Taymor's trademark is her innovative use of masks, puppetry, imaginative scenic design, and live actors in theater that draws on literature and folklore from around the world, especially from traditions in Japan, Indonesia, Mexico, Europe, and Africa. In her film work she has filled the screen with similar vibrant images as well as edgy depictions of violence and hard-hitting characterizations.

Taymor is difficult to place in a creative niche: in addition to a lengthy list of theatrical and film credits including direction, design, and production, she has also authored screenplays and nonfiction books. For example, she coauthored *Julie Taymor, Playing with Fire: Theater, Opera, Film*, a book documenting her career, which *Opera News* critic Patrick J. Smith deemed "fascinating," and Sean Abbott in *American Theater* called "sumptuous." She has also won kudos and awards for her theater work, including a 1998 Tony Award for her production of *The Lion King*, the first time a woman walked away with that impressive honor for a Broadway musical. Taymor's achievement lay in transforming what could be a kid's show into a format that audiences of all ages could enjoy without feeling patronized. "Julie Taymor is the new lion queen of Broadway," wrote Robert Brustein in *New Republic* at the time, "universally acclaimed for having built a bridge between the avant-garde and the commercial theater." Writing in *Entertainment Weekly*, Steve Daly likewise noted that Taymor's "pageant of visual splendors has redefined stage spectacle." Her filmed adaptation of William Shakespeare's lesser-known play, *Titus Andronicus*, earned her a nomination for best screenplay in the Edgar Allan Poe Awards. Her biopic of the Mexican painter, Frida Kahlo, was nominated for six Oscars and Taymor herself was also nominated for a Golden Lion Award for directing from the Venice film festival.

However, Taymor has also suffered her fair share of failures and critical rebukes. Anthony Tommasini, for example, reviewing her 2004 production of Mozart's *Die Zauberfloete* for the Metropolitan Opera, felt it was "so packed with stage tricks, so peopled with puppets, kite-flyers, dancers and extras of sundry description, that the exceptionally fine music . . . was overwhelmed." Taymor was once pelted by a tomato-wielding opera buff for her 1996 production of Richard Wagner's opera, *The Flying Dutchman* for the Los Angeles Opera.

An Early Sense of Spectacle

Even her detractors, however, admit Taymor's genius, her high style and sense of theater and drama. It is no accident that Taymor has such eclectic taste in theater. she has been involved in the stage in one way or another she was a young child and she has studied theater around the world, from Paris to Bali. Taymor, who grew up in the Boston suburb of Newton, Massachusetts, loved theater as a child and enjoyed putting on juvenile plays in the family backyard with her siblings. She participated in children's theater programs, becoming the youngest member of Boston's experimental Theater Workshop at age eleven. After graduating from high school at age sixteen, Taymor decided to go to France to study mime with Jacques LeCoq. In Paris, she discovered the expressive potential of masks and puppets, which have figured prominently in her work ever since. After completing her undergraduate degree at Oberlin College in 1974, Taymor earned a Watson traveling fellowship to study in Indonesia and Japan, and she remained in Java and Bali for four years. The performances she saw in Bali, where theater is part of everyday life, transformed her conception of theater and inspired her to form her own company while abroad, Teatr Loh, or theater of the source. Taymor's time in Bali was not without difficulty, however. There were earthquakes, motor accidents, a bout of malaria, and even a case of gangrene for the young American to survive. But all these experiences confirmed in Taymor the importance of theater as a communal ritual.

Sir Anthony Hopkins stars in the 1999 film drama *Titus.* (Directed by Julie Taymor. The Kobal Collection. Reproduced by permission.)

Returning to the United States in 1980, Taymor worked with playwright Elizabeth Swados on *The Haggadah* for the New York Shakespeare Festival. This experience introduced her work to a growing audience and paved the way for a succession of notable works, including the puppets for the American Repertory Theatre's production of *The King Stag* in 1984. Her production of *Juan Darién: A Carnival Mass,* however, established her reputation on the New York theater scene. The play, inspired by a short story by Uruguayan writer Horacio Quiroga and featuring music by Taymor's life companion, composer Elliot Goldenthal, tells the story of an orphaned jaguar cub who is adopted by a village mother who is grieving for her own dead child, turns into a human for a time, but when rejected by human society returns to its jaguar form to take vengeance on the village. Critics praised Taymor's use of masks and puppets to express the magical and surrealistic elements in the play. Reviewing a 1996 reprise production in *Time,* Richard Zoglin called the play a "visually dazzling and utterly original piece of stagecraft."

The Lion King and Beyond

Increasingly admired as a designer and director, Taymor achieved widespread fame for the stage adaptation of the Walt Disney animated movie *The Lion King.* Taymor felt the story—in which the cub Simba unwittingly causes his father's death, is banished by his evil uncle Scar, and finally overcomes his false guilt and returns to kill Scar and reclaim his kingdom—had much potential. But she had no wish to treat the material in the sentimentalized manner typical of children's theater. Instead, she chose to incorporate elements from folk rituals and spectacle.

The result was a stunning Broadway success for Taymor. "Let it be said at once that 'The Lion King' is a great show," wrote *Newsweek* critic Jack Kroll, "not just for the parents and kids who will flock to it . . . but for anyone drawn to a landmark event in American entertainment." One of the most expensive musicals ever financed, *The Lion King* was a triumphant showcase for all Taymor's work, from

Balinese dance to Javanese shadow play, masks and puppets, and most of all, Taymor's irrepressible creativity. "It's Taymor's visual magic that's unprecedented in Broadway musicals," Kroll further remarked. Thiswizardry ranges from stampeding wildebeests to a fiery cosmos of stars which slowly forms the features of the dead lion, Mufasa. "A wealth of invention yields a feast for the eye," wrote T.M. Hartmann in *Back Stage*, "as Taymor juxtaposes animals and humans through masks, puppets, and techniques that she traces back as far back as cave paintings." *Time* reviewer Richard Zoglin called the musical a "gorgeous, gasp-inducing spectacle," a show that "appeals to our primal, childlike excitement in the power of theater to make us see things afresh." And David Richards, writing in the *Washington Post* called it, simply, a "monster hit."

With the fame and financial independence that she earned for *The Lion King* Taymor went on to focus on a more controversial project, a film adaptation of Shakespeare's *Titus Andronicus*, which she had earlier directed for the stage. It is one of Shakespeare's least-known and least admired plays; dealing with themes of extreme violence, it is not often produced. Speaking with Douglas Eby on the online *TalentDevelop.com*, Taymor explained that her motivation for adapting and filming *Titus* was its surprising relevance: "Our entertainment industry thrives on the graphic details of murders, rapes and villainy, yet it is rare to find film or play that not only reflects on these dark events but also turns them inside out, probing and challenging our fundamental beliefs on morality and justice." And speaking with Daly of *Entertainment Weekly*, Taymor said, "I love revenge stories. . . . They're full of strong emotions."

Taymor's adaptation, which blurs time periods and uses startling visual elements, was widely admired. Writing in *Variety*, Deborah Young mentioned the "vivid images . . . that left an indelible mark" on the film. Similarly Leah Rozen noted in *People* that Taymor "fills her debut film with striking images."

A dance sequence from the 1997 stage production of *The Lion King.* (Photograph by Kathy Willens. AP Images.)

Salma Hayek stars as Mexican artist Frida Kahlo in the 2002 film biography *Frida*. (Directed by Julie Taymor. Miramax/Dimension/The Kobal Collection/Sorel, Peter.)

Todd McCarthy, writing in *Variety*, declared, "Theatrical wizard Julie Taymor strides boldly into the feature film arena with 'Titus' and emerges with a conditional victory." McCarthy felt that while Taymor had made Shakespeare's tale of revenge in Rome "accessible and exceedingly vivid," he also thought the film was "too rarefied and demanding to cross over to the wider audience that has made hits of several Shakespeare adaptations in recent years." Rozen also had reservations about *Titus*, finding that "it engages one's eyes more than one's heart and mind." Similarly, *Entertainment Weekly* critic Lisa Schwarzbaum found the film to be simply a "sampling of stagy scenes barreling to a gruesome climax." However, *Time* magazine critic Corliss was much more positive in his assessment, calling the film a "complex weave of word and image," and an adaptation of the original play that makes it "vivid, relevant and of elevating scariness."

Of Painters and Monsters

Taymor's next project was the film *Frida*, which was about the life and work of Mexican painter Frida

Kahlo, who lived from 1907-1954. The artist lived in pain for much of her life, having suffered from polio in childhood and having sustained severe abdominal and spinal injuries in a tramcar accident. Married to the famous mural painter Diego Rivera, Kahlo associated with both avant-garde artists and revolutionary politicians, including an affair with Bolshevik revolutionary leader Leon Trotsky. Her paintings, often depicting views of her own tormented body, are noted for their intense emotion and their surreal blend of realistic and symbolic elements. Starring Salma Hayek, the film was released in 2002.

Writing in the *New Yorker*, David Denby noted that *Frida* "has a rambunctious spirit and a liberated sense of color." *Variety* contributor Young similarly praised Taymor's "robust and imaginative direction" in this "heroic love story and survivor's tale." David Noh, however, voiced the concern of several critics in his *Film Journal International* review of *Frida*: "Taymor speeds through Kahlo's life with her usual verve and color. Much of *Frida* is impressive and striking, flavored by Taymor's undeniable visual skill, but her efforts are rather stymied [by] a pedestrian script." Similar criticism came from *Hollywood Reporter* contributor Kirk Honeycutt, who felt the film was a "fairly conventional biopic rather than the artistic statement one might anticipate given Julie Taymor's theatrical background." Stronger criticism came from *Time* critic Richard Schickel, who found *Frida* a "trivializing movie." However, *New Republic* film writer Stanley Kauffmann, found more to like in the film. "Many elements of *Frida* . . . are extraordinary," Kauffmann wrote, "but the prime marvel is that Taymor has, so to speak, turned the film over to her actors." Kauffmann concluded, "Taymor's triumph is that her film, despite its distance from us in many ways, is pertinent and enthralling." Even detractors of the film, such as Philip Kerr writing in the *New Statesman*, had to allow that "the film is well shot, and attractive to look at."

Taymor also kept her hand in the theater, with her Broadway production of *The Green Bird*, a "fractured fairy tale for adults," as *Time* critic Zoglin noted. Based on a fable by Carlo Gozzi, the play had earlier been produced by Taymor Off Broadway. For Charles Isherwood, writing in *Variety*, *The Green Bird* was a "perfectly charming alternative to Broadway's more glitzy family entertainments." And *New Republic* critic Brustein found the same production "an unmitigated delight for eyes and ears."

In 2006, Taymor returned to the world of opera, directing the premier of *Grendel*, composed by her companion Goldenthal, and for which she coauthored the libretto. Adapted from the John Gardner novel, which in turn was an adaptation of the epic *Beowulf*, *Grendel* tells of a huge monster that once terrorized a Danish kingdom. The hero, Beowulf, is dispatched to kill the monster. Here, however, the tale is related from the point of view of Grendel, "a pensive, suffering soul trapped in the body of a beast," as *New York Times* critic Tommasini noted. An elaborate and expensive production at $2.8 million, *Grendel* was delayed in production when some of the intricate staging did not function properly. Several critics complained that the staging, in fact, outshone the music. *New York* contributor, Peter G. Davis, for example, observed that "the stage is constantly animated by Taymor's trademark puppetry, flying figures, exotic epic creatures, and fantastically deformed grotesques." Davis went on

Eric Owens, in costume, rehearsing a scene from the 2006 stage production of *Grendel*. (Photograph by Stefano Paltera. AP Images.)

Taymor speaking at a news conference at the Metropolitan Opera House in New York City in February, 2006. (Photograph courtesy of AP Images, 2006.)

to note that "if sheer eye-popping spectacle now defines what a new opera should be about, then *Grendel* measures up handily. . . . What a pity that the music gets in the way and finally defeats the project." Similarly, Tommasini wrote: "Opera has long embraced spectacle, but isn't it supposed to be a music-driven art form?"

If you enjoy the works of Julie Taymor, you may also want to check out the following:

The film version of *The Lion King*, 1994, and the books *Grendel*, by John Gardner, 1971, and *A Biography of Frida Kahlo*, by Hayden Herrera, 1983.

Taymor, however, was too busy working on new projects to be bothered by the critics. In 2005 she took on directorial duties for a film about two lovers in London during the 1960s. *All You Need Is Love* was scheduled to have a Beatles flair to it, with eighteen songs by the British group featured in the film. Meanwhile a plethora of other stage and screen projects await for this creator whom *Time* writer Zoglin termed the "theater's champion beguiler."

■ Biographical and Critical Sources

BOOKS

Contemporary Theatre, Film, and Television, Volume 20, Thomson Gale (Detroit, MI), 1999.

Taymor, Julie, and Eileen Blumenthal, *Julie Taymor, Playing with Fire: Theater, Opera, Film*, Henry M. Abrams Books (New York, NY), 1999.

PERIODICALS

American Theatre, April, 1996, Sean Abbott, review of *Julie Taymor, Playing with Fire: Theater, Opera, Film*, p. 30; p. 30; September, 1998, Sylviane Gold, "The Possession of Julie Taymor," pp. 20-26; October, 1998, Adrienne Martini, "Serious Adventures," p. 38; December, 1999, Mel Gussow, "Mask On, Mask Off," p. 10; July-August, 2000, review of *Julie Taymor, Playing with Fire*, p. 71; November, 2000, p. 12.

Back Stage, December 6, 1996, Irene Backalenick, review of *Juan Darién: A Carnival Mass*, p. 40; November 14, 1997, T.M. Hartmann, "A Wealth of Invention, a Passion for Integrity: Julie Is the Lion Taymor," p. 18; April 21, 2000, Victor Gluck, review of *The Green Bird*, p. 31; April 5, 2001, Michael Green, review of *The King Stag*, p. 22.

Cineaste, summer, 2000, Maria De Luca and Mary Lindroth, "Mayhem, Madness, Method: An Interview with Julie Taymor," p. 28.

Daily Variety, April 19, 2000, p. 2; October 23, 2000, pp. 15, 19.

Dallas Morning News, August 15, 2000, Al Brumley, "'Titus' Is Slam-Bang Shakespeare"; October 29, 2002, Philip Wuntch, review of *Frida*.

Drama Review, Vol. 43, no. 3, 1999, pp. 36-55.

Entertainment Weekly, December 5, 1997, Jess Cagle, review of *The Lion King*, pp. 72-73; June 5, 1998, p. 73; January 14, 2000, Lisa Schwarzbaum, review of *Titus*, p. 49; February 11, 2000, Steve Daly, "Julie Madly Deeply," pp. 43-46; November 1, 2002, Lisa Schwarzbaum, review of *Frida*, p. 50.

Film Journal International, October, 2002, Maria Garcia, "Portrait of Frida," pp. 14-15; November, 2002, David Noh, review of *Frida*, pp. 31-32.

Harper's Bazaar, November, 1996, Gerard Raymond, "Making Faces," p. 149; May, 2000, p. 118.

Hollywood Reporter, August 3, 2002, Stephen Galloway, "Artistic Rivalry," pp. 8-10; August 30, 2002, Kirk Honeycutt, review of *Titus*, pp. 11-12; January, 2003, "The Composer-Director Relationship," pp. S12-S15; March 24, 2003, Donna Perlmutter, review of *The Flying Dutchman*, p. 63.

Interview, January, 2000, Alan Cumming, "Taymor . . . Not Tamer," p. 34.

Maclean's, January 23, 2000, John Bemrose, review of *Titus*, p. 54.

New Republic, February 2, 1998, Robert Brustein, "The Lion Queen," pp. 25-26; May 15, 2000, Robert Brustein, "Women in the Theater," p. 32; November 18, 2002, Stanley Kauffmann, review of *Frida*, p. 26.

New Statesman, March 3, 2003, Philip Kerr, review of *Frida*, p. 44.

Newsweek, November 24, 1997, Jack Kroll, review of *The Lion King*, pp. 70-71.

New York, July 3, 206, Alicia Zuckerman, "The Monster in the Room," p. 102; July 31, 2006, Peter G. Davis, review of *Grendel*, p. 79.

New Yorker, November 11, 2002, David Denby, review of *Frida*.

New York Times, October 11, 2004, Anthony Tommasini, review of *Die Zauberfloete*; July 13, 2006, Anthony Tommasini, review of *Grendel*.

Opera News, May, 1993, Patrick J. Smith, "New Masks for Old Myths: Julie Taymor Brings Her Theatrical Invention to Opera, Transforming Stravinsky's 'Oedipus Rex'," p. 30; January 20, 1996, Patrick J. Smith, review of *Julie Taymor, Playing with Fire*, p. 43; September, 2004, David Cote, "The Alchemist," p. 38.

People Weekly, January 26, 1998, Nancy Matsumoto, "Pride of the Lions: Julie Taymor Turns 'The Lion King' into Eye-popping Art with Heart," pp. 88-91; January 31, 2000, Leah Rozen, review of *Titus*, p. 31.

San Jose Mercury News, October 28, 2002, Bruce Newman, review of *Frida*.

Smithsonian, February, 1993, Miriam Horn, "A Director Who Can Conjure up Magic Onstage," pp. 62-71.

Stereo Review's Sound and Vision, November, 2000, p. 145.

Theatre Crafts International, March, 1998, Ellen Lampert Greaux, "It's Good to Be King," pp. 42-49.

Time, December 16, 1996, Richard Zoglin, "No Dancing Teapots," p. 85; July 28, 1997, pp. 64-68; November 24, 1997, Richard Zoglin, review of *The Lion King*, p. 103; December 27, 1999, Richard Corliss, review of *Titus*, p. 166; May 1, 2000, Richard Zoglin, review of *The Green Bird*, p. 78; November 4, 2002, Richard Schickel, review of *Frida*, p. 83.

Variety, August 11, 1997, Tad Simons, review of *The Lion King*, p. 64; January 3, 2000, Todd McCarthy, review of *Titus*, p. 79; April 24, 2000, Charles Isherwood, review of *The Green Bird*, p. 37; September 9, 2002, Deborah Young, review of *Frida*, p. 29; February 4, 2005, Nicole LaPorte, "Taymor's Falling in 'Love'," p. 1; June 19, 2006, Alan Rich, review of *Grendel*, p. 49.

Victoria, November, 2000, Claire Whitcomb, "Julie Taymor: Sorceress of the Stage," p. 40.

Village Voice, February 2, 1996, p. 69; March 19, 1996, p. 82; December 17, 1996, Michael Feingold, "Feral Flying," p. 89; December 28, 1999, p. 121.

Washington Post, December 28, 1997, David Richards, "The Pride of Broadway: Julie Taymor Turns 'The Lion King' into Brilliant Theater," p. G1; November 17, 2000.

ONLINE

Bloomberg.com, http://www.bloomberg.com/ (June 9, 2006), David Mermelstein, "Taymor's Flash Tops Goldenthal's Score in L.A. Opera 'Grendel.'"

BroadwayWorld.com, http://www.broadwayworld.com/ (September 4, 2006), "Taymor's 'Grendel' Delays L.A. Opera Premiere to June 1."

Internet Movie Database, http://www.imdb.com/ (September 26, 2006), "Julie Taymor."

Oberlin College Web site, http://www.oberlin.edu/ (September 26, 2006), Betty Gabrielli, "Julie Taymor Continues the Artistic Journey, Begun at Oberlin, with The Lion King"

TalentDevelop.com, http://talentdevelop.com/ (September 26, 2006), Douglas Eby, "Julie Taymor on Making 'Titus.'"*

(Photograph by Stuart Ramson. AP Images.)

Lily Tuck

■ Personal

Born October 10, 1938, in Paris, France; divorced first husband; married second husband (died, 2002); children: three sons. *Education:* Radcliffe College, B.A.; the Sorbonne, M.A.

■ Addresses

Home—New York, NY. *Agent*—Georges Borchardt, Inc., 136 East 57th St., New York, NY 10022.

■ Career

Writer.

■ Awards, Honors

PEN/Faulkner Award nomination, 2000, for *Siam: or, The Woman Who Shot a Man*; National Book Award, 2004, for *The News from Paraguay*.

■ Writings

Interviewing Matisse: or, The Woman Who Died Standing Up (novel), Knopf (New York), 1991.
The Woman Who Walked on Water (novel), Riverhead Books (New York), 1997.
Siam; or, The Woman Who Shot a Man (novel), Overlook Press (Woodstock, NY), 1999.
Limbo, and Other Places I Have Lived (short stories), HarperCollins, 2002.
The News from Paraguay (novel), HarperCollins, 2004.

Contributor of stories to periodicals, including *Kenyon Review, New Yorker,* and *Ploughshares.*

■ Sidelights

Lily Tuck is a novelist and short story writer whose works focus on individuals who are trying to create a place for themselves in foreign lands under sometimes dangerous circumstances. Tuck was the surprise winner of the 2004 National Book Award in fiction for her fourth novel, *The News from Paraguay.* Tuck's win caused ripples inside the American literary world, for she was a relatively unknown writer and the National Book Foundation committee seemed to have bypassed novels published that year by much more prominent names.

On the Run

Tuck was born in France in 1938, to which her parents had fled after Nazi dictator Adolf Hitler came to power five years before in their native

Tuck holding the National Book Award she received for her 2004 novel *The News from Paraguay.* (Photograph by Stuart Ramson. AP Images.)

Germany. When Nazi troops invaded France in 1940, her family was forced into a second exile, and this time went to South America. Tuck was sent to schools in Lima, Peru, and Montevideo, Uruguay, while her father served in the forces of the French Foreign Legion for a time. "My childhood, although not unhappy, was a solitary one," Tuck remarked to an interviewer on *Bookbrowse.com.* "I was an only child and my parents had to move a lot—first from Germany, then France, then South America—to escape the war and persecution. This also meant that I had to change schools several times and learn different languages. The result of this, I think, is that I had to rely on my imagination for company and entertainment. It also forced me to read a lot."

When her parents divorced, Tuck and her mother settled in New York City. "I was used to being the outsider and being lonely," she told Wendy Smith in *Publishers Weekly.* "It bothered me to a certain extent, but it was what I expected. That's probably the reason I'm a writer." Tuck began penning stories in earnest and even entertained thoughts of becom-

ing an author. Recalling a chance meeting she had during a train ride to her grandparents, Tuck stated to *America's Intelligence Wire* contributor Hillel Italie, "I was in the dining car when a man said to me, 'What do you want to be when you grow up little girl?' and I said, 'A writer,' and he said, 'Isn't that interesting? I'm a writer, too.' And he wrote his name on a piece of paper and said, 'When you write something let me know and I'll try and help you.' I was thrilled. I thought my career was made." When Tuck later shared the encounter with her grandmother, she promptly tore up the paper. "To this day, I don't know who the man was."

As a young woman, Tuck earned a degree from Radcliffe College, and married at a relatively early age. Her husband was independently wealthy, and for a time they lived in Thailand in the 1960s, where he attempted to launch a business venture. She had three sons in five years, but was divorced from her husband and returned to France. She earned a master's degree in American literature from the Sorbonne, Paris's famed university, and began writing a story based on the actual case of a rather well-known American living in Thailand who had gone missing.

Tuck had known that man, Jim Thompson, personally. He was a Princeton-trained architect who settled in Thailand in the late 1940s, after a stint with the forerunner of the Central Intelligence Agency. In the 1950s and 1960s, Thompson became a well-known figure in Thailand thanks to his revival of the country's ancient silk weaving industry. He disappeared one day in 1967 after going out for a hike in the highlands that bordered Malaysia. The unsolved mystery has intrigued many for decades, and various theories have usually linked his disappearance to his former career in U.S. Army intelligence.

Publishes Critically Acclaimed Novels

Tuck devoted herself to the Thompson story, and then shopped the manuscript around to various publishers. "I spent seven years on it and then couldn't get it published," she told Smith. By 1977, she had married a second time and settled in New York City. Returning to her craft, she decided to take an intensive writing workshop run by Gordon Lish, a onetime editor at *Esquire* who had helped shape the prose of short-story master Raymond Carver. As she related to Smith, "What he taught me . . . is to be incredibly grammatical, to spell everything properly, to be logical. That was one of his big things, that every sentence has to follow the next sentence. This is one of the reasons I don't revise very much, because the sentence has to be as perfect as I can get it, and that leads me to the next sentence, so I don't write these long, big drafts where everything is this hodgepodge and then I fix it later." The tutelage helped, and she finished what she feels is her most experimental novel, *Interviewing Matisse: or, The Woman Who Died Standing Up,* which Knopf published in 1991.

Interviewing Matisse consists entirely of dialogue that takes place during a four-hour, late-night telephone conversation between Molly, a middle-aged artist who lives in Connecticut, and Lily, a New Yorker. Molly, who dominates the interaction, has just learned that their mutual friend, Inez, was found dead in her apartment, standing propped up in the corner and wearing nothing but underwear and galoshes. Shocked by the news, Molly and Lily

INTERVIEWING MATISSE

OR THE WOMAN WHO DIED STANDING UP

A NOVEL BY LILY TUCK

AUTHOR OF **THE NEWS FROM PARAGUAY** NATIONAL BOOK AWARD WINNER

Two women cope badly with the death of one of their friends in this 1991 novel. (Harper Perennial, 2006. Hardcover edition of this book was published in 1991. Used by permission of Alfred A. Knopf, a division of Random House, Inc.)

reminisce about Inez and soon begin wandering from subject to subject—including their lovers, family members, mutual friends, the art world, travel, and restaurants. At times it appears as though the two are not listening to each other, but are engaged in separate monologues. They also share stories of other people who have died, especially those who committed suicide or were victims of bizarre accidents.

In a discussion of famous people they have met, Molly recalls an interview that her former lover conducted with aging French painter Henri Matisse. Molly, then a young woman, photographed the artist and swam in his pool. As she describes the experience to Lily, Molly is searching through her desk for the interview. When she finds it, she is surprised to discover that Matisse spoke little about art and mainly about trivial matters, such as how to cook an egg. This theme is repeated throughout the novel, with both women attempting to focus on meaningful issues, but always returning to superficial topics. Critics were generally impressed with the stream-of-consciousness quality of the discourse, although some found the voices too much alike, or the content uninteresting. Kendall Mitchell, writing in the *Chicago Tribune*, appreciated Tuck's "ear for the exact way people talk at each other" and found the work "a startlingly inventive tour de force." Although *New York Times* contributor Michiko Kakutani had trouble distinguishing between the two characters, she called *Interviewing Matisse* "a most impressive first novel—sharp, funny, and strangely affecting."

In her second novel, *The Woman Who Walked on the Water,* Tuck crafts a spare narrative about a well-to-do woman's quest for enlightenment. Adele is an affluent Connecticut woman who abandons almost everything in her comfortable life to follow an uncompromising Indian guru, whom she meets on a visit to the cathedral in Chartres, France. Adele's spiritual quest leads her to take long, challenging swims in the ocean. One day she fails to return from her swim. Tuck "leaves much to the imagination," said *Booklist* contributor Donna Seaman. "This compelling and enigmatic tale is not unlike a Zen koan, a paradox fashioned to inspire sustained, even circular meditation." Noting that Tuck "has taken stylistic risks and emerged triumphant," A *Publishers Weekly* reviewer went on to say, "Her stark prose and allegory-inside-allegory narrative tug the reader, like an ancient Eastern conundrum, toward a 'realization which is beyond understanding.'. . . This deftly and deceptively simple book is wondrously deep."

Siam; or, The Woman Who Shot a Man is an "assured and absorbing third novel," in the estimation of a *Publishers Weekly* contributor. The story begins in

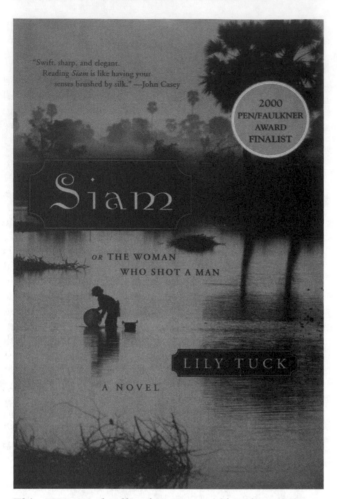

This 1999 novel tells of a young wife who moves to Thailand with her husband and becomes obsessed with a missing American. (Plume, 2000. Cover photograph copyright © Nik Wheeler/Black Star. Used by permission of Penguin Group (USA) Inc.)

1967, on the day U.S. bombers begin attacking North Vietnam from bases in Thailand. Claire, a twenty-five-year-old from Boston, has just arrived in Bangkok with her husband, James, whom she scarcely knows. His work as an engineer at the aircraft base in Nakhom Phanom keeps him away from home much of the time, leaving Claire to drift through the mysteries of Thailand, American policy, and her own unformed self. She develops a deep suspicion of everyone around her and a fascination with a missing American entrepreneur. "Her vivid, unromanticized picture of Bangkok in the late '60s," concluded the *Publishers Weekly* reviewer, "is a fitting backdrop for a haunting story about the end of innocence." *Siam* even earned Tuck a nomination for a PEN/Faulkner Award for Fiction in 1999.

Limbo, and Other Places I Have Lived, a collection of short stories, appeared in 2002. In the work, "Tuck efficiently and eloquently chronicles the lives of women who undergo both geographical and emotional displacement," according to a *Publishers Weekly* critic. Set in such exotic locales as Peru, Cambodia, and Italy, the fourteen tales examine themes of solitude, dislocation, love, obsession, and nostalgia. "Traveling with Tuck is a metaphysical adventure, endowed with richly uncommon observations that reveal uncertain emotions," observed *Booklist* reviewer Carol Haggas.

Receives National Book Award

Tuck's 2004 novel, *The News from Paraguay*, is the fictional story of Eliza Lynch, a Paris courtesan of Irish birth who was the real-life mistress of Paraguay's dictator, Francisco Solano López, known as Franco. The story moves from their first meeting in Paris in 1854, when she is the mistress of a Russian noble and he is the son of Paraguay's president, to their later life in Paraguay and Solano's disastrous instigation of a war with Brazil, Argentina, and "Banda Oriental" (later Uruguay), that decimated the country in the 1860s. "The author's research is impressive . . . but never overbearing as she explores the life of a spoiled kept woman in a foreign land," noted a Publishers Weekly contributor. Though *The News from Paraguay*, garnered the National Book Award, the work received decidedly mixed reviews. "Franco is not an implausible dictator, but he is exceptionally repugnant, and Tuck never makes clear what greater truth his repugnance conveys," wrote Time critic Lev Grossman. "As a result, *The News from Paraguay* remains a beautifully written but curiously cold and creepy novel." Similarly, Entertainment Weekly critic Jennifer Reese deemed the work a "vivid, intriguing, but disjointed novel."

When Tuck won the National Book Award for 2004 for her work—and with it, a $10,000 prize—she caused somewhat of a stir when she admitted in her acceptance speech she had never been to Paraguay. The Paraguayan government immediately issued an invitation, and the news of a book about Solano—still a national hero to many Paraguayans, partly for standing up to far mightier South American superpowers of his time despite his reputation for brutality—and its author's imminent visit began to attract attention in the press. Though it had not yet been published in Spanish, Paraguay's official language, Tuck's novel and its depiction of the dictator stirred a contentious public debate.

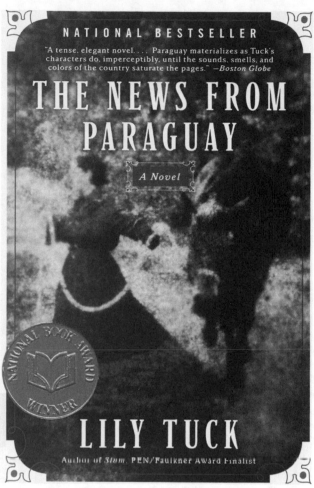

NATIONAL BESTSELLER

"A tense, elegant novel. . . . Paraguay materializes as Tuck's characters do, imperceptibly, until the sounds, smells, and colors of the country saturate the pages." —*Boston Globe*

THE NEWS FROM PARAGUAY

A Novel

LILY TUCK

Author of *Siam*, PEN/Faulkner Award Finalist

The story of Ella Lynch, mistress of Paraguayan dictator Francisco Solano, is recounted in this 2004 novel. (Rebecca Floyd, illustrator. Harper Perennial, 2005. Copyright © 2004 by Lily Tuck. Reproduced by permission of HarperCollins Publishers.)

If you enjoy the works of Lily Tuck, you may also want to check out the following books:

Minfong Ho, *Rice without Rain*, 1990.
Tomas Elroy Martinez, *Santa Evita*, 1996.
Madison Smartt Bell, *The Stone that the Builder Refused*, 2004.

Historians noted, however, that Solano's record as a statesman was indeed a blemished one, and that Tuck's book was a work of fiction, after all. She nearly canceled her trip, but in the end went, was feted, and was supplied with a police bodyguard just in case. "I'm glad I didn't come before I wrote the book," she told Larry Rohter in the *New York Times*, "because I would have been overwhelmed by all the factions and their points of view. I am a quiet person, not a politician, so I don't know if I would even have started to write if I knew all of the issues that were at stake."

Tuck believes that the themes of dislocation and rootlessness that she examines in her work is a direct result of having lived in different countries. As she told Smith in *Publishers Weekly*, "My life has been so dictated by political events. I didn't starve to death, I wasn't tortured, I was well taken care of, but there was always this undercurrent of my mother and father having lost everything. I feel very anchored in one sense with my family, but in another I feel that my life is such an accident, I could have ended up in a million different places: France, Germany, South America."

■ Biographical and Critical Sources

BOOKS

Contemporary Literary Criticism, Volume 70, Thomson Gale (Detroit, MI), 1992, pp. 117-121.
Newsmakers, Thomson Gale (Detroit, MI), 2006.

PERIODICALS

America's Intelligence Wire, November 26, 2004, Hillel Italie, "Native Parisian Lily Tuck Explores the Roots of Rootlessness."
Book, January-February, 2002, Penelope Mesic, review of *Limbo, and Other Places I Have Lived*, p. 72.
Booklist, February 15, 1996, Donna Seaman, review of *The Woman Who Walked on the Water*, p. 993; October 1, 1999, Neal Wyatt, review of *Siam: or, The Woman Who Shot a Man*, p. 344; January 1, 2002, Carol Haggas, review of *Limbo, and Other Places I Have Lived*, pp. 814-815; March 15, 2004, Brad Hooper, review of *The News from Paraguay*, p. 1268.
Chicago Tribune, May 19, 1991, p. 7.
Entertainment Weekly, December 3, 2004, Jennifer Reese, review of *The News from Paraguay*, p. 94.
Kirkus Reviews, January 1, 1996; December 15, 2001, review of *Limbo, and Other Places I Have Lived*, p. 1719; February 15, 2004, review of *The News from Paraguay*, p. 153.

Library Journal, March 15, 1991, pp. 118-119; March 1, 1996, p. 107.

New York Times, March 22, 1991, p. C31; January 7, 2000, p. 49; January 29, 2002, p. E10; November 18, 2004, p. A25; November 30, 2004, p. B2; February 17, 2005, p. A4.

New York Times Book Review, April 14, 1991, p. 20; April 28, 1996, p. 23; February 10, 2002, p. 26.

Publishers Weekly, February 1, 1991, review of *Interviewing Matisse: or, The Woman Who Died Standing Up,* p. 64; January 8, 1996, review of *The Woman Who Walked on Water,* p. 55; September 27, 1999, review of *Siam,* p. 67; December 10, 2001, review of *Limbo, and Other Places I Have Lived,* pp. 51-52; May 3, 2004, review of *The News from Paraguay,* p. 172; June 7, 2004, Wendy Smith, "Lily Tuck: At Home as a Foreigner," pp. 27-28.

Seattle Post-Intelligencer, March 18, 2005, p. 24.

Time, November 29, 2004, Lev Grossman, "One Deserved to Win, the Other . . . The National Book Award for Fiction Goes to a Saga about a Dictator," p. 146.

ONLINE

Bookbrowse.com, http://www.bookbrowse.com/author_interviews/ (September 1, 2006), "Lily Tuck Talks about Her Book, *The News from Paraguay.*"*

(Photograph copyright © Sarah Weeks. Used with permission of Pippen Properties Inc.)

Sarah Weeks

■ Personal

Born in Ann Arbor, MI; daughter of a college professor and a homemaker. Children: Gabe, Nat (sons). *Education:* Graduated from Hampshire College and New York University.

■ Addresses

Home—New York, NY. *E-mail*—authorweeks@aol.com.

■ Career

Singer, songwriter, and children's book author. Member of adjunct faculty, New School University, New York, NY; program presenter at schools and libraries; founding member of A.R.T. (Authors Readers Theatre). Has written lyrics for Sesame Street and the Olsen Twins.

■ Writings

FOR YOUNG ADULTS

Regular Guy, Laura Geringer Books (New York, NY), 1999.

Guy Time, HarperCollins (New York, NY), 2000.

My Guy, Laura Geringer Books (New York, NY), 2001.

Guy Wire, Laura Geringer Books (New York, NY), 2002.

Get Well Soon, or Else! ("Boyds Will Be Boyds" series), Scholastic (New York, NY), 2004.

Beware of Mad Dog ("Boyds Will Be Boyds" series), Scholastic (New York, NY), 2004.

Danger! Boys Dancing! ("Boyds Will Be Boyds" series), Scholastic (New York, NY), 2004.

So B. It, Laura Geringer Books (New York, NY), 2004.

Jumping the Scratch, Laura Geringer Books (New York, NY), 2006.

Fink's Funk ("Boyds Will Be Boyds" series), Scholastic (New York, NY), 2006.

Contributor to *Tripping over the Lunch Lady,* Puffin (New York, NY), 2006.

PICTURE BOOKS

Hurricane City, illustrated by James Warhola, HarperCollins (New York, NY), 1993.

Follow the Moon, illustrated by Suzanne Duranceau, HarperCollins (New York, NY), 1995.

Red Ribbon, illustrated by Jeffrey Greene, Laura Geringer Books (New York, NY), 1995.

Noodles, illustrated by David A. Carter, Laura Geringer Books (New York, NY), 1996.

(And vocalist) *Little Factory* (with computer disk), animation by Byron Barton, Laura Geringer Books (New York, NY), 1998.

Mrs. McNosh Hangs up Her Wash, illustrated by Nadine Bernard Westcott, Laura Geringer Books (New York, NY), 1998.

Splish Splash, illustrated by Ashley Wolff, HarperCollins (New York, NY), 1999.

Piece of Jungle, illustrated by Suzanne Duranceau, Laura Geringer Books (New York, NY), 1999.

Happy Birthday, Frankie, illustrated by Warren Linn, Laura Geringer Books (New York, NY), 1999.

Drip, Drop, illustrated by Jane Manning, HarperCollins (New York, NY), 2000.

Mrs. McNosh and the Great Big Squash, illustrated by Nadine Bernard Westcott, HarperFestival (New York, NY), 2000.

Bite Me, I'm a Shape, illustrated by Jef Kaminsky, Random House (New York, NY), 2002.

Bite Me, I'm a Book, illustrated by Jef Kaminsky, Random House (New York, NY), 2002.

My Somebody Special, illustrated by Ashley Wolff, Harcourt (San Diego, CA), 2002.

Angel Face, illustrated by David Diaz, Atheneum (New York, NY), 2002.

Oh My Gosh, Mrs. McNosh!, illustrated by Nadine Bernard Westcott, HarperCollins (New York, NY), 2002.

Two Eggs, Please, illustrated by Betsy Lewin, Atheneum (New York, NY), 2003.

(And vocalist) *Without You* (includes CD), illustrated by Suzanne Duranceau, Laura Geringer Books (New York, NY), 2003.

(And vocalist) *Crocodile Smile: Ten Songs of the Earth as the Animals See It* (songbook; includes CD), HarperCollins (New York, NY), 2003.

If I Were a Lion, illustrated by Heather M. Solomon, Atheneum (New York, NY), 2004.

Paper Parade, illustrated by Ed Briant, Atheneum (New York, NY), 2004.

Baa-Choo!, illustrated by Jane Manning, HarperCollins (New York, NY), 2004.

I'm a Pig, illustrated by Holly Berry, Laura Geringer Books (New York, NY), 2005.

Be Mine, Be Mine, Sweet Valentine, illustrated by Fumi Kosaka, Laura Geringer Books (New York, NY), 2006.

Counting Ovejas, illustrated by David Diaz, Atheneum (New York, NY), 2006.

Overboard!, illustrated by Sam Williams, Harcourt (Orlando, FL), 2006.

Pip Squeak, illustrated by Jane Manning, Laura Geringer Books (New York, NY), 2007.

Bunny Fun, illustrated by Sam Williams, Harcourt (Orlando, FL), 2007.

Peek in My Pocket, illustrated by David A. Carter, Harcourt (Orlando, FL), 2007.

Ella, Of Course!, illustrated by Doug Cushman, Harcourt (Orlando, FL), 2007.

■ Adaptations

The "Guy" novels were adapted by a feature film by Disney Studios.

■ Sidelights

Sarah Weeks is an acclaimed author of books for children and young adults. Her middle-grade novels, such as the works in the "Guy" and "Boyds Will Be Boyds" series, have been popular with preteen readers. In addition, her young adult works *So B. It* and *Jumping the Scratch* have been praised by readers and critics alike.

Weeks was born and raised in Ann Arbor, Michigan. Her father, an English professor at the University of Michigan, and her mother, a homemaker, encouraged her love of literature. As Weeks noted on her Web site: "I loved to be read out loud to and I have very pleasant memories of sitting at the dinner table as my father read a section of the newspaper to us or something that he was teaching in his class. He really loved books and words and he passed that on to my brother and sister and me. My mother read to me every night at bedtime and my parents took us to the library all the time when we were kids."

A Performer and Author

Upon graduating from high school, Weeks studied at Hampshire College, a liberal arts school in Massachusetts, then moved to New York City. After working as a singer and songwriter in New York theatre for over two decades, Weeks branched into a new career in 1993 when she published *Hurricane City,* her first book for children. Many of her picture books, such as *Two Eggs, Please* and *If I Were a Lion,* feature rhyming texts that have been praised by critics for their energetic, rhythmic appeal. In addition, Weeks has created illustrated songbooks, such as *Crocodile Smile, Follow the Moon,* and *Without You,* which include recordings of her performances. "From the time I was a little girl, the two things I enjoyed most were music and writing," Weeks stated on her Web site. "I still feel that way."

Mrs. McNosh Hangs up Her Wash introduces the quirky heroine of several picture books by Weeks, all featuring what *Booklist* reviewer Shelley Townsend-Hudson dubbed "delightful" cartoon illustrations by Nadine Bernard Westcott. *My Somebody Special,* an "ultimately reassuring tale" that focuses on young children's worries over attending nursery school according to *Booklist* contributor Julie Cummins, follows an animal cast as each creature waits for the arrival of their "somebody special" at the end of the day. In *Angel Face* a young boy wanders off while picking blackberries with his mother, who sends Old Crow out in search of her "angel-faced" son; the crow has a different perspective on humankind, however, and becomes perplexed when he finds only a white-faced child asleep in the woods. In *Kirkus Reviews* a contributor praised *Angel Face* as "a tribute to the unique beauty of every child," while in *Booklist* Ilene Cooper noted that the "evocative text and storybook images touch the heart." Commenting on Weeks's recording of the book's lyrical text, a *Publishers Weekly* reviewer wrote that the author "sings the verses in a clear, appealing voice of impressive range."

The "Guy" Series

Weeks introduces eleven-year-old Guy Strang in *Regular Guy.* Suffering the classic teen frustration of uncooperative and totally-not-with-it hippy-era parents, Guy becomes convinced that he is actually adopted, and when a nerdy schoolmate is discovered to have been born on the same day and in the same hospital, he decides to check these alternate parents out. The story's "lessons in understanding emerge lightly," according to a *Horn Book* contributor, while a *Publishers Weekly* critic noted that "the climactic showdown is a virtual chain reaction of buffoonery." Guy becomes even more frustrated in *Guy Time,* when his parents separate, his dad moves out of state, and he is left with a mom who has started dating again. With the help of best friend and co-conspirator Buzz, he begins a letter-writing campaign that, while not causing his parents to reunite, at least brings his father closer. Meanwhile, Guy begins to have romance problems of his own in a novel that *School Library Journal* reviewer Terrie

Dorio wrote "captures the intense feeling" of a young teen "trying to deal with the process of growing up." In *Publishers Weekly,* a reviewer called *Guy Time* "simultaneously funny and poignant," while *Booklist* contributor Chris Sherman praised Weeks's novel as "a satisfying, funny story."

Guy's adventures continue in *My Guy,* in which Guy's mom becomes engaged to the totally unacceptable professional-clown father of the meanest girl in Guy's school, and *Guy Wire,* wherein Buzz's bicycling accident puts him in the hospital and causes fourteen-year-old Guy to learn about the true value of friendship. Reviewing *Guy Wire* in *Booklist,* Francisca Goldsmith commended Weeks for her ability to balance a "realistic and cheerful" text with a story line that "will give thoughtful readers much to ponder."

Works for Young Adults

Weeks's young-adult novel *So B. It* finds twelve-year-old Heidi It living with her mentally disabled mother in a tiny apartment, where the pair are watched over by housebound and caring neighbor Bernadette. When Heidi begins to question how circumstances brought her and her mother to this point, she finds some old photographs that prompt her to leave home in search of information about her family. Her journey takes her from her home in Nevada all the way to Liberty, New York, where she "relies on her luck, instinct, and the people she meets on the way," according to *School Library Journal* reviewer Martha B. Salvadore. In *Horn Book,* Kitty Flynn called *So B. It* a "well-told story tinged with loss," while Debbie Carton praised Weeks's prose in *Booklist* as "lovely writing—real, touching, and pared cleanly down to the essentials." On her Web site, Weeks called *So B. It* her most serious work. "The novel has its funny moments, but there are also some very sad moments, and Heidi is a deeper, more emotional character than any other I've written," the author stated. "In the end I wouldn't say *So B. It* is a sad story, though; I think it's a very hopeful story."

A boy learns to deal with tragedy and loss in *Jumping the Scratch,* a "powerful story of a child's pain," according to a critic in *Kirkus Reviews.* When his father runs off, Jamie and his mother move in with his Aunt Sapphy in her trailer home. Sapphy, the victim of an accident at her factory job, suffers from a type of amnesia that prevents her from forming short-term memories. Jamie, on the other hand, is

SARAH WEEKS

So B. It

A NOVEL

A confused Heidi It tracks down her family history in this 2004 novel. (Alicia Mikles, designer. HarperCollins Publishers, 2004. Cover art copyright © Anna Palma/Corbis. Jacket copyright © 2004 by HarperCollins Publishers. Used by permission of HarperCollins Publishers.)

read something and that triggers a story idea. Once I have an idea, the story doesn't always come out right away. Sometimes it has to sit in my head for a long time, being turned over and over again until I understand it well enough to start putting it down on paper."

If you enjoy the works of Sarah Weeks, you may also want to check out the following books:

Katherine Hannigan, *Ida B: . . . and Her Plans to Maximize Fun, Avoid Disaster, and (Possibly) Save the World,* 2004.
Karen Karbo, *Minerva Clark Gets a Clue,* 2005.
Ellen Wittlinger, *Blind Faith,* 2006.

A prolific and versatile author, Weeks sees no reason to limit her works to a particular audience. "It's nice being able to write both picture books and novels because it means that I'm always shifting around, doing different things," she commented on her Web site. "One day I might be working on a rhyming book about a clothesline, the next day a song about a penguin and the day after that a serious book about a girl who goes on a long journey in search of herself. Variety. That's what keeps life interesting."

haunted by a terrible memory, and he begins to heal with the help of a sympathetic classmate; his "emotional reaction to the incident he was trying to suppress shakes Sapphy and returns her memory," observed *Booklist* contributor Ilene Cooper. "Giving Sapphy amnesia gave me an excuse to explore that interesting quirk of memory a little," Weeks commented on her Web site. "It also provided a satisfying balance between Jamie, who wants so badly to be able to forget, and Sapphy who, because of her accident at the cherry factory, can't form new memories, and as a result is like a record with a scratch, unable to move forward. Thinking about it in that way helped me to find the title for the book—*Jumping the Scratch,*

Weeks acknowledges that the writing process is a mysterious one. "I'm not ever sure where the ideas come from," she wrote on her Web site. "Sometimes they seem to pop into my head out of thin air, and other times I see something, or hear something, or

■ Biographical and Critical Sources

PERIODICALS

Booklist, December 1, 1994, Carolyn Phelan, review of *Crocodile Smile,* p. 675; April 15, 1998, Shelley Townsend-Hudson, review of *Mrs. Nosh Hangs up Her Wash,* p. 1455; March 15, 1999, Carolyn Phelan, review of *Splish, Splash!,* p. 1339; January 1, 2000, Michael Cart, review of *Happy Birthday, Frankie,* p. 938; July, 2000, Gillian Engberg, review of *Drip, Drop,* p. 2046; August, 2000, Chris Sherman, review of *Guy Time,* p. 2142; October 1, 2000, Gillian Engberg, review of *Mrs. McNosh and the Great Big Squash,* p. 350; August, 2001, Shelle Rosenfeld, review of *My Guy,* p. 2123; February 1, 2002, Ilene Cooper, review of *Angel Face,* p. 946; May 1, 2002, Shelly Townsend-Warner, review of *Oh My Gosh, Mrs. McNosh!,* p. 1537; August, 2002, Francisca Goldsmith, review of *Guy Wire,* p. 1965, and Julie Cummins, review of *My Somebody Special,* p. 1977; March 15, 2004, Jennifer Mattson, review of *If I Were a Lion,* p. 1311; June 1, 2004, Debbie Carton, review of *So B. It,* p. 1731; August, 2004, Hazel Rochman, review of *Baa-Choo!,* p. 1946; February 1, 2006, Ilene Cooper, review of *Jumping the Scratch,* p. 51.

Horn Book, May, 1999, review of *Regular Guy,* p. 340; May, 2000, review of *Guy Time,* p. 323; July, 2001, review of *My Guy,* p. 462; July-August, 2004, Lolly Robinson, review of *Paper Parade,* p. 443, and Kitty Flynn, review of *So B. It,* p. 462.

Kirkus Reviews, March 1, 2002, review of *Angel Face,* p. 347; April 1, 2002, review of *My Somebody Special* and *Oh, My Gosh, Mrs. McNosh!,* p. 501; September 15, 2003, review of *Without You,* p. 1184; February 1, 2004, review of *If I Were a Lion,* p. 139; February 9, 2004, review of *If I Were a Lion,* p. 79; April 15, 2004, review of *Paper Parade,* p. 402; May 15, 2004, review of *So B. It,* p. 499; April 15, 2006, review of *Jumping the Scratch,* p. 418.

Kliatt, May, 2004, Claire Rosser, review of *So B. It,* p. 15.

New York Times Book Review, September 16, 2001, review of *My Guy,* p. 26; January 18, 2004, John Schwartz, "The Breakfast Club," review of *Two Eggs, Please,* p. 18.

Publishers Weekly, August 15, 1994, review of *Crocodile Smile,* p. 27; June 19, 1995, review of *Follow the Moon,* p. 26; July 24, 1995, review of *Red Ribbon,* p. 64; November 23, 1998, review of *Little Factory,* p. 65; June 21, 1999, review of *Regular Guy,* p. 68; August 2, 1999, review of *Happy Birthday Frankie,* p. 82; December 20, 1999, interview with Weeks, p. 23; June 19, 2000, review of *Guy Time,* p. 80; February 11, 2002, review of *Angel Face,* p. 185; April 15, 2002, review of *My Somebody Special,* p. 62; November 17, 2003, review of *Without You,* p. 62; May 3, 2004, review of *So B. It,* p. 190.

School Library Journal, June, 2000, Terrie Dorio, review of *Guy Time,* p. 155; September, 2000, Martha Topol, review of *Drip, Drop,* p. 211; December, 2000, Adele Greenlee, review of *Mrs. McNosh and the Great Big Squash,* p. 127; May, 2001, Linda Binder, review of *My Guy,* p. 160; May, 2002, Lisa Dennis, review of *My Somebody Special,* p. 130; June, 2002, Faith Brautigam, review of *Oh My Gosh, Mrs. McNosh!,* p. 114; September, 2002, Be Astengo, review of *Guy Wire,* p. 236; October, 2003, Lauralyn Persson, review of *Without You,* p. 141; April, 2004, Laurie Edwards, review of *If I Were a Lion,* p. 126; June, 2004, Roxanne Burg, review of *Paper Parade,* and Donna Marie Wagner, review of *Two Eggs, Please,* p. 121; July, 2004, Maria B. Salvadore, review of *So B. It,* p. 114; May, 2006, Connie Tyrrell Burns, review of *So B. It,* p. 138.

ONLINE

HarperChildrens Web site, http://www.harperchildrens.com/ (March 7, 2005), "Sarah Weeks."

Sarah Weeks Home Page, http://www.sarahweeks.com/ (September 1, 2006).*

Michael Westmore

(Photograph by Albert L. Ortega/WireImagecom.)

■ Personal

Born March 22, 1938, in Los Angeles, CA; son of Mont (a makeup artist) and Edith (a hairdresser) Westmore; married Marion Bergeson; children: McKenzie, Michael, Jr. *Education:* University of California, Santa Barbara, B.A., 1961.

■ Addresses

Home—Los Angeles, CA. *Office*—c/o CBS Studios, 7800 Beverly Blvd., Los Angeles, CA. 90036.

■ Career

Makeup designer and artist. Universal Studios, makeup artist, 1959-70; freelance makeup artist, 1970—; Paramount Studios, makeup supervisor for "Star Trek" television series, 1987-2005, and movies, 1987—. Makeup artist on films, including, *Rocky,* 1976; *Rocky II,* 1979; *Raging Bull,* 1980; *Blade Runner,* 1982; *First Blood,* 1982; *Rocky III* 1982; *2010,* 1984; *The Iceman,* 1984; *Mask,* 1985; *The Clan of the Cave Bear,* 1986; *Annihilator,* 1986; *Stripped to Kill,* 1987; *Masters of the Universe,* 1987; *Roxanne,* 1987; *Project X,* 1987; *Johnny Handsome,* 1989; *Rocky V,* 1990; *Star Trek: Generations Star Trek: First Contact,* 1996; *Star Trek: Insurrection,* 1998; *Along Came a Spider,* 2001; *Star Trek: Nemesis,* 2002, among others. Makeup designer and artist for television shows, including, *The Munsters,* 1964; *Eleanor and Franklin,* 1976; *The Day After,* 1983; *Why Me?,* 1984; *The Three Wishes of Billy Grier,* 1984; *Amazing Stories,* 1987; *Star Trek: The Next Generation,* 1987; *Babe Ruth,* 1992; *Star Trek: Deep Space Nine,* 1993; *Star Trek: Voyager,* 1995; *Enterprise,* 2001. *Exhibitions:* Works have been exhibited at various museums, including the California Museum of Science and Industry.

■ Awards, Honors

Academy Award, Best Makeup, 1986, for *Mask;* Emmy Award, Outstanding Achievement in Makeup, for *Eleanor and Franklin* (with Del Armstrong), 1976, *Why Me?,* 1984; Emmy Awards, with others, for Outstanding Achievement in Makeup, for *The Three Wishes of Billie Greer,*1985, *Amazing Stories,* 1987, *Star Trek: The Next Generation,* 1988 and 1992, *Star Trek: Deep Space Nine,* 1993 and 1994, *Star Trek: Voyager,* 1996.

■ Writings

The Art of Theatrical Makeup for Stage and Screen, McGraw-Hill (New York, NY), 1973.

(With Joe Nazzaro) *"Star Trek: The Next Generation" Make-up FX Journal,* Titan Books (Sittingbourne, Kent, England), 1994.

(With others) *Star Trek Aliens & Artifacts,* Pocket Books (New York, NY), 2000.

Also produced and performed on videos, including *Looking Your Best: With Michael Westmore,* 1990, and *The Hollywood Makeover,* 2000, with Shirley Jones.

■ Sidelights

Michael Westmore is, in the words of *Smithsonian* contributor Jake Page, "a reigning scion of a greasepaint dynasty that stretches back to Hollywood's golden age, a family of eccentric and tempestuous makeup geniuses who have adorned, disguised and altered an astounding number of the world's most recognizable faces." Westmore is, in fact, the third generation of Westmores who have provided Hollywood stars with both beautiful and beastly appearances. He has helped to glamorize actors such as Liz Taylor, Farrah Fawcett, and Cher, but has also provided more gruesome effects: a spray of blood and a broken nose for boxer Jake La-Motta in *Raging Bull,* the contorted facial features in *Mask,* for which he won an Academy Award,, and a host of aliens for the "Star Trek" series, both television and film, for which he has been makeup supervisor since 1987.

Westmore deals in illusion, but these are fleeting visions that involve painstaking labor: his aging process for the star of the movie *2010,* for example, took less than a minute of film time, but cost Westmore a month or hard work to construct and almost six hours to apply. Westmore has worked in both film and television in a career that started in 1961; for his television work he has received forty Emmy nominations, and has won nine. Five of these have been for "Star Trek" programs.

Greasepaint Dynasty

Westmore, born in 1938, indeed comes from a long line of makeup designers. His grandfather, George Westmore, began the dynasty in 1917 when, shortly after emigrating from England, he settled in Hollywood. Although Max Factor had, in 1909, been the first makeup artist to the fledgling American film industry, George Westmore soon became an indispensable part of the industry, as well, working with stars such as Douglas Fairbanks and Mary

Eric Stoltz in the 1984 film *Mask.* (Directed by Peter Bogdanovich. Courtesy of Universal/The Kobal Collection.)

Pickford. His six sons followed in his footsteps. In addition to Michael Westmore's father, Mont, there were the twins Perc and Ern, Wally, Bud, and Frank. At one time, almost all the studios in Hollywood had a Westmore in charge of makeup. Westmore's uncle, Wally, who worked at Paramount for forty-five years, developed the morphing technique for the 1932 movie, *Dr. Jekyll and Mr. Hyde,* an effect that was, at its time, quite revolutionary. Westmore's father, in addition to doing the makeup for the Hollywood classic, *Gone with the Wind,* was also responsible for turning a former gigolo, Rudolf Valentino, into a superstar with his makeup techniques.

Michael Westmore's two older brothers, Monty, Jr., and Marvin, also followed in the family business, as have his own children and his nephews. Speaking with David Van Biema in *People* magazine, Westmore noted that he and his brothers "tried to figure how much collective time the family has put into the business. . . . We came up with something like 300 years." Westmore was a small child when his father died, and he was raised by his mother, who worked as a hairdresser in the movie industry, putting in long hours over a six-day week. He was brought up mostly by the family housekeeper, Kate.

His uncles, especially Perc and Bud, were close to the child as he grew up. On Saturdays he would wander the soundstages at Warner Bros. Studios. "It was great," Westmore recalled for Van Biema. "Those were the days when Doris Day and Dennis Morgan were making musicals. The studio was my playground."

However, when it came time for college, Westmore decided to major in art history at the University of California, Santa Barbara. He had dreams of becoming an archaeologist, but upon graduation his uncle Bud offered him an internship at Universal Studios under famed makeup artist John Chambers, who would later create the characters for the 1968 film, *Planet of the Apes.* During his apprenticeship period, Westmore worked on television shows such as *The Munsters,* and when his uncle left Universal, Westmore basically took his place. However, as he noted

to Tim Clark, writing in *Variety,* "I wasn't really interested in lipstick and powder. . . . I wanted to really get into the creative end of it."

Sets Out on His Own

Westmore decided to leave Universal in 1971, and work as a freelancer. Until he became firmly established, he resorted to a variety of sources for income, including the creation of Halloween masks and consulting plastic surgeons to restore the image and self-image of people who have been severely scarred by accidents, birthmarks, cleft lips, and cancer excisions. The year 1976 proved a turning point for him, winning his first Emmy for his work on the television drama, *Franklin and Eleanor,* and doing the makeup for Sylvester Stallone on *Rocky.*

Westmore works on Mary Thompson's makeup for *Star Trek: The Next Generation.* (Photograph by Julie Markes, 1993. AP Images.)

Daryl Hannah stars in the 1985 film *Clan of the Cave Bear.* (Directed by Michael Chapman. Courtesy of JonesFilm/Warner Bros/The Kobal Collection.)

Westmore would go on to do the makeup on four of the five films in the "Rocky" series. The 1980 movie *Raging Bull,* however, firmly established Westmore as a makeup designer as well as artist. Westmore still considers this Martin Scorsese film one of his favorite jobs. "I was with Robert [De Niro] for eighteen months," Westmore told Clark. "Every frame of the movie, I was either putting a butterfly stitch on him or some other appliance." In part due to his creative work on that film, an Oscar was established for the category of makeup in 1981. Westmore would win it four years later for his work on *Mask,* directed by Peter Bogdanovich, and starring Cher as the mother of a teenage son whose face has been horribly disfigured by a rare disease. Westmore developed numerous latex heads for that film.

Westmore has also made the *Guinness Book of Records,* for his Herculean labors on the 1983 television drama, *The Day After.* The story details the effects of a nuclear war on a Kansas town; part of Westmore's job on that film was to create the effects of radiation burns on 1,500 extras in just twelve hours. In 1986, he took on another gargantuan job

of special effects makeup, creating the characters for *The Clan of the Cave Bear.*

Moves to "Star Trek"

In 1987, Paramount Pictures offered Westmore the position as makeup supervisor for their television series, *Star Trek: The Next Generation.* "For a multitalented makeup artist, Star Trek was a plum job," noted Page, "demanding the use of all Michael's tricks and creativity." His job was to deal not only with the cast of regulars, such as Patrick Stewart in the role of Capt. Jean-Luc Picard, but also to create the look for all new performers in the series, be they human or alien. Initially, he and one assistant put in eighteen-hour days getting the right look for the series; in subsequent years the staff grew to six fulltime assistants with as many as fifty part-timers brought in during heavy production times. Westmore's aliens have graced these series, including *Star Trek: The Next Generation, Star Trek: Deep Space Nine, Star Trek: Voyager,* and *Enterprise.* He was with the show from 1987 until it was finally cancelled in the entire head, which is bald and no hair on it at all." Westmore's son, Michael, Jr., a film editor and electronics guru, was brought in to solve the more technical difficulties with some of the these aliens.

If you enjoy the works of Michael Westmore, you may also want to check out the following books:

Anthony Timpone, *Men, Makeup & Monsters: Hollywood's Masters of Illusion and Fx*, 1996.
Ron Miller, *Special Effects: An Introduction to Movie Magic*, 2006.
Steve Wolf, *The Secret Science behind Movie Stunts & Special Effects*, 2007.

Westmore also supervised special makeup effects and design on "Star Trek" movies, including *Star Trek: Generations, Star Trek: First Contact, Star Trek: Insurrection*, and the 2002 *Star Trek: Nemesis*. Westmore has created hundreds of hours of television and film material for "Star Trek," and also many hundred different characters. But as he told Scott Essman for *StarTrek.com*, it is the work he feels called to: "It's really been a lot of work and I've enjoyed all of it. I can't say that I've really had any bad experiences. I've made the most of them, even when it's bad. . . . I'm doing something that I like doing. I'm not having to go to work in a factory. I get to do something that I had dreams of as a child." Page summed up Westmore's long career in the *Smithsonian*: "Aliens exuding humanity, monsters both terrible and lovable, and the beautiful faces of . . . stars—wonderful illusions forever etched in our brains. All it takes is some good genes . . . and a bit of Westmore magic."

■ Biographical and Critical Sources

BOOKS

Westmore, Frank, *The Westmores of Hollywood*, Berkley Books (New York, NY), 1978.

PERIODICALS

Entertainment Weekly, September 7, 2001, Benjamin Svetkey, "Keep on Trekkin'," p. 74.

Armin Shimerman in full makeup for the *Star Trek: Deep Space Nine* television show. (Courtesy of Paramount TV/The Kobal Collection.)

2005. Each new series could demand up to two hundred original faces, for which Westmore and his crew would develop designs and appliances, or pieces of anatomy and effects to be glued on.

"I have almost a light touch," Westmore told Deborah Fisher in *StarTrek.com*, "a soft touch whether it's alien good or bad. . . . Even my bad aliens don't telegraph and give things away too soon." While working on the television series, Westmore had a studio at the Paramount lot where his plaster casts were made and rubber appliances created. Westmore explained the categories of aliens to a contributor for *BBC Online:* "We have the straight humans, and then we have what we know as the mild humanoids, and that usually means maybe just a little something on the nose. Then we get into what we call a medium humanoid, and that would be possibly a forehead with maybe the nose attached to it. A partial alien would be the full face with hair and a wig, and then I've got the full alien, which is

Patrick Stewart and Alice Krige in the 1996 science fiction film *Star Trek: First Contact.* (Courtesy of Paramount/The Kobal Collection/ Marks, Elliot.)

People, November 17, 1986, David Van Biema, "Hollywood's Westmore Clan Makes Up (Literally) the Town's Greasepaint Dynasty," p. 95.

Smithsonian, May, 2000, Jake Page, "Beauty and the Beasts," p. 110.

Variety, May 27, 2002, Tim Clark, "Emmy-Winning Makeup Maestro: Michael Westmore," p. S8.

ONLINE

BBC Online, http://www.bbc.co.uk/ (September 7, 2006), "Star Trek Interviews: Michael Westmore."

Internet Movie Database, http://www.imdb.com/ (September 6, 2006), "Michael Westmore (I)."

Memory Alpha, http://www.memory-alpha.org/ (September 6, 2006), "Michael Westmore."

SciFiPulse, http://www.scifipulse.net/ (November 14, 2002), Ian M. Cullen "The Art of Alien Faces."

StarTrek.com, http://www.startrek.com/ (July 3, 2000), Deborah Fisher, "Spotlight: Michael Westmore—The Man behind the Mask"; (May 21, 2003), Scott Essman, "Westmore on Westmore: A Career in Make-up"; (September 6, 2006), "Michael Westmore," and "Making Enterprise: Make-up Supervisor Michael Westmore."*

Connie Willis

(Photograph by Connie Willis. Reproduced by permission.)

■ Personal

Born December 31, 1945, in Denver, CO; daughter of William (a lineman) and LaMarlys Trimmer (a homemaker); married Courtney W. Willis (a physics professor), August 23, 1967; children: Cordelia. *Education:* Colorado State College (now University of Northern Colorado), B.A., 1967.

■ Addresses

Home—Greeley, CO. *Agent*—Ralph Vicinanza, 111 8th Ave., Ste. 1501, New York, NY 10011.

■ Career

Writer and educator. Branford Public Schools, Branford, CT, teacher of fifth and seventh grades, 1967-69; freelance writer, 1969—; Colorado artist-in-residence.

■ Member

Science Fiction Writers of America.

■ Awards, Honors

National Endowment for the Humanities grant, 1980; Hugo Awards, World Science Fiction Convention, 1982, for novelette "Fire Watch," 1988, for novella "The Last of the Winnebagos," 1993, for novel *Doomsday Book* and for short story "Even the Queen," 1994, for short story "Death on the Nile," 1997, for short story "The Soul Selects Her Own Society . . .," 1999, for novel *To Say Nothing of the Dog,* 2000, for novella "The Winds of Marble Arch"; John W. Campbell Memorial Award, World Science Fiction Convention, 1988, for novel *Lincoln's Dreams;* Nebula Awards, Science Fiction Writers of America, both 1982, for "Fire Watch" and short story "A Letter from the Clearys," 1988, for "The Last of the Winnebagos," 1989, for novelette "At the Rialto," 1992, for novel *Doomsday Book* and short story "Even the Queen"; shortlisted for Arthur C. Clarke Award, 2002, for *Passage;* Hugo Award nomination for Best Novella, 2004, and Nebula Award nomination for best novella, 2005, both for *Just like the Ones We Used to Know;* Locus Award for Best Fantasy and Science Fiction Writer of the Nineties; Alex Award, American Library Association, for *To Say Nothing of the Dog;* Hugo Award, 2006, for best novella, for *Inside Job.*

■ Writings

SCIENCE FICTION NOVELS

(With Cynthia Felice) *Water Witch,* Ace Books (New York, NY), 1980.

Lincoln's Dreams, Bantam (New York, NY), 1988.

(With Cynthia Felice) *Light Raid,* Ace Books (New York, NY), 1989.

Doomsday Book, Bantam (New York, NY), 1992.

Uncharted Territory, Spectra (New York, NY), 1994.

Remake, M.V. Ziesing (Shingletown, CA), 1994.

Bellwether, Bantam (New York, NY), 1996.

(With Cynthia Felice) *Promised Land,* Ace Books (New York, NY), 1997.

To Say Nothing of the Dog; or, How We Found the Bishop's Bird Stump at Last, Bantam (New York, NY), 1997.

Passage, Bantam (New York, NY), 2001.

D.A., Subterranean Press (Burton, MI), 2007.

OTHER

Fire Watch (science fiction stories), Bluejay (New York, NY), 1984.

(With others) *Berserker Base,* Tor Books (New York, NY), 1985.

Impossible Things (science fiction stories), Bantam (New York, NY), 1993.

(Editor) *The New Hugo Winners,* Volume 3, Baen Books (New York, NY), 1994.

Even the Queen and Other Short Stories (sound recording), 1997.

Miracle, and Other Christmas Stories, Bantam (New York, NY), 1999.

(Editor and author of commentary) *Nebula Awards 33: The Year's Best SF and Fantasy Chosen by the Science-Fiction and Fantasy Writers of America,* Harcourt (New York, NY), 1999.

(Editor, with Sheila Williams) *A Woman's Liberation: A Choice of Futures by and about Women,* Warner Books (New York, NY), 2001.

Inside Job (novella), Subterranean Press (Burton, MI), 2005.

The Winds of Marble Arch and Other Stories: A Connie Willis Compendium, Subterranean Press (Burton, MI), 2007.

Also author of the novella *Just like the Ones We Used to Know,* published in *Isaac Asimov's Science Fiction Magazine,* 2003. Contributor of stories to science fiction magazines, including *Omni* and *Isaac Asimov's Science Fiction Magazine.* Contributor of stories to anthologies, including *New Skies: An Anthology of Today's Science Fiction,* edited by Patrick Nielsen Hayden, Tor, 2003, and *Year's Best Fantasy 6,* edited by David G. Hartwell and Kathryn Cramer, Tachyon Publications, 2006.

■ **Adaptations**

Willis's short story "Just Like the Ones We Used to Know" was adapted for television as *Snow Wonder,* CBS, 2005.

■ **Sidelights**

The recipient of numerous Hugo and Nebula Awards, as well as the first American to be short-listed for the 2002 Arthur C. Clarke science fiction award, Connie Willis has written novels and stories that have been acclaimed not only by critics and readers but also by her fellow science-fiction writers. Willis is the author of such noted works as the short story "Even the Queen," the novella "The Last of the Winnebagos," and the novel *Doomsday Book.* She is "one of the least predictable" writers in the field, Don D'Ammassa noted in *Twentieth-Century Science-Fiction Writers,* with works "ranging from science fiction to fantasy to horror." As a result, the critic explained, "Willis has established a reputation as one of the most reliably skillful writers in the genre,

NEBULA AND HUGO AWARD-WINNING AUTHOR OF
DOOMSDAY BOOK AND *TO SAY NOTHING OF THE DOG*

CONNIE WILLIS

TWELVE POWERFUL STORIES FROM ONE OF SCIENCE FICTION'S MOST DAZZLING IMAGINATIONS

FIRE WATCH

BANTAM BOOKS

This 1984 collection gathers Weeks's early short stories.
(Cover art copyright © 1998 by John Jude Palencar. Reproduced by permission of Bantam Books, a division of Random House, Inc.)

particularly at shorter length." "The more carefully one scrutinizes her work, the odder it all seems," observed a contributor in *Science Fiction Writers*. "Willis knows quite a lot of science and uses it correctly, but her work—despite all the awards she has received from science fiction fans—is only marginally science fiction. Her central motivation is often to explore such feelings as nostalgia, memory, regret, turning points, pain, and reconciliation. The science fiction elements provide a matrix, or an enabling metaphor, within which these human feelings can be analyzed and understood."

Willis was born in Colorado in 1945, and spent her childhood there. When she was twelve years old, her mother died, and "the world ended," the author wrote in *Locus*. "Like Katherine Ann Porter said in *Pale Horse, Pale Rider*, a knife came and cut my life in half." Willis took comfort in literature; as she told a *Locus* interviewer, "What saved me was the books I had read and the books I went back to read." Willis added, "I had read *A Fine and Private Place* by Peter S. Beagle, which says such wonderful things about death and has such an uplifting attitude, and James Agee's *A Death in the Family*, which is all about the stunning shock and how you adjust to it, and Katherine Anne Porter, and Emily Dickinson. . . . These authors were the only people telling the truth." At age thirteen she discovered Robert Heinlein's classic novel *Have Space Suit, Will Travel*. Willis became hooked on science fiction in general and Heinlein in particular. *Have Space Suit, Will Travel* "was funny, exciting, full of literary allusions (every other science-fiction writer is also besotted with books) and absolutely limitless," she explained to Linda DuVal in the *Writer*. Willis hoped to write similar works some day, and dreamed of having her own stories appear in one of the various "Year's Best Science Fiction" collections she enjoyed.

A woman is haunted by dreams of the American Civil War in this 1988 novel. (Bantam, 1992. Cover art copyright © 1992 by Jean-Francois Poderin. Reproduced by permission of Bantam Books, a division of Random House, Inc.)

Becoming a Writer

After graduating from high school, Willis attended Colorado State College (now the University of Northern Colorado), where she studied English and elementary education. She always planned to become a writer, but figured that she would need a regular job to support herself until she broke into the business. She earned her degree in 1967, the same year that she married Courtney Willis, and began teaching in Connecticut. She left teaching two years later when she had a baby, and planned to write at home while raising her daughter, Cordelia. For the next eight years she wrote science fiction, but only made a single sale in the genre. To combat the rejection slips, she also wrote "tawdry" confession stories for magazines such as *True Ro-*

mance and *True Confessions*. While the pieces were not what she really wanted to write, they gave her good experience as well as publication credits. As she explained in *Locus*, the "positive side" of writing confessions was that "I did nothing for ten years but plot, because there was nothing else to do. In the Confessions, there's no room for innovation or experimental literature or elaborate Jamesian characterizations or anything, so you just do plot. I do think it really helped me learn how to structure my stories."

Willis persisted, and by 1980 she was publishing short stories in science fiction magazines and anthologies; she also collaborated with Cynthia Felice on a novel, *Water Witch*. Willis has always believed that the short story form is at the heart of the science fiction genre. She told Nick Gevers in *Interzone*: "I think this is because in the short forms, you are glimpsing worlds through a keyhole (or maybe a better analogy is that you're seeing the landscape lit up for just a second during a lightning flash) and you don't get bogged down with world-building and world-explaining and world-saving, none of which are as dazzling as the short, sharp vision you see in Vonnegut's 'Harrison Bergeron,' or Bradbury's 'The Golden Apples of the Sun' or Sonya Dorman's 'When I Was Miss Dow.'"

It was with her short stories that Willis finally made a breakthrough. Her 1982 novelette "Fire Watch" earned both the Hugo and Nebula Awards—given by science fiction fans and writers, respectively—while the same year her short story "A Letter to the Clearys" also swept science fiction's highest honors. "Fire Watch" is set in a future where history students conduct research by actually travelling back in time; one student is sent back to witness the London Blitz of World War II, where he battles alongside the volunteers who are trying to prevent the destruction of St. Paul's Cathedral. But the story is about more than war and time travel; as Gerald Jonas observed in the *New York Times Book Review*, Willis "is concerned with things that last and things that don't—and with admirable economy, she uses time travel to explore the distinction." Similarly, "A Letter from the Clearys" is about more than portraying the world after a nuclear war. In examining how a young woman struggles to deal with the aftermath of a nuclear holocaust, "Willis illustrates the strongest point of her fiction, her ability to create utterly convincing characters," D'Ammassa stated. Both these stories were published in the author's first story collection, titled *Fire Watch*. Writing of the collection's eleven stories, a *Publishers Weekly* critic noted that "Willis's range is impressive" and called *Fire Watch* "an exciting collection by one of the best new SF writers." Jonas similarly remarked that Willis's writing "is fresh, subtle and deeply moving," while *Booklist*'s Roland Green concluded that the author's technique and "impressive command of the language make for accomplished readability."

Willis's first solo novel, *Lincoln's Dreams*, focuses on Annie, a young woman plagued by dreams about the U.S. Civil War, and Jeff, a researcher who helps identify the source of those dreams. The nightmares are so detailed that they could only be the dreams of someone else—most likely Confederate General Robert E. Lee. In a *New York Times Book Review* article, Gerald Jonas said the book "literally gave me dreams—strange narrative fantasies that left me with a not unpleasant sense of being on the verge of some important revelation. As the book itself did." Willis conceals nothing, and the mystery of

Lincoln's Dreams is solved. David Brin indicated in the *Los Angeles Times Book Review* that "whether writing drama or witty humor or, in this case, a poignant examination of duty, Willis conveys through her characters a sense of transcendent pity that few modern authors ever attempt."

Doomsday Book Wins Hugo and Nebula

Willis followed *Lincoln's Dreams* with *Doomsday Book*, a time-travel novel set in England in both the mid-twenty-first century and the fourteenth century. Against the wishes of her tutor, Oxford history student Kivrin decides to travel back to the year 1320. An error in the time-travel procedure sends her back to 1348 instead, a time when the Black Death was raging throughout England. Kivrin

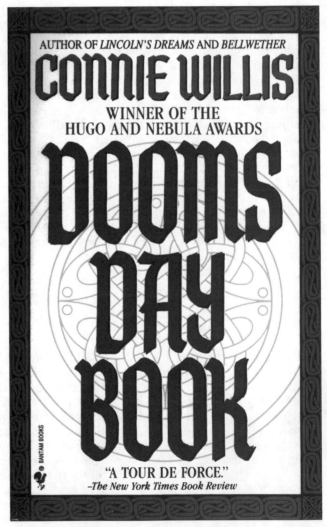

AUTHOR OF *LINCOLN'S DREAMS* AND *BELLWETHER*

CONNIE WILLIS
WINNER OF THE HUGO AND NEBULA AWARDS

DOOMS DAY BOOK

BANTAM BOOKS

"A TOUR DE FORCE."
—*The New York Times Book Review*

A student travels back in time to 14th century England in this 1992 novel. (Bantam, 1993. Reproduced by permission of Bantam Books, a division of Random House, Inc.)

This humorous 1994 novel is set on the planet Bhoote, which is not all it seems to be. (Bantam Books, 1994. Cover art copyright © 1994 by Gary Ruddell. Reproduced by permission of Bantam Books, a division of Random House, Inc.)

becomes deeply involved with the people of the era and in fighting the epidemic. Meanwhile, a plague also breaks out in the world from which Kivrin had traveled, revealing that although science has progressed in its ability to combat contagious disease the human reaction to it has not. While noting some errors in Willis's historical research, *New Statesman & Society* critic David V. Barrett nevertheless called *Doomsday Book* "one of the harshest yet most beautiful novels I have read for years." A *Publishers Weekly* reviewer found the novel to be "an intelligent and satisfying blend of classic science fiction and historical reconstruction," and concluded: "This book finds villains and heroes in all ages, and love, too, which Kivrin hears in the revealing and quietly touching deathbed confession of a village priest."

Willis's *Uncharted Territory* is a farce set in the far future. On the backwater world of Bhoote, two gently feuding planetary surveyors and a visiting "socioexozoologist" who is studying alien mating customs are taken on a horseback tour of the planet by a larcenous native guide who makes up violations of native customs, and the fines that accompany them, as they proceed. The slapstick narrative eventually leads to a revelation about the geology of Bhoote. A critic for *Publishers Weekly* described *Uncharted Territory* as "a pleasant diversion," while noting "there's little for the reader to take away." However, Carl Hays observed in *Booklist:* "Willis proves unsurpassed in SF in her ability to unload, within a short but thoroughly satisfying narrative space, a full literary bag of tricks ranging from wry dialogue to extraterrestrial intrigue."

Willis shifted tone again with the 1994 title *Remake*. In a near-future Hollywood, traditional moviemaking has been replaced by computer graphics. Tom, the narrator of the story, is in charge of mining old films to create new ones, often starring dead actors. It is also his job to make sure the remakes adhere to the politically correct attitudes of the times. Tom falls in love with Alis, a young woman who has come to Hollywood to become a star in the kind of movies that are no longer made. Oddly, Alis begins turning up as a dancer in the old movies Tom watches to create new ones. To pursue his love, Tom must unravel this mystery. "Willis's writing, as usual, is transparently clean and deft," a *Publishers Weekly* writer commented. Gary K. Wolfe, writing in *Locus,* compared *Remake* to "a good cocktail-party debate about old movies," and noted that much of the book's charm comes from "Willis's own random opinions and observations about the movies she loves." *Science Fiction Age* contributor Martha Soukup referred to *Remake* as a movie in her review, writing that "Willis in this movie is all tricky plot, social satire, and snappy, appealing dialogue at a hundred miles an hour."

According to a *Publishers Weekly* critic in a review of Willis's *Bellwether:* "In Willis's fifth solo novel, her practiced screwball style yields a clever story which, while imperfect, is a sheer pleasure to read." *Bellwether* takes place in the near future at a corporation known as Hi-Tek. Sociologist/statistician Sandy Foster is joined by a mail girl and an expert in chaos theory in her research into the source of fads. According to a *Publishers Weekly* critic, "where the story's headed becomes transparent too early. . . . But none of that counts much against this bright romantic comedy, where the real pleasure is the thick layers of detail . . . and the wryly disdainful commentary on human stupidity."

HUGO AND NEBULA AWARD-WINNING AUTHOR OF *DOOMSDAY BOOK*

CONNIE WILLIS

bellwether

"ONE OF SCIENCE FICTION'S BEST WRITERS." —*The Denver Post*

BANTAM BOOKS

A high-tech corporate trio tries to discover the source of fads in this humorous 1996 novel. (Bantam, 1996. Cover art copyright © 1996 by Bruce Jensen. Reproduced by permission of Bantam Books, a division of Random House, Inc.)

In *To Say Nothing of the Dog; or, How We Found the Bishop's Bird Stump at Last* Willis returns to England and the theme of time travel. The plot revolves around time-traveler Ned Henry, a wealthy man who wants to rebuild Coventry Cathedral by scavenging the past, and a supposed vacation back to 1888 where Ned discovers that he must correct an incongruity in time with the help of love interest and fellow time-traveler Verity Kindle. "What a stitch!" proclaimed Sally Estes in *Booklist*. Estes continued: "Take an excursion though time, add chaos theory, romance, plenty of humor, a dollop of mystery, and a spoof of the Victorian novel and you end up with what seems like a comedy of errors but is actually a grand scheme 'involving the entire course of history and all of time and space.'" A

Publishers Weekly writer commented: "While thematically not the major novel that Willis's much-acclaimed *Doomsday Book* was, her newest shares its universe as well as its near flawlessness of plot, character and prose." *To Say Nothing of the Dog* "establishes Willis not only as SF's premiere living humorist, but possibly as the genre's premiere humorist ever," wrote Wolfe in *Locus*. Michael Berry wrote in the *San Francisco Sunday Examiner and Chronicle:* "Few writers can match Willis' blend of comedy and science fiction. *To Say Nothing of the Dog* finds her in top form."

Addresses the Subject of Death

Passage, Willis's 2001 novel, focuses on a topic that has long been of interest to the author: how people deal with death. The book tells the story of neurologist Richard Wright and psychologist Joanna Lander, who are studying the phenomena of Near Death Experiences by inducting test subjects into simulated near-death states through the use of psychoactive drugs. After several of their test subjects drop out of the experiment, Joanna goes under herself and finds herself reliving memories of the *Titanic.* After each session, the anxiety Joanna experiences grows, and she must solve the mystery of why she sees what she sees, as well as try to understand why people experience what they do so near to death. "With memorable characters, believable science, and convincing hospital ambiance . . . [*Passage*] will rock readers back on their heels," wrote Estes in *Booklist.* Jackie Cassada of the *Library Journal* praised Willis for "constructing an unforgettable tale of courage and self-sacrifice." According to Dori De-Sapin in the *School Library Journal,* "This novel will draw not only science fiction fans, but also those who have wondered about their own passage from this existence into the next."

In an interview with *Publishers Weekly* contributor Dorman T. Shindler, Willis explained that instead of focusing on death on a "Hallmark card level," as she referred to stories that treat death as something not to be worried about, Willis wanted to show that "whatever death brings, it's huge, it's major, it's terrifying! And it's awesome (in the old fashioned sense of the word.)" So in *Passage,* though the characters' experiences might be surreal, they never physically communicate with the dead, and they feel what it must be like to be alone at the time of death.

In 2005, Willis published a novella titled *Inside Job.* The author again deals with the paranormal by following the story of skeptical magazine publisher

"THE MOST HILARIOUS BOOK OF ITS KIND SINCE JOHN IRVING'S *THE WATER-METHOD MAN* AND *A CONFEDERACY OF DUNCES* BY JOHN KENNEDY TOOLE."*

CONNIE WILLIS

TO SAY NOTHING OF THE DOG

This 1997 time-travel novel follows Ned Henry as he tries to fix the past. (Cover art copyright © 1998 by Eric Dinyer. Reproduced by permission of Bantam Books, a division of Random House, Inc.)

Rob and ex-actress Kildy as they become involved with a psychic channeler named Ariaura. While Kildy and Rob try to figure out if Ariaura is a fake, the channeler accuses the couple of trying to destroy her career. Several critics responded positively to *Inside Job,* finding that the author's writing is intensified in this shorter form, enhancing the story and character development. "Willis grows even better in her short fiction, bringing to this novella both richness and integrity," wrote Jackie Cassada in a review for the *Library Journal.* Others thought the book was smart, informative, and appealing to Willis's continually growing group of fans. *Inside Job* is "highly enjoyable, somewhat educational and will

leave readers happy at the end," observed one *Publishers Weekly* contributor.

In addition to her solo novels, Willis has collaborated on three novels with Felice, and she has also published several collections of stories. In a review of Willis's third collaboration with Felice, 1997's *Promised Land,* a *Publishers Weekly* critic remarked: "Since they first teamed up, in *Water Witch,* Willis and Felice have been a solidly successful pair known for smoothly mixing SF adventure with humor and light romance." The reviewer considered *Promised Land,* a young woman's coming-of-age story set on a desolate colony planet, to be no exception: "Lively characters, a well-defined setting and sure-handed storytelling add up to a novel that's bound to capture readers' imaginations." Commenting in *Booklist* on Willis's collection *Impossible Things,* Carl Hays stated, "Ranging in style from biting satire to speculative history, Willis' second collection of short fiction displays a versatility of form and conception few in the genre can match." Willis's third collection, *Miracle, and Other Christmas Stories,* provides strange twists on some traditional Christmas icons, including Frank Capra's *It's a Wonderful Life* and Charles Dickens's *A Christmas Carol.* Other stories include a man who is redeemed when he is trapped inside a toy store, the reappearance of Joseph and Mary in the modern world, and a contemporary parable of the three wise men. A writer for *Publishers Weekly* stated: "The witty, literate Willis offers a wonderfully enjoyable ode to Christmas with this collection of eight fantastic seasonal titles." Charles de Lint, reviewing the title for the *Magazine of Fantasy and Science Fiction,* concluded: "Willis invariably delivers a good story and she does it eight times here."

If you enjoy the works of Connie Willis, you may also want to check out the following books:

Robert Aspirin, *Myth Directions,* 1982.
Paula Danziger, *This Place Has No Atmosphere,* 1986.
Douglas Adams, *The Hitchhiker's Guide to the Galaxy,* 1995.

"All I ever wanted to be was a science fiction writer," she told Shindler. She explained in the same interview: "My characters are always trying to figure out the world, and they never have enough information. Everything depends on their understanding the situation; yet it's a situation much too big and complicated for them to understand. That, to me, is the human condition in a nutshell." "For Willis, science fiction is not about science but about the relationship between science and humanity," observed *Library Journal* contributor Wilda Williams. "Science fiction is a very literary field," the author told DuVal, "full of humor, marvelously inventive and very philosophical." As an author, "you can write about anything you want—social satire, political issues, adventure, mystery, even romance. I've never felt constrained by it."

■ **Biographical and Critical Sources**

BOOKS

Contemporary Novelists, 7th edition, St. James Press (Detroit, MI), 2001.

St. James Guide to Fantasy Writers, St. James Press (Detroit, MI), 1996.

St. James Guide to Science Fiction Writers, 4th edition, St. James Press (Detroit, MI), 1996.

Science Fiction Writers, 2nd edition, Scribner (New York, NY), 1999.

PERIODICALS

Booklist, February 15, 1985, Roland Green, review of *Fire Watch*, p. 824; June 15, 1992, Roland Green, review of *Doomsday Book*, p. 1811; December 15, 1993, Carl Hays, review of *Impossible Things*, p. 741; May 1, 1994, Carl Hays, review of *Uncharted Territory*, p. 1586; July, 1997, Laurie Hartshorn, review of *Even the Queen and Other Short Stories*, p. 1829; January 1, 1998, Sally Estes, review of *To Say Nothing of the Dog; or, How We Found the Bishop's Bird Stump at Last*, p. 786; April 15, 1999, Roland Green, review of *Nebula Awards 33: The Year's Best SF and Fantasy Chosen by the Science-Fiction and Fantasy Writers of America*, p. 1518; November 15, 1999, Roland Green, review of *Miracle, and Other Christmas Stories*, p. 609; March 15, 2001, Sally Estes, review of *Passage*, p. 1361; August 2001, Regina Schroeder, review of *A Woman's Liberation: A Choice of Futures by and about Women*, p. 2102; June 1, 2005, Ray Olson, review of *Inside Job*, p. 1770.

Bookpage, May, 2001, review of *Passage*, p. 31.

Bookseller, April 5, 2002, "Brits Dominate SF Prize," p. 27.

Denver Post, April 20, 2001, Dorman T. Shindler, review of *Passage*.

Detroit Free Press, June 3, 2001, review of *Passage*, p. 4E.

Globe & Mail (Toronto, Ontario, Canada), May 26, 2001, review of *Passage*, p. D17.

Interzone, November, 2001, Nick Gevers, "Farce Retrospective: An Interview with Connie Willis."

Kirkus Reviews, September 1, 1999, review of *Miracle, and Other Christmas Stories*, p. 1345; March 1, 2001, review of *Passage*.

Kliatt, July, 2003, review of *To Say Nothing of the Dog*, p. 6.

Library Journal, February 15, 1997, Susan Hamburger, review of *The Promised Land*, p. 165; December, 1998, review of *To Say Nothing of the Dog*, p. 188; April 1, 1999, Laurel Bliss, review of *Nebula Awards 33*, p. 132; April 15, 2001, Jackie Cassada, review of *Passage*, p. 135, and Wilda Williams, "Crossing the Final Frontier," p. 136; July, 2001, Nancy Pearl, "Summer Book Report," p. 160; January, 2002, review of *Passage*, p. 51; August 5, 2005, Jackie Cassada, review of *Inside Job*, p. 76.

Library Journal, December, 1994, review of *Remake*, p. 139; August 1, 2005, Jackie Cassada, review of *Inside Job*, p. 76.

Locus, March, 1992, Gary K. Wolfe, review of *Doomsday Book*, p. 27; July, 1992, p. 36; June, 1994, Gary K. Wolfe, review of *Uncharted Territory*, p. 62; January, 1995, Gary K. Wolfe, review of *Remake*, p. 21; November, 1997, Faren Miller, review of *To Say Nothing of the Dog*, p. 19; January, 1998, Gary K. Wolfe, review of *To Say Nothing of the Dog*, p. 15; January, 2003, "Connie Willis: The Facts of Death."

Los Angeles Times Book Review, February 7, 1988, David Brin, review of *Lincoln's Dreams*, p. 11.

Magazine of Fantasy and Science Fiction, May, 1995, Charles de Lint, review of *Remake*, pp. 35-36; April, 1996, review of *Bellwether*, p. 33; August, 2000, Charles de Lint, review of *Miracle, and Other Christmas Stories*, p. 24.

Mythprint, August, 2001, Paula DiSante, "A Foot in the Door of Hereafter," p. 4.

New Scientist, May 4, 2002, review of *Passage*, p. 58.

New Statesman & Society, November 27, 1992, David V. Barrett, "Out of Time," review of *Doomsday Book*, p. 38.

New York Times Book Review, March 10, 1985, Gerald Jonas, review of *Fire Watch*, p. 31; June 7, 1987, Gerald Jonas, review of *Lincoln's Dreams*, p. 18; August 14, 1994, p. 30; December 21, 1997, Gerald Jonas, review of *To Say Nothing of the Dog*, p. 21.

Publishers Weekly, January 18, 1985, review of *Fire Watch*, p. 64; April 14, 1989, Sybil Steinberg, review of *Light Raid*, p. 54; May 4, 1992, review of *Doomsday Book*, p. 54; November 29, 1993, review of *Impossible Things*, p. 59; June 6, 1994, review of

Uncharted Territory, p. 62; December 19, 1994, review of *Remake,* p. 51; January 29, 1996, review of *Bellwether,* p. 96; January 27, 1997, review of *The Promised Land,* p. 82; October 27, 1997, review of *To Say Nothing of the Dog,* p. 56; March 8, 1999, review of *Nebula Awards 33,* p. 51; October 25, 1999, review of *Miracle, and Other Christmas Stories,* p. 55; March 12, 2001, review of *Passage,* p. 67; May 21, 2001, Dorman T. Shindler, "Connie Willis: The Truths of Science Fiction," p. 76; July 30, 2001, review of *A Woman's Liberation,* p. 66; May 30, 2005, review of *Inside Job,* p. 44.

San Francisco Sunday Examiner and Chronicle, January 18, 1998, Michael Berry, review of *To Say Nothing of the Dog.*

School Library Journal, August, 2001, Dori DeSpain, review of *Passage,* p. 211.

Science Fiction Age, March, 1995, Martha Soukup, "Connie Willis Visits Future Hollywood for a Thought-Provoking *Remake,*"p. 10.

U.S. News & World Report, June 18, 2001, "Top Picks," p. 58.

Voice of Youth Advocates, October, 1987, p. 182; April, 1998, Mary B. McCarthy, review of *To Say Nothing of the Dog,* p. 62; June, 1994, Margaret Miles, review of *Impossible Things,* p. 102; August, 1996, Kathleen Beck, review of *Bellwether,* p. 173; April, 2000, review of *Miracle, and Other Christmas Stories,* p. 51; April, 2002, review of *A Woman's Liberation,* p. 16.

Writer, November, 2004, Linda DuVal, "Transcending Genres," p. 24.

Washington Post Book World, May 24, 1987, Gregory Feeley, "Cyberpunks and Humanists," p. 6; July 31, 1988; May 28, 1989; June 28, 1992, John Clute, review of *Doomsday Book,* p. 8; June 26, 1994, Sullivan, Tim, review of *Uncharted Territory,* p. 11.

Wilson Library Bulletin, September, 1992, Gene LaFaille, "Science Fiction Universe," pp. 98-99.

Women's Review of Books, March, 2002, Donna Minkeowitz, review of *A Woman's Liberation,* p. 9.

ONLINE

Agony, http://trashotron.com/agony/ (October 23, 2005), Rick Kleffel, review of *Inside Job.*

Connie Willis Home Page, http:// www.geocities.com/Wellesley/5595/willis/willis.html (December 4, 2005).

Connie Willis.net, http://www.sftv.org/cw/ (January 26, 2007).

Cybling.com, http://www.cybling.com/ (August, 1998), online interview with Connie Willis.

Infinity Plus, http:// www.infinityplus.co.uk/ (December 4, 2005), interview with Connie Willis.

OmniVisions Online Chat, http:// www.hourwolf.com/ (December 4, 1997), interview with Connie Willis.

Salon.com, http://www.salon.com/ (December 23, 1999), Polly Shulman, "Tempting Fate."

SciFi.com, http://www.scifi.com/ (December 4, 2005), interview with Connie Willis.*

Author/Artist Index

The following index gives the number of the volume in
which an author/artist's biographical sketch appears: